THE
AMERICAN JEW

A Composite Portrait

EDITED BY

OSCAR I. JANOWSKY

Harper & Brothers Publishers

NEW YORK AND LONDON

To the memory of

LOUIS DEMBITZ BRANDEIS

whose life was a synthesis of
Americanism and Zionism

Hadassah dedicates this book

CONTENTS

PREFACE   ix
    Margaret G. Doniger
    Chairman, National Education Committee, Hadassah

I. HISTORICAL BACKGROUND   1
    Oscar I. Janowsky
    Associate Professor of History, College of the City of New York

II. JUDAISM AND THE SYNAGOGUE   28
    David de Sola Pool
    Rabbi, Shearith Israel, The Spanish-Portuguese Synagogue, New York

III. JEWISH EDUCATION—ACHIEVEMENTS AND NEEDS   56
    I. B. Berkson
    Lecturer in Education, College of the City of New York

IV. THE CULTURAL SCENE: LITERARY EXPRESSION   92
    Marie Syrkin
    Associate Editor, *Jewish Frontier*

V. HEBREW IN JEWISH CULTURE   122
    Abraham S. Halkin
    Assistant Professor of Hebrew, Brooklyn College

VI. STRUCTURE OF THE JEWISH COMMUNITY   134
    Abraham G. Duker
    Editor in Research Institute on Peace and Post-War Problems, American Jewish Committee

VII. ECONOMIC TRENDS   161
    Nathan Reich
    Assistant Professor of Economics, Hunter College

VIII. ANTI-SEMITISM   183
     Jacob J. Weinstein
     Rabbi, K. A. M. Temple, Chicago

  IX. CURRENT PHILOSOPHIES OF JEWISH LIFE ✓   205
     Milton Steinberg
     Rabbi, Park Avenue Synagogue, New York

   X. ZIONISM IN AMERICAN JEWISH LIFE   231
     Sulamith Schwartz
     Editor, *Hadassah Newsletter*

  XI. CONCLUSION   251
     Oscar I. Janowsky

     EVALUATION OF THE PORTRAIT OF AMERICAN
     JEWISH LIVING

   I. THE JEWISH COMMUNITY AND THE OUTSIDE WORLD ✓ 261
     George N. Shuster
     President, Hunter College

  II. THE NATIONAL BEING AND THE JEWISH
     COMMUNITY ✓   270
     Horace M. Kallen
     Professor of Philosophy and Psychology, Graduate Faculty,
        New School for Social Research, New York

     SELECTED BIBLIOGRAPHY   287

     CONTRIBUTORS TO THIS VOLUME   299

     INDEX   305

PREFACE

IN TIMES of crisis, there is an instinctive urge among groups as among individuals to gain a deeper insight into the pattern of their living. Confronted by the threat of disaster, we come to recognize that knowledge of what we are and what we stand for is no longer a purely intellectual concern but a weapon in the struggle for survival.

Today, with the entire democratic order under challenge and attack, men and women everywhere are probing accepted institutions and time-honored ways of life and re-evaluating these in the light of the problems of our day. In this spirit, we Americans are turning with intensified earnestness to a study of our history, re-examining its fundamental concepts and traditions in order to discover direction and guidance in the shaping of present-day policy and action.

The threat to democratic ideals and institutions now so unmistakable was apparent a decade ago to those who saw in the seemingly unrelated acts of totalitarian powers the pattern of fascism itself. To the Jew in particular that relationship had become tragically clear. He sensed in the Nazi program and its principles not only the immediate threat to his own survival but the ultimate challenge to democracy and to the moral bases of civilization.

It was the awareness of that threat, and a compelling sense of obligation to make manifest its full significance and implications which led Hadassah, the Women's Zionist Organization of America, to expand the scope of its education program so as to include a comprehensive survey of contemporary Jewish life and Jewish values in the light of changing world forces. The publication several years ago of "Jewish Survival in the World Today" by Abraham G. Duker marked the first step in that program. The present volume, dealing specifically with the American scene, is the second.

In this book, we have attempted to survey, analyze and interpret the functioning of the Jewish group of America. Drawn in broad outline, this "composite portrait" has sought to discern the character, trends and values inherent in American Jewish life. We have indicated variants and shadings for we recognize that it is the sum total of divergences as well as similarities which make for the full-dimensioned portrait.

Our survey begins with a historical background of present day American Jewry which serves as introduction to the discussion as a whole. The subsequent chapters examine the varying facets of Jewish life—its religious, cultural, educational, philanthropic and communal activities, indicating in each instance animating ideals, both Jewish and general. It then proceeds to an analysis of anti-Semitism and of economic factors as they affect the Jewish group. The two final chapters deal with conceptions or ideologies of Jewish living and with the pervasive influence of Zionism. To round out the picture, the volume concludes with an evaluation by two distinguished American scholars—an evaluation not of the book but of the portrait of American Jewish living which the book attempts to reproduce.

In presenting this "composite portrait" of the American Jew to the general public, we do so in the belief that the attempt of any group to understand itself has significance to the whole society of which it forms a part. We are encouraged in this belief by the increasing acceptance of the fact that the United States is itself a composite of values contributed by its many groups. A respect for the distinct contribution of each group is an essential and distin-

guishing characteristic of American democracy. In fact, it is this
stress on the interplay, the merging rather than the submerging
of ideals and traditions which has made America the symbol of
unequivocal opposition to the enforced uniformity of totalitarianism.

It is hoped that this volume, begun as an educational project
within Hadassah, will find a warm and responsive audience
among all Americans; that it will fill a long-felt need for a comprehensive and readable analysis of American Jewish life, and
thus help to provide for the Jew a guide to participation, for the
non-Jew a basis of understanding.

This book owes its being to the sustained and devoted efforts of
the members of the Hadassah Education Advisory Committee
—to Dr. I. B. Berkson, Dr. Oscar I. Janowsky, Rabbi Milton
Steinberg and Marie Syrkin, who for upwards of a year met at
frequent intervals to organize and direct the preparation of the
materials now incorporated in this volume. The task of editing
has been the responsibility of Dr. Janowsky who has made of
this symposium an integrated whole.

In a broader sense, this book owes its being also to Henrietta
Szold who, as founder, implanted the principle that education
is an inseparable part of the Zionist effort; to Jessie E. Sampter
and her successors who formulated and directed the educational
projects of Hadassah; and to Rose G. Jacobs who was primarily
responsible for the initiation of the present expanded education
program.

Although not immediately related to this specific project, the
writer and the members of the National Board wish to acknowl-
edge a deep indebtedness to Dr. Mordecai M. Kaplan, whose
courageous and constructive approach to the problems of contemporary Jewish life has profoundly influenced a whole generation of those engaged in the field of Jewish education.

MARGARET G. DONIGER

EDITOR'S NOTE

THE EDITING of a volume involves a dual function: first, the planning of the contents and the selection of contributors; and second, the arrangement of the material in the unified and co-ordinated form of a book. The latter function was my responsibility.

The conception and design of the book as well as the choice of contributors was a task of the first magnitude. It was necessary first to visualize in broad outline the contours of the volume and the contents of the individual chapters, and then to select the proper person for each assignment. This task was performed by the Education Advisory Committee, working in cooperation with the Chairman of the National Education Committee of Hadassah.

In my own work of getting the material into final shape, I had the constant and invaluable aid of Mrs. Sundel Doniger and of the members of the Education Advisory Committee who read critically every manuscript. I am grateful to the contributors for their exemplary co-operation. Mrs. David de Sola Pool read the entire manuscript and Mr. Mortimer Hays, Dr. Harry S. Linfield and Professor Michael Kraus read individual chapters. The book has profited from their comments and constructive criticism. The index is the work of Miss Sophie Udin, librarian and director of the Zionist Archives and Library in New York City. Finally, I wish to express my appreciation of the unfailing courtesy and co-operation which I have received from Mr. Edward C. Aswell of Harper & Brothers.

Although this book has been prepared and published under the sponsorship of Hadassah, each author bears sole responsibility for his or her opinions and interpretations.

OSCAR I. JANOWSKY

THE AMERICAN JEW

HISTORICAL BACKGROUND

Oscar I. Janowsky

INTRODUCTION

"IT IS in the nature of man that where he sees a past he hopes still for a future." These are the words of a distinguished Hungarian statesman of the nineteenth century, and we might add with equal pertinence, that a living group which seeks to appraise the present and to mold the future must of necessity probe its roots in the past.

The casual observer of Jewish life in the United States (and not a few who play at Jewish leadership are casual observers) despairs of the future, because he knows nothing of the past. He surveys the Jewish scene of today with an inexpert eye. He looks in from without and not infrequently looks down from above. Like the traveler whose speeding car has just rounded the summit of a mountain, he catches only hasty glimpses. The growth on the hillsides is in a state of confusion and neglect. Withering trunks stand precariously in rocky soil, and branches are falling away. The underbrush grows wild and obscures all paths. The traveler concludes that the rolling country and the valley below have seen better days. He cannot distinguish between transplanted shoots which never struck deep roots, and sturdy saplings which the native soil and climate have reared. He lacks the time and concentration to observe that, in the distance, men and women are clearing paths and nursing plants which give promise for the future.

The casual observer of Jewish life sees only irrational multiplication of institutions and confusion of ideologies. Unacquainted with the past, he knows nothing of the successive layers of imported institutions, and of the process of selection which has been at work for nearly three centuries. If we are to understand the Jewish present in this country, and give direction to the fashioning of the future, we must inquire whence came the millions of America's Jews? Why did they come? What did they bring with them in their immigrants' knapsacks? How did they fit into the new environment? How and by whom were Jewish institutions designed?

A tour of the American Jewish past might well begin with a visit to the Statue of Liberty in New York Bay. The sonnet cast at the base of the statue reads in part:

> Mother of Exiles. From her beacon-hand
> Glows world-wide welcome; . . .
>
>   .   .   .   .   .   .
>
> "Keep, ancient lands, your storied pomp!" Cries she,
> With silent lips. "Give me your tired, your poor,
> Your huddled masses yearning to breathe free,
> The wretched refuse of your teeming shore,
> Send these, the homeless, tempest-tost to me,
> I lift my lamp beside the golden door!"*

These words, written by Emma Lazarus, a celebrated New York Jewess, are a fitting monument for the whole American people, but the immediate inspiration undoubtedly was the mass immigration of the persecuted Russian Jews. Compassion for the hapless victims of Tsarist fury deepened her appreciation of America as a haven for the homeless, just as the tolerant national-

* See "The New Colossus," in *The Poems of Emma Lazarus,* I, Boston, 1889, pp. 202-3.

ism of the New World led her to espouse the cause of a Jewish Palestine.

The Jews of the United States were among the millions of exiles who flocked to the New World. They were the tired, the poor, the huddled masses, the wretched, the homeless, the tempest-tost. They began coming as straggling individuals in a trickle which was barely noticed, and ended in a mighty torrent when a whole people, two million strong, found a homeland in the United States, in the short span of forty years (1881-1920).

ORIGINS AND GROWTH OF THE JEWISH POPULATION IN THE UNITED STATES

The Sephardic *(Spanish-Portuguese) Period*

A Jewish thread runs through the entire history of America, although the word "Jew" is barely mentioned in our history books. In the very discovery of the New World, Columbus was aided by Marranos, converted Jews who were high in the counsels of the Spanish court. The American historian, Herbert B. Adams, concludes in a happy phrase, when referring to the legend of Isabella's crown jewels, "Not jewels but Jews were the real financial basis of the first expedition of Columbus."* Yet, the narrowness of an intolerant age postponed for more than a century the open recognition of Jewish organized life in America. The gory inquisition perpetuated in Spanish and Portuguese America the hatreds and savagery of the Old World. But a breeze of freedom and tolerance blew up on the north Atlantic seaboard, where the Dutch and the English made their homes.

The first Jewish community in the United States was established at New Amsterdam, soon to be renamed New York. Twenty-three men, women and children, fugitives from South American bigotry, sailed into what is today New York harbor in September, 1654, but without the welcome which Emma Laz-

* Adams, H. B., *Columbus and His Discovery of America*, Johns Hopkins University Studies in Historical and Political Science, Tenth Series, X-XI, Baltimore, 1892, p. 486.

arus later discerned in the "Mother of Exiles." Like most refugees, they were poor, and their meager belongings had to be sold at auction to pay for their passage. But they were bold and self-reliant; they had to be, as pioneers who must depend on their own resources. The Dutch Governor, Peter Stuyvesant, would gladly have driven them forth, but wiser counsels prevailed in Holland, and he was obliged to allow them a grudging tolerance. Their political and economic rights were limited. Even the right of public worship was denied, for the bigot knows only too well that freedom is contagious. The establishment of a synagogue might have emboldened Lutherans and Catholics to rear their Churches, and the pattern of religious uniformity would have been torn to tatters. The newcomers, however, soon took root in the soil of America, not through the purchase of real estate, which Stuyvesant tried unsuccessfully to prevent, but through the laying out of a cemetery, part of which remains to this day.

Exactly ten years after the arrival of the Jews in New Amsterdam, control of the territory passed to the English, and the future of the Jews in North America was inextricably and permanently joined with the fortunes of the British settlers, who sought new homes and a new life overseas. The status of the Jews as an organized group was soon normalized through the recognition of the right of public worship, and before the seventeenth century had come to an end, the Jewish community of New York possessed a rallying center, a synagogue situated near lower Broadway.

During the century and a half preceding the adoption of the American constitution, Jews filtered into other seaboard settlements. But it would take us far afield to pursue individual Jews or isolated families. We are concerned primarily with the history of Jewish life in the United States, and the life of a group is evidenced in its institutions.

Rhode Island was the only New England colony which tolerated a permanent Jewish community in the seventeenth century. The

Puritans protested vigorously enough against religious requirements which they considered erroneous or oppressive, but they
were sufficiently part of their age to deny tolerance to dissenters
in their midst. Roger Williams, the guiding genius of Rhode Island, however, consistently maintained the belief in the separation
of church and state. The charter of the colony, secured in 1663,
declared that no person should be "any wise molested, punished,
disquieted, or called in question, for any differences in opinione
in matters of religion. . . ."* The Jews found this religious climate congenial, and a thriving community took root in Newport,
more than a hundred years before the American Revolution.

Jews found it possible to settle in organized communities in two
of the southern colonies and in Pennsylvania. In these regions,
liberals exerted strong influence in favor of religious toleration,
and an equally potent factor was the desire of the promoters of
colonization to attract serious-minded and hard-working immigrants. The Fundamental Constitutions of Carolina, drafted by
the great English liberal, John Locke, in 1669, contained provisions
guaranteeing religious toleration to "Jews, heathens and other
dissenters . . . ," and provided that ". . . any seven or more
persons, agreeing in any religion, shall constitute a church. . . ."†
This constitution did not remain in force for long, but the principle of religious toleration was not abandoned, and Jews immigrated into Charleston in numbers sufficient to organize a religious
community in 1750.

When Georgia was founded, partly as a humanitarian venture
to rehabilitate hapless debtors and oppressed German Protestants,
the Jews assumed that true humanitarianism could hardly exclude
their own poor and persecuted. A shipload of *Sephardic* Jews, and
another of German origin, therefore, reached the model colony
soon after the arrival of the first governor, James Oglethorpe. The
philanthropic trustees in London, as well as the settlers on the

* MacDonald, William (editor), *Select Charters and Other Documents Illustrative of
American History*, 1606-1775, New York, 1899, p. 128.
† MacDonald, cited, p. 165.

spot, were scandalized by the arrival of the unwelcome guests, and demanded their exclusion. But Oglethorpe made his own decisions and permitted the Jews to remain and to found the institutions necessary for group life.

A Jewish community was organized at Philadelphia about 1745. More than a half century previously, William Penn, an English upper-class Quaker, who had himself tasted the harshness of religious intolerance, inaugurated his "holy experiment" in Pennsylvania. Religious liberty was guaranteed not only to Christians of every description but to all who "acknowledged one Almighty and Eternal God to be the Creator, Upholder, and Ruler of the World."* Jews settled in several Pennsylvania towns during the eighteenth century, but they could not muster sufficient strength to build a single synagogue, until the dislocations of the American Revolution brought refugees to Philadelphia from New York and other towns. The effects of the Revolution were likewise instrumental in breaking down religious barriers in Virginia, where the sixth organized Jewish community took shape at Richmond in 1790.

At the time of the founding of the Republic, the Jewish population, concentrated chiefly in a half dozen seaboard centers, numbered between 2000 and 3000,† in a total population of about 4,000,000, or less than one-tenth of 1 per cent (1 in a thousand). During the following half-century, the Jews increased some 400 per cent, a rate of growth somewhat higher than that of the general population. By 1840, immigration and natural increase had raised the Jewish population to about 15,000 in a total of 17,000,000, still less than one in a thousand. The old Jewish centers had grown in numbers, new communities had sprung up in the east-

---

* See Greene, E. B., *The Foundations of American Nationality*, N. Y., 1922, p. 173.

† It should be remembered that all Jewish statistics in the United States, even those of the present, are estimates. We have no absolutely accurate statistics, because the census looks upon Jews as a religious group, and the decennial census makes no inquiries about religion. On the question whether such inquiries are desirable, see Linfield, H. S., *State Population Census By Faith*, N. Y.; Jewish Statistical Bureau, 1941.

ern states, and Jews had established themselves in the frontier towns, across the Appalachian Mountains and in the Mississippi Valley. Such communities as New Orleans, Louisville, Cincinnati, and Cleveland, date from this period.

If one were to examine closely the Jewish population at the time of the American Revolution, or even as late as 1840, one would discover a considerable number of German Jews, and even a sprinkling of East European origin. But the majority were *Sephardim,* tracing descent from Spanish and Portuguese exiles. The tone of Jewish life and leadership was in most instances provided by the predominant element which was wealthy and quite contemptuous of the poor and unpolished immigrants from Central and Eastern Europe. It is for this reason that the period which we have surveyed has been designated the *Sephardic* or Spanish period of American-Jewish history.

The German Immigration

During the generation following 1840, the United States passed through a period of expansion unique in the annals of history. The frontier was swept westward and southward until the present boundaries were reached. Railroad trunk lines and local branches girded the continent, annihilating distance and affording easy access to regions where land was plentiful and new life beckoned. Ocean transportation was revolutionized, so that the crossing could be effected by steamer in nine or ten days. Population increased with startling rapidity, largely because the desire for freedom and economic betterment, which had formerly impelled Englishmen to seek new homes overseas, now operated with equal force upon Irishmen, Germans and others.

German immigration was particularly numerous, and among the masses of Germans who settled in the United States during the nineteenth century were close to 200,000 Jews. Anti-Jewish prejudice, like autocratic government, died hard in Germany, and scores of thousands fled to escape grinding poverty, oppressive disabilities or, as in Bavaria, limitation upon the number of Jewish marriages.

Some of the German Jews settled on the Atlantic coast. Others moved on into the interior, and founded or developed such Jewish communities as Chicago, Cincinnati, Memphis, St. Paul and Indianapolis. The Middle West was then undergoing rapid development, and large numbers of Christian-German immigrants were settling on the land to till the soil, as they had done in their old homeland. In similar manner, the German Jews, who had long been accustomed to peddling and trading, took up the functions of middlemen among their former countrymen.

The German Jews began migrating to the United States before 1840, but perhaps a majority of them arrived during the two decades preceding the Civil War. As Jewish disabilities were swept away in their old homeland and economic conditions improved, mass emigration ceased. However, the character of American Jewry was quickly transformed. The *Sephardim* constituted but a fraction of the Jewish population, which remained overwhelmingly German until the 1880's, when the eastern wave of immigration set in. The forty years, from 1840 to 1880, might well be designated the German period of American-Jewish history. The religious, philanthropic and fraternal organizations which are associated with the German Jews were founded and largely developed during this period.

The Jewish population of the United States began its phenomenal growth during the years 1840-1880. In forty years, the number of Jews leaped from some 15,000 to about 250,000. The total population of the country likewise grew rapidly—from about 17,000,000 to some 50,000,000—but immigration enabled the Jews to increase at a rate nearly eight times as fast. In 1880, the American Jews comprised one-half of 1 per cent of the population of the United States.

The East European Immigration

During the last two decades of the nineteenth century, the agrarian frontier of the United States vanished. Good arable land ceased to be available for the hardy pioneer who braved the wilderness. But a new frontier appeared—the industrial frontier of the factory, the mine and the teeming city. The United States entered upon an era of rapid industrialization, which transformed the *extensive* economy of the country—a horizontal expansion, as it were—into an *intensive* economy. And just as previously there had been a crying need for labor to till the vast new lands, so limitless opportunities began to beckon to those who possessed the hardihood to man the machines.

However, the old sources of immigration appeared to dry up. Germany had been unified and was itself undergoing a phenomenal industrial transformation, which absorbed all available labor. Even Ireland, whose people had emigrated in such overwhelming numbers, was beginning to solve its virulent land problem. The starving tenants, who had formerly sought relief in flight to the United States, found new strength in unity and organization, which wrung concessions from the absentee landlords. The people of Northern and Western Europe no longer knocked at the gates of the New World in large masses, but their place was taken by the millions of Southern and Eastern Europe—by Italians, Poles, Russians, South Slavs and Jews.

Much nonsense has been written about the inferior quality of the immigrants from Southern and Eastern Europe. Even an historian of academic distinction has said, "Much of the immigration since 1880 has been of what may be called an unnatural character . . . the road to America has been made so easy that it no longer requires any special fortitude and courage to make the transit . . . the highly colored accounts . . . have tended to draw over many who are merely weakly restless and inefficient."*

* Fish, C. R., *The Development of American Nationality* (revised edition), New York, 1918, p. 512.

Obviously the learned professor never made the steerage journey across the Atlantic, nor did he experience the toil of sweatshop or mine. He certainly did not appreciate the "special fortitude and courage" required to tear oneself away from homeland and family, and to strike out into the unknown. The immigration from Southern and Eastern Europe was motivated by causes which were fundamentally no different from those which had affected Puritans, Germans and Irish. It was the desire for economic betterment, or freedom from persecution, or both, which led South and East Europeans, as it had previously impelled northerners and westerners, to seek a new life in the Land of Freedom and Promise.

The tidal wave of immigration which swept over the shores of the north Atlantic between 1880 and 1920 included two million Jews. The pogroms of 1881 are properly assigned as a reason for the mass migration of Jews from Tsarist Russia. But poverty and discrimination, though less sensational, were no less potent, and they affected Galician and Rumanian as well as Russian Jews. The *Bilu* movement with its slogan, "House of Jacob come let us go," revealed admirably the state of mind of Russian Jewry. Some migrated to Palestine. Others sought a haven in the New World.

The immigration of Jews into the United States increased markedly during the 1880's and 1890's, but the peak was reached during the years of turmoil and pogroms, which accompanied and followed the Russian Revolution of 1905. Masses of men and women, often in excess of 100,000 per year (when the total annual immigration was about 1,000,000) poured into a few eastern ports, notably New York, and were swallowed by the gaping factories, where they toiled and sweated and starved to save the few dollars necessary to reunite families, or to rescue more distant relations from the Tsarist inferno.

In 1920, the Jewish population stood at about 3,500,000 in a total population of about 106,000,000. In the forty years which witnessed the doubling of the total population, the Jews grew to be fourteen times their number (250,000) of 1880. Only one-half of 1 per cent of the population of the country when the eastern migration began, the Jews reached a proportion of 3½ per cent in 1920.

After the first World War, the United States Government embarked upon a policy of drastic restriction of all immigration, and the flood at once narrowed to a trickle. Thereafter the Jewish population continued to grow, but no longer at so rapid a rate. At the last census of religious bodies (1936), the Jewish population of the United States was estimated at about 4,777,000.*

INTEGRATION OF THE JEWS INTO AMERICAN SOCIETY

Political Adjustment

We have now traced the bare chronology of Jewish history in the United States. We have seen the Jews on the march, cut loose from their old moorings and gradually, painfully finding new anchorage in America. We must now look a bit more closely to see how they adjusted themselves to their new surroundings and struck roots in the new homeland.

The number of organized Jewish communities was small in colonial America, but individual Jews or families found their way practically into every colony prior to the American Revolution. This was especially true after 1740, when the British Parliament authorized the naturalization of Jews in the American colonies. The civil rights of residence, and of earning a livelihood without molestation, were thus achieved. But this constituted toleration rather than full equality. Religious tests, especially for holding office, were common, and although at times disregarded and Jews sat in several local legislative bodies, political equality was not achieved until after the Revolution.

The Constitution of the United States removed all religious disabilities, so far as the Federal Government was concerned.

* See United States Department of Commerce, *Census of Religious Bodies,* 1936, Bulletin No. 72, *Jewish Congregations,* p. 1; Linfield, H. S., "The Jewish Population of the United States," in *The American Jewish Year Book,* Vol. 43 (5702), Philadelphia, 1941, pp. 654-673.

Article VI, section 3, provided that "no religious test shall ever be required as a qualification to any office or public trust under the United States." The first amendment to the Constitution guaranteed the free exercise of all faiths, and prohibited Congress from establishing any church as the privileged religion of the nation. But the restrictions which individual states had imposed remained in force, and a long struggle had to be waged before local conservatism was overcome.

When the thirteen colonies repudiated British sovereignty and asserted their independence, new constitutions had to be drafted, and this afforded the opportunity to eliminate religious disqualifications. James Madison and Thomas Jefferson led the liberal forces in Virginia to victory in a conflict for religious equality which had a profound effect upon the entire country. No religious test for office was required in the New York Constitution. Pennsylvania soon removed the provision that members of the legislature affirm the divine inspiration of the New Testament. South Carolina first granted equal rights to all Protestants, but after a few years this was modified to include Jews. Thomas Kennedy of Maryland, who had not "the slightest acquaintance with any Jew in the world, . . ."* braved bitter opposition in his successful struggle to remove (in 1826) a religious test which had kept Jews from public office. Similar disqualifications remained on the statute books of a number of states—North Carolina until 1868 and New Hampshire until 1877—but common practice proved more liberal than formal law, and by the second quarter of the nineteenth century, the overwhelming majority of the Jews of the country enjoyed full political and civil equality.

Economic Adjustment

Religious differences delayed for a time the absorption of the Jews into the political life of their new homeland. No such handi-

* Quoted in Levinger, L. J., *A History of the Jews in the United States*, Cincinnati, 1930, p. 138.

cap hindered their full participation in the economic development of the country. The resources of the New World afforded unlimited opportunities, and the successive waves of immigrants quickly achieved economic usefulness, both to themselves and to their adopted country.

The early settlers were successful merchants, with valuable trade connections in England, Holland and the West Indies. They plied their trade in the seaboard towns, of which Newport, Rhode Island, was a leading entrepôt, especially in the eighteenth century. Some of the Jews figured prominently in the commercial life of the colonies. To cite but one example, Aaron Lopez of Newport owned a considerable number of ships at the time of the Revolution, and was widely known and respected among the mercantile aristocracy of the time. Ezra Stiles, a leading clergyman and President of Yale University, referred to Lopez in his Diary as ". . . a Merchant of the first Eminence; for Honor and Extent of Commerce probably surpassed by no Merchant in America. . . ."*

The German Jews who arrived in the nineteenth century were in the main poor petty-traders. As a rule, they began modestly enough with packs on their backs, or with horse and wagon. Industry, business acumen and thrift soon enabled the itinerant peddlers to open retail stores and, in time, many a great business establishment evolved from these small beginnings.

The families which have built some of our great merchandising firms may be traced to the German immigrants of the mid-nineteenth century. The Straus family is perhaps best known. Lazarus Straus emigrated from western Germany in the 1850's and, after a decade of peddling and retailing in Georgia, he settled in New York. His two elder sons, Isidor and Nathan Straus, built up the Macy and Abraham & Straus department stores.†

The German Jews were quickly absorbed in the American middle class, and considerable numbers of East European immi-

---

* *The Literary Diary of Ezra Stiles,* edited by Dexter, F. B., III, N. Y., 1901, p. 24.

† Another illustration is afforded by the Gimbel firm, the centenary of the founding of which at Vincennes, Indiana, was recently celebrated.

grants began to repeat the economic cycle of their Americanized coreligionists. They peddled and opened stores, and not a few achieved business success. But their numbers were much too great to be absorbed quickly in the middle class. Moreover, when the East European Jews arrived, machine industry was growing rapidly, and they possessed neither the capital nor the business contacts to compete successfully with the native employers. The bulk of the new immigrants, therefore, became an industrial proletariat, earning their livelihood as machine hands, chiefly in the needle trades.

However, the East European Jews did not remain a static and immobile proletariat. The industry and business ability, which had served the German Jews so well, asserted itself again, and before long the newcomers began to rival the native owning element in the light industry of the large cities. Considerable numbers of the second generation also took to schooling with avidity, and penetrated into the professions and into the rapidly growing white-collar classes.

Social and Cultural Adjustment

Thus, the successive waves of Jewish immigrants found freedom of economic enterprise in the United States almost from the beginning, and the political disabilities were gradually eliminated. The Jews responded to this treatment with enthusiasm. They quickly identified themselves with their new homeland and eagerly shared the dangers and sacrifices entailed in its defense and general welfare.

A small group, a minority, is always obliged to defend its position, because the intolerant elements among the majority often impugn its motives and cast aspersions upon its achievements. Jews have, therefore, resorted to apologetics, and Jewish apologists have been at great pains to prove that in every crisis which our country has faced, Jews have played their part and discharged their duty loyally. We are reminded time and again that the cause of the American Revolution was dear to the hearts of the Jews. They advanced funds when bankruptcy dogged the footsteps of the Patriots. Haym Salomon, an immigrant from Poland, threw himself into the cause with such abandon, that he risked his life and spent his entire fortune. Robert Morris, the financier of the Revolution, leaned heavily upon Salomon. He served as paymaster of the French troops; he negotiated the war subsidies from France and Holland; and he helped tide over impoverished members of the Continental Congress, such as James Madison.

In every crisis, the armed forces of the nation counted their Jewish fighting men and their Jewish dead. While no complete figures are available, at least forty Jews have been identified in the armies of the Revolution, at a time when the total Jewish population was under 3000. In the Civil War, more than 7000 staked their lives in the Union and Confederate armies. They served in the Spanish American War in the army, in the navy, and among the "Rough Riders" of Theodore Roosevelt. And painstaking estimates have established that in the first World War, more than 200,000 Jews served with the colors, 40,000 as volunteers. They constituted more than 4 per cent of the armed forces, when the Jewish population was hardly above 3 per cent of the total. Ten thousand Jews were commissioned officers. They had their share of casualties and of citations for valor.*

These facts occasion no surprise to anyone who has studied Jewish history. They are worth relating, but not in apology, for apologetics is a tiresome and fruitless sport. They are recalled here chiefly to show how thoroughly the Jews adjusted themselves to the life of free America. And this identification must be viewed in relation to the background of the immigrants. The *Sephardic* Jews had learned from gruesome experience to associate the state with the dreaded inquisition. To the German immigrants, govern-

---

* See Leavitt, Julian, "American Jews in the World War," in *The American Jewish Year Book*, Vol. 21 (5680), Philadelphia, 1919, pp. 141-155.

ment had meant discrimination and haughty contempt. And the fugitives from Russia remembered with horror the visitations of a savage or brutalized soldiery. But once in the United States, the Jews underwent a phenomenal psychological transformation. Some of the German immigrants who served in the Civil War, and many of the Eastern Europeans who served in the first World War, had but half learned the English language, and were only dimly conscious of the meaning of American civilization and culture. Yet, they felt part of their adopted homeland, and rallied to its defense.

The American pattern of tolerance and good will captured the imagination of the Jews at an early date. During eras of persecution, the Jew's psychic defense was contempt for the oppressor, and for the religion which appeared to sanction inhumanity. In free America, he learned to respect the faith of his neighbor, and expected equal regard for Judaism. Judah Touro (1775-1854), who removed from Newport to New Orleans, was the first great Jewish philanthropist in the United States. The founder of a synagogue, his devotion to Judaism did not preclude generosity to Christian fellow citizens. When a Universalist Church was foreclosed and sold at auction, he purchased the property and turned it over to the congregation rent free.*

To dismiss such liberality as merely the eagerness of a minority to please, would be to reveal a lack of understanding of the tolerant spirit of young America. When in need, the Jews did not hesitate to appeal to Christians for assistance. Shortly after the Revolution, when the young congregation of Philadelphia, *Mikveh Israel,* found itself in financial straits, aid was requested from non-Jews, and it was forthcoming, Benjamin Franklin heading the list with a contribution of five pounds. Such was adjustment at its best, Jews and non-Jews modifying ancient antipathies and learning to live together in harmony and mutual respect.

---

* This was far from an isolated case. In 1711, when a public subscription was raised for the steeple of Trinity Church in New York, several Jews contributed.

The identification of Jews with their adopted country was perhaps best expressed in homely verse, read when the Bunker Hill monument was dedicated at Boston in 1843. The building of the monument was made possible by substantial contributions from Judah Touro and Amos Lawrence, a non-Jew of Boston. The following lines were widely quoted:

> Amos and Judah—venerated names!
> Patriarch and prophet press their equal claims,
> Like generous coursers, running neck and neck,
> Each aids the work by giving it a check.
> Christian and Jew, they carry out a plan—
> For though of a different faith, each is in heart a man.

It was this basic equality which rendered true adjustment possible. The Jew was eager to identify himself with his country, and the non-Jew was ready to accept him on equal terms. Small wonder that Jewish names figure prominently in the growth and achievements of the United States. Numerous men and women have risen to high station in political and economic life, in the armed forces, in the ranks of labor, in literature, in the arts, and in the sciences. Perhaps the most celebrated Jewish name in American history is Louis D. Brandeis, first Jew to serve as Justice of the Supreme Court of the United States, and a powerful influence among the liberal forces of the country. He identified himself closely with American Jewry, and was an ardent Zionist.

We have stressed the underlying friendliness which the Jews found in the American environment, and which enabled them to become thoroughly integrated with the life of the country. It must not be assumed, however, that intolerance was totally in eclipse. Every age had its bigots, masquerading under various names—Nativist, Ku Klux Klan, Social Justice—and inveighing against "aliens," or Catholics, or Jews. In times of economic or political crisis, these dark forces have been able to exert considerable influence, but the democratic spirit has not yet failed to cast them off with disdain. Anti-Semitism cannot be ignored, and will be treated in a subsequent chapter. But it must be noted that its virus, while at times discoloring the surface, has never infected the main stream of American Jewish history.

THE JEWISH COMMUNITY—INSTITUTIONAL LIFE

The United States has thus afforded a home to masses of fugitives from European intolerance, and the Jews as individuals have found no serious difficulty in adjusting themselves to the American environment. What of their distinctive group life or, for want of a better term, what of the Jewish community in the United States?

In the course of nearly three centuries, the Jews have developed a great variety of institutions to serve their specialized needs as a group. There are religious bodies, educational establishments, philanthropic and social welfare agencies, fraternal societies, economic organizations, national cultural associations, federations for overseas relief and reconstruction, and goodwill or self-defense committees. The number of organized Jewish groups runs literally into the thousands, and their total annual disbursements have been estimated at well over $100,000,000, a figure which would compare favorably with the budgets of the smaller states of the world, particularly if military expenditures were deducted.

A critical analysis of Jewish institutional life is provided in subsequent chapters. Here we desire only to examine the nature of the Jewish community, and to probe into the discordant elements which have affected its unity.

German versus East European Jews

For two generations, the Jews of the United States have been popularly differentiated by the terms "German" and "East European." The words signify country, or region of origin, but the implications have run deeper. When the East European Jews arrived, their German brethren had already adjusted themselves to the American scene. They had become part of the middle class, while the East Europeans gravitated toward the proletariat. They were the donors, the newcomers, the recipients of charity. The German Jews were in contact with American social and cultural life, while the more recent immigrants were massed in a few large cities where the cultural *milieu* was more self-contained. And economic and social cleavages were hardened by ideological formulas.

It is a common human failing to regard oneself as superior to one's neighbor. This weakness has expressed itself in a widespread popular prejudice against immigrants from Eastern and Southern Europe.* The German Jews, immigrants of a preceding generation, could hardly remain immune to this bias, especially when recent arrivals were poor, outlandish in dress and appearance and untutored in American ways. Their justification of this bias was an afterthought, but it appeared plausible. Had not the German Jews avoided metropolitan ghettos and courageously scattered through the land? Had they not built the great philanthropic associations and fraternal orders which united Jewry? Had they not become Americanized quickly and almost imperceptibly?

This attitude was perhaps inevitable; it is certainly understandable, especially when one remembers that the German Jews had themselves been the victims of scorn and ostracism at the hands of the haughty *Sephardim.*† But it has no basis in history. Pretensions of superiority of German over East European Jews have no more validity than the Nazi chatter about "Aryan" preeminence. All Jews—*Sephardim,* Germans, and East Europeans—reacted to conditions which prevailed in America at the time of their arrival. All built institutions to meet their special needs, and every group contributed to the fashioning of the American Jewish community of today.

* See above, p. 9.
† See, for example, Lebeson, A. L., *Jewish Pioneers in America,* New York, 1931, pp. 116, 172-174, 195, 286.

Evolution of the Jewish Community

When the *Sephardic* immigrants arrived on the eastern seaboard, religious denominationalism was a distinctive feature of American life, and the church was the center of a good deal of the social and cultural activities of the time. The Jews, therefore, established a synagogual community. All Jewish group interests revolved about the synagogue and, if conditions had been favorable, a broad religious and cultural autonomy might have developed. But the basis was lacking for a variegated Jewish cultural life. The *Sephardic* Jews, or their ancestors, had been Marranos whose Jewish knowledge consisted mainly of fugitive memories, for Jewish learning and lore had largely faded from their consciousness. Charity could not serve as a stimulus for group activity and for inter-communal collaboration, because widespread and persistent poverty was not in evidence among this class of Jews. Local need, as it arose, was met by each individual congregation.

The communities of the various towns became in essence self-contained units, a tendency which was encouraged by the difficulties of communication in colonial America. Only on rare occasions do we find co-operative efforts, as when the congregations of New York, Philadelphia, Charleston, and Richmond addressed a joint letter of congratulation to Washington, when he was elected President of the Republic. Otherwise, the local synagogue met the Jewish needs of the individual. Prayer, the reading of the Bible, observance of the ritual and burial in a Jewish cemetery constituted Judaism. Since the day of the public school had not yet dawned, the congregation made provision for the secular as well as religious education of Jewish children. Beyond that, the *Sephardic* Jews were permeated with the prevailing secular culture of the time.

The German Jews, who immigrated about the middle of the nineteenth century, changed the character of American Jewry. They spread through the length and breadth of the land. They built great and lasting institutions which enriched Jewish com-

munal living. But all this was achieved not out of deliberate purpose, or special gifts of vision. Conditions prescribed the course
of action, and necessity was the mother of invention.

The German immigrants were in the main poor peddlers and
petty traders. As such, they were obliged to scatter and to seek
their livelihood in isolated little groups, for there was not room
in the eastern cities for scores of thousands in retail trade. As immigrants and Jews, they were not welcome in the non-Jewish fraternal organizations. They had to build their own *Landsmanschaften* and Orders and, dispersed in small groups over the land, it was
necessary to unite in national bodies, in order to render their work
effective.

Large numbers of the scattered German immigrants required
financial aid before they could become self-sustaining. Parochial
charity could not meet their needs, and synagogual sponsorship
would have proved a handicap because the congregations were
then torn by factional strife over the issue of religious reform.
Philanthropy, to be effective, had to be organized independently
of the synagogues and, where possible, the appeal had to reach
beyond the local community.

The German Jews met the challenge of the environment. They
built hospitals, orphan asylums, benevolent associations, and then
united these efforts in city-wide federations. They established
Y. M. H. A.'s, the first in New York in 1874, and they organized
lodges like the B'nai B'rith, which originated in 1843 in New
York, and branched out quickly into other parts of the country.
Nor were religious institutions ignored. Congregations and temples multiplied and in the 1870's, Isaac M. Wise, the leading
advocate of religious Reform, brought together many of the
reform groups into the Union of American Hebrew Congregations, and soon thereafter he inaugurated the Hebrew Union
College.

The German Jews thus broadened the base of Jewish living
in the United States. The term "Jew" signified more than mem-

bership in a synagogue, or observance of the ritual. It meant concern with Jewish communal conditions, such as poverty and dependency. It brought to mind unique fraternal and social institutions. Perhaps the greatest contribution of the German Jews consisted in their efforts to unite on a national scale, and to co-ordinate the work of the local groups. In the place of small, self-contained, independent "Jewries," as it were, which the *Sephardim* knew, an American Jewry emerged.*

However, Jewish living during the German period lacked depth, because the cultural content of Judaism was circumscribed. The masses of the German Jews were lacking in Jewish knowledge. Even in their old homeland, Jewish learning was in eclipse, and conditions in the New World were hardly favorable to a renascence. Religious reform, too, dispensed with much of Jewish tradition and custom, and severed the thread of continuity with the less distant past. For the mass of the Jews, therefore, Jewish living became the observance of a limited ritual and communal charity. It remained for the East European Jews to enrich the content and deepen the color of Jewish group life.

The exodus from Eastern Europe was a people's migration. Whole communities were transplanted, young and old, rich and poor, learned and ignorant. The newcomers had not been "merely weakly restless and inefficient"† in their old homes. They had experienced a deep political and cultural awakening, and had rebelled against the savagery of Tsarism. They had not only fled from persecution. Like the Puritans of a previous age, they came in search of a new home. And they possessed in full measure the courage, hardihood, and flexibility to become adjusted to the rigors of factory life. Middlemen and scholars learned new trades, mastered the intricacies of machine production and struggled successfully with the complex life of industrialism.

The genius for organization exhibited by the East Europeans

---

* It is hardly necessary to point out that improved means of communications, notably the building of railroads, made this possible.

† See above, p. 9.

was no less remarkable than that of the German Jews. The latter had come in an era of free capitalism and employed their talents to build great business enterprises. The Russian, Polish, Galician, and Rumanian Jews found in urban America a rampant industrialism, which provided work in factories under sub-human conditions. The vitality and resourcefulness of the pioneer—the pride of America—quickly asserted itself. The lowly immigrants organized gigantic trade unions and waged economic warfare with skill and determination. The great strikes of the needle industries exhibited discipline, tenacity, and leadership of the highest order. Even the rank and file understood that higher wages, shorter hours, and decent working conditions, while indispensable, were not sufficient as the goals of organized labor. They supported leaders who experimented with social insurance, arbitration and stability of employment. Some of America's most socially-minded and forward-looking trade unions were built by the East European Jews.

Jewish religious, cultural, and philanthropic institutions remained under the leadership of the German element for more than a generation. The immigrants accepted gratefully the proffered aid of their Americanized and more fortunately situated coreligionists. But they did not surrender their conception of Jewish living. The stately temples appeared too cold and forbidding to satisfy the religious needs of the masses, and a multitude of unpretentious synagogues sprouted like mushrooms. Dignified and decorous prayer was not enough. The *hassidim* (pietists) reproduced in America their unique joyfulness, and others looked to the house of prayer as a center of study and learning.

The East European Jews organized their own *landsmanschaften* and social welfare agencies for mutual aid and overseas relief, their own study circles, *talmud torahs* and *yeshivahs*. They built theaters and a formidable press, large and influential dailies as well as periodicals in the Yiddish and Hebrew languages. Writers of ability produced drama, fiction, poetry, and literary criticism in the vernacular, and the masses read the works with avidity. Zionist societies appeared, and co-operated with similar bodies in other countries, in furthering the national revival of the Jews, especially in Palestine. In time, the Eastern Jews penetrated the beautiful but culturally wanting halls of the Y. M. H. A.'s and fraternal orders, and began a process of education which is still in progress.

Even organized large-scale philanthropy and defense of Jewish rights abroad—unique contributions of the German Jews—were basically affected. During the nineteenth century, the Board of Delegates of American Israelites, and later the American Jewish Committee, had acknowledged the sense of kinship of America's Jews with their oppressed brethren in Russia, Rumania, and elsewhere. They had protested against persecution, and furnished financial aid to the stricken. The East European Jews championed the view that protests and provision for food and shelter were laudable but inadequate. They argued that once the effort is made to remove disabilities and sustain life of Jews abroad, American Jewry must concern itself with the needs of Jews, not only as individuals but as a national-cultural group; that the Jewish group required a national homeland in Palestine, and national-cultural equality in Eastern Europe.

This view encountered vigorous opposition, but in the end it prevailed. During the course of the first World War, it was debated thoroughly, and when the Peace Conference met, Louis Marshall, the undisputed leader of the anti-nationalist, mainly German element, co-operated in pleading for Palestine and minority rights, with Louis D. Brandeis, Julian W. Mack, and Stephen S. Wise, who had organized the American Jewish Congress and made the cause of the Eastern Jews their own.

Relation of Jewish Community to American Life

The multiplication of cultural institutions, which resulted from the mass immigration of Eastern Jews, extended the scope of

Jewish group life and involved a reappraisal of the relationship of the Jewish community to American society and culture. The national conflicts of Europe had aroused in some Americans a reaction of suspicion to all special group loyalties, save in religion, and religion was presumed to concern itself solely with worship and theology. In point of fact, the tolerant spirit of American life never required such rigid uniformity, but the patronizing attitude toward the newcomer resulted in misunderstanding.

It was assumed that the immigrant brought no culture with him, no institutions, no way of life. He was an empty vessel into which one could pour Americanism to the brim. With a superior and condescending air the high-pressure agencies demanded that the "aliens" abandon their "uncouth" manners, their "foreign" customs, their "un-American" appearance and their old world languages, which were viewed as jargons. They were to be "civilized" in a hurry.

The Eastern Jews, along with other immigrants, resented the attitude of the super-patriots. Perhaps because they had suffered from persecution in the Old World, they sensed the true meaning of Americanization and distinguished it sharply from Prussianization and Russification. The Prussian Junker and the Tsarist official sought to assimilate Poles or Jews by suppressing their languages and cultures. Americanization, however, is positive, and not negative. It requires that the immigrant learn the English language, and identify himself with the American way of life. But every American is free to maintain another, a supplementary language or culture.

The Eastern Jews eagerly sought to become Americanized. Adult men and women, who spent their days in factories, flocked to evening schools to learn English, American history, and civics. They sent their children to the public school. They became naturalized, and took part in the political and social life of their new homeland. But they were loath to discard their Jewish heritage.

For them, adjustment to American life involved a fusion of the best of both cultures.

Today, this position is being vindicated. Liberal-minded thinkers recognize that the immigrant brings a culture with him, one that has value both to himself and to America. The newcomer who abandons most readily his old mode of life does not make the best citizen. Conscious and rapid change creates personal and family demoralization, and produces the psychological maladjustment one finds not infrequently among children of immigrants. Americanism is not a one-way process, but a reciprocal one. The immigrants who preserve their group and cultural loyalties adjust themselves most readily to their new environment, and they enrich American life.

Conclusion

Any attempt to appraise the relative importance of each of the three layers of the American Jewish population would be puerile and futile. One should rather view the contributions of each, both to America and to the Jewish community, in historical perspective. Then it will be observed that every wave of immigrants simply reproduced the communal life which they had known in the Old World. All sought eagerly to become part of their adopted country, and all tried loyally to preserve Judaism. But they could hardly have been expected to do otherwise than build in their own image. The *Sephardic* ex-Marrano built a Judaism which he knew, one of ritual and prayer. The German Jew imitated the religious experimentation of the reform movement of his old home, and expanded communal living to include charity and fraternal societies as well as religion. The East European Jew, who had been part of a group steeped in tradition, learning and lore, stressed cultural values, and endowed the community with the cohesive force of group consciousness.

In each case, the institutions established were largely transplanted from the Old World, and adjustments were necessary before they could take root in the new soil. Neither a *Sephardic*, nor a German, nor an East European Jewish community has been reproduced in the United States, but we have a product of all three, and of the American environment. There has been a process of pruning and grafting and of soil enrichment. The tender shoot planted by the *Sephardim* has grown into a sturdy tree, but many of its spreading branches were grafted upon it by the enterprising Germans, and much of the life-sustaining fluid which preserves its suppleness and vitality can readily be recognized as that which animated and preserved Russian, Babylonian and Palestinian Jewry. The Jewish community of the United States is the product of an evolutionary process which is still in progress, and which is fashioning an American Jewry.

II

JUDAISM AND THE SYNAGOGUE

—

David de Sola Pool

THE SYNAGOGUE AND THE JEWISH COMMUNITY

AMERICAN Jewry has long been a composite of three well-defined groups. The *Sephardim* became in time a self-contained community, prosperous and largely loyal to their synagogue. The German Jews, in their eagerness to discover the essence of Judaism and to translate it into modern terms, experimented with religious reform. The masses from Eastern Europe made the attempt, at least during the first generation, to maintain a rigorous Orthodoxy.

What was it that held together the Jewish community in the early years of American history? The answer can be given in one word—the synagogue. One must not think of the early American synagogue as a magnificent building. The first synagogue built in New York City was a structure thirty-five feet square and twenty-one feet high. In that little synagogue, which stood on Mill Street for almost a century from 1730 to 1825, all New York Jewry worshipped.

The community had a simple organization. The leader was the *hazan* (reader) and he was assisted by the *shammash* (beadle), a bustling functionary with many and varied duties to perform. The care of the synagogue was his task and he must needs see to the cessation of work on the eve of the Sabbath and festivals and the timely awakening, long before dawn, of worshipers during the penitential period. In New York City, which gives the clearest and longest continuous picture of historical development, and in other communities as well, the group lived in close proximity to the synagogue, especially during the early period. But as the city expanded, the residents scattered, and by the beginning of the nineteenth century, most of the Jews lived at a distance from their one house of worship. In its last period, the Mill Street Synagogue was largely deserted of neighborhood congregants. The same centrifugal movement affected all the early synagogues of New York, so that none of their buildings has survived. Therefore, although one may recognize the synagogue as being the central cohesive force in early American Jewish life, one must also allow for the disruptive fact of American distances.

The little community sensed the danger of disorganization, and reached out to hold on to the Jews who were drawing away from immediate contact with the synagogue. Thus in 1736, the New York congregation declared that "we are not able to defray the charge of the congregation without the help and assistance of our brethren dwelling in the country, and by the consent of the majority of this congregation [we] order that every family or private person that carries on trade in the country and is in circumstances shall pay yearly for the use of this congregation to the Parnas for the time being the sum of forty shillings."*

The perils of dispersion ran deeper, for Jews were moving out into the vast hinterland. To leave the few towns where there were synagogues was to move physically out of Jewish life. There are numerous examples of Jewish pioneers who settled in the early days in New Haven, or St. Louis, or Louisville, or other towns and, for want of Jewish community life, were quickly absorbed into the Christian population. Indeed, some Jews of the seaboard towns, in which Jewish community life flourished, found it dif-

* *Publications of the American Jewish Historical Society*, XXI, 1913, p. 36.

ficult to comply with Jewish ritual requirements, especially when traveling. Peter Kalm, a Swedish botanist, describing conditions in New York in the middle of the eighteenth century, writes of the Jews: "They commonly eat no pork. Yet I have been told by several men of credit that many of them (especially among the young Jews) when traveling did not make the least difficulty about eating this, or any other meat that was put before them."*

The Jewish congregations made vigorous efforts to stem the tide of disintegration which the rarefaction of the community was encouraging. Warning signals were flashed to the scattered and straying members to stay within the fold. For example, during the latter half of the eighteenth century, the *Sephardic* congregation of New York repeatedly admonished the wayward that laxity in ritual observance would result in exclusion from office or honor in the congregation and, on occasion, total expulsion from the community and denial of Jewish burial were threatened. A prescript of 1757 is perhaps typical. It read, "Whosoever for the future continues to act contrary to our Holy Law by breaking any of the principal commandments [and in these were included 'trading on the Sabbath, eating of forbidden meats, and other heinous crimes'] will not be deemed a member of the congregation, have none of the *mitzvoth* [religious functions] of the synagogue conferred on him, and when dead will not be buried according to the manner of our brethren."†

These attempts to put constraints about the community and hold it together by force and in a single congregation always failed because of the American spirit and conditions of life. They were challenged not alone by individual defections, but as the community grew larger, by organized secessions. By 1825, the Jewish population of New York City had grown too large to be contained in the one little synagogue building which was only

---

* Kalm, Peter, *Travels in North America*: Reprinted in the *Manual of the Common Council of New York*, 1869, pp. 841-2; Daly, Charles P., *Settlement of the Jews in North America*, N. Y., 1893, p. 50.

† *Publications of the American Jewish Historical Society*, XXI, 1913, p. 74.

thirty-five feet square. Moreover, the Jews who were then arriving in larger numbers from Germany, England and Holland were
accustomed to the *Ashkenazic* (German) ritual. They wanted to
preserve their own pronunciation of Hebrew, their own melodies,
and their own traditional customs.

Furthermore, bringing with them a strict European standard
of Orthodoxy, they regarded the American congregation as in
some ways religiously negligent. They found a synagogue pre-
sided over by a *hazan* while they were accustomed to the leadership of a rabbi. Most of them settled in the residential district two
miles distance from the synagogue. The result was a secession in
1825, and the establishment of a second synagogue, *B'nai Jeshurun,* into which came English, Dutch and German Jews, with the
German element predominating. In its turn, *B'nai Jeshurun* gave
birth to a new off-shoot when three years later, in 1828, *Anshe
Chesed* was organized, and in the years immediately following,
other synagogues proliferated by secession. The determining factor in these divisions and reorganizations was diversity of background and country of origin, for German Jews were not thoroughly comfortable in a congregation of *Sephardic* or English
background, nor were Polish Jews altogether at home in a German synagogue.

Once the way was shown for the community to spread out into
numerous synagogues, the pull of decentralization became ir-
resistible, and all efforts to unite the fragments proved ineffective.
When unity could no longer be maintained around one synagogue, the attempt was made to build a cohesive *kehillah* (community) through control of the cemetery, of *shechitah* (ritual
slaughtering), *kosher* meat and Passover supplies, and of Jewish
charity, but this was all unavailing. All these functions originally
had been centered solely in the American synagogue and had
helped make it the focal point of an organized community. In the
eighteenth century, one could not be given Jewish burial in New
York City without the help of the synagogue, which adminis-

tered the sole cemetery and everything else that went with a funeral. In the nineteenth century, this became the function of competing synagogues, and in our day, it is a service which may be rendered independently of any synagogue.

In the eighteenth century, the synagogue held a monopoly on the control of *kashruth* (ritually prepared food). The one *shochet* (ritual slaughterer) was a paid official of the congregation. The preparation of *kosher* meat for the whole community was controlled, supervised and guaranteed by the synagogue. In the nineteenth century, the synagogue lost control of this essential of organized Jewish religious life. Similarly, in the eighteenth century, the production of *matzoth* (unleavened bread) and of other Passover fare was in the hands of the religious community. Today it is a purely commercial undertaking.

In the eighteenth century, all Jewish philanthropy was centered in the synagogue. Every transient poor person, every needy or aged ailing person, every poor widow and orphan, was cared for by the community through the synagogue. In the nineteenth century, as the community grew and the number of synagogues multiplied, philanthropy assumed the character of a completely independent, and often technically non-sectarian, specialized undertaking. In this way, the synagogue lost its position of centrality in American Jewish life. One could live and die as a Jew without ever turning to the synagogue, or being in any way dependent on it.

Thus, the Jewish community was reduced to fragments. The synagogue proved unable to maintain the all-embracing authority of its early days, and no other agency emerged with sufficient strength to afford comprehensive unity. But it would be a mistake to assume that this process was the result of wilful negligence or deliberate design on the part of American Jews. The determining factors must be sought in the conditions of life in the New World.

America was remote from the Old World. Europe was reached

by a three months' ocean trip, not without danger, and the Jewish pioneers were virtually cut off from the strong historic communities overseas, except for the arrival of individual immigrants. From time to time, emissaries came representing Palestinian institutions and various Jewish causes, but until about the year 1825, Judaism had to be a home-grown product of the United States. For the first two centuries of American Jewish life, there was neither rabbinical leadership, nor deep knowledge of Judaism among the laity.

Until the nineteenth century, American Jews were entirely without any higher Jewish education. The synagogue was led by a *hazan*, who in the early days was often a layman with a pleasant voice and some knowledge of Hebrew. There was no rabbi. In the absence of the rabbi, the *hazan* sometimes preached, or a notable layman would be called on to do the preaching on special occasions. When a question of ritual arose which required more knowledge than the *hazan* possessed, usually the community called on a learned layman. The rabbi is a very late arrival in the United States. An occasional itinerant rabbi would appear toward the end of the 1700's, usually seeking funds for institutions or individuals abroad. But it was only with the coming of the larger German immigration in the first third of the nineteenth century that rabbis began to settle. No Jewish scholars were produced in this country until late in the nineteenth century.

Jewish religious life has also been affected by the rather free social contact among the white population of America, which has prevailed with but occasional exceptions. In the inbred European ghetto, religious negligence had been more difficult than religious observance. Outside the ghetto, and especially in the dynamic environment of America, religious observance became more difficult.

In Savannah, Charleston, New York, Newport and other old communities, Jews and Gentiles lived together, worked together, did business together, played together, joined political clubs together, and lived their lives together, except in the distinctive aspects of religion. This freedom in social relations inevitably facilitated laxity in religious observance and a high proportion of intermarriage. The early small communities, faced with this problem in a severe form, had to make up their minds whether to recognize mixed marriage or completely to disbar it. As it increased and the community felt itself more and more weakened, communal regulations were passed prohibiting the proselytization of any non-Jew to Judaism. This radical step may have restrained some who contemplated marriage outside the fold. It undoubtedly was instrumental in inducing many others to sever all connections with the Jewish community.

The separation of church and state served further to limit the authority of the synagogue and to dissolve the natural cohesiveness of the community. The lay state has assumed many of the functions formerly discharged by church or synagogue, and what authority remains in the religious congregation rests on the good-will of a voluntary membership. Constraint is out of the question, for no one can be compelled to belong to a synagogue or religious community. There cannot even be in the United States a parallel to the German *Kultusgemeinde* or French *consistoire*.

This brief characterization of the history of the Jewish community in the United States reveals a continuous process of decentralization which has deprived the synagogue of the central position which it occupied in the early days. But it must be emphasized that Jewish religious life has progressed despite the forces of disintegration. Individuals on the periphery of Jewish living have fallen away in considerable numbers. Organized unity has vanished and uniformity of belief or practice has proved unattainable. Jewish spiritual life, however, endures in a variety of forms.

ORTHODOXY

Orthodoxy, the main stream of historical tradition, has been the Judaism of the overwhelming majority of Jews in the United

States. Yet, the term "Orthodoxy" does not accurately apply to this historical Judaism, because it means the profession of what is regarded as the right opinion, especially with respect to theological doctrines. A better term would be "orthopraxy," meaning correct practice of the regulations and customs of the religion. For orthodoxy in Judaism has never been seriously concerned about shadings of belief. It has found room for every type of Jew from the most rationalistic to the most mystical.

Because orthodox Judaism is based on authoritative written codes, it has an essential unity the world over. But local religious customs, many of them dating back many centuries, and with acquired authority of tradition, give it outward diversity in different lands. Orthodox Judaism in the United States in our own generation is far from identical with orthodox Judaism anywhere else. To some types of trans-oceanic Orthodoxy, it is hardly recognizable as such. For instance, Orthodoxy in the United States is not concerned with *payoth* (ear-locks), or the typical long black coat, or the *shaitel* (wig) for married women. An American synagogue can be orthodox even though the ladies' gallery may not be blocked off by a curtain or lattice work, or the reading desk set in the center of the synagogue. American Orthodoxy has tacitly almost forgotten the prohibition of shaving, the law forbidding the mixture of materials in one's garments, and hundreds of similar Jewish laws which in other ages and lands had unquestioned authority.

Moreover, within American Orthodoxy, there are different types and variations. Orthodoxy with an East European Yiddish background differs from the German variety, which is different in its turn from *Sephardic* Orthodoxy. There are still other forms, all transplanted to the United States and living side by side, each defined by its own group.

Thus, orthodox Judaism is not hide-bound and petrified. It is fluid, yielding to the currents of life. And it has always been so. In different ages and different countries, varying standards of Orthodoxy have prevailed. In Italy Orthodoxy has not proscribed the organ in the synagogue, and in England Chief Rabbi Adler allowed the mixed choir. In Paris the Consistoire permitted riding to synagogue by subway on the Sabbath, while in Shanghai the jinrikisha but not the automobile is permitted for this purpose. Often, the heterodoxy of one generation becomes the orthodoxy of another. Even the standard legal code of Judaism, the *Shulhan Aruch*, as printed, contains throughout two variations of Orthodoxy—one that of the *Sephardim*; the other more rigorous, that of Moses Isserles, the spokesman of Polish Jewry.

Needless to say, not all American orthodox Jews live up to their standards of Orthodoxy. Throughout the United States, especially outside of the largest cities, Orthodoxy is often a name rather than a representation of religious practices. In the very small communities, few are in a position to observe such cardinal traditions of Jewish life as the Sabbath or the dietary laws. Even in the larger communities, most Jewish businesses are open on Saturday. Yet, the great majority of American Jews are classed as orthodox, because their early training was orthodox, because the synagogue which they attend is orthodox, and because their home pays more or less respect to the Jewish dietary laws. Throughout the United States one can find large numbers of Jews who resort to orthodox ritual only on such occasions as a wedding, a funeral, or the celebration on Passover. These can be considered as at best only passively orthodox.

The strength of orthodox Judaism is its intensive and unbroken traditionalism. It clings to Hebrew as a sacred tongue, to the Hebrew Bible as its ultimate authority, to the Law of Moses as a way of life, to the admonitions of the Prophets for its ethics, to the outpourings of the Psalms for much of its liturgy. The intellectual foundation of Orthodoxy rests on the obligation of constant study of the Bible and rabbinical teachings by both old and young. Restoration in Zion is integral in its Messianic hope. Because of this intensive and unbroken traditionalism, Orthodoxy has held unswervingly to its course in the line marked by Moses, the Prophets and the Rabbis. But it is extremely difficult to maintain an ancient Hebraic tradition in modern times, outside of Palestine and outside of an essentially Jewish environment. Emancipation from the ghetto meant the dissolution of a social order in which intensive Jewish religious life was comparatively easy, and absorption in an environment permeated by western secular influences.

Since 1880, Orthodoxy in the United States has been overwhelmingly an East European type of Judaism, identified, for the most part, with first generation immigrants, whose synagogues have reproduced those of the Old World. The service in such synagogues, as a rule fervent and of a highly spiritual character, is usually much too long. Because of its length, parts of the service are read hurriedly and unceremoniously. As a result, the congregant cannot maintain a continued mood of rapt devotion, and the synagogue suffers at times from a lack of decorum which tends to alienate the young American generation.

There are other factors which have reduced the number of worshipers in the old-type orthodox synagogue. Its religious leaders quickly lost their influence. Coming to this country at a mature age, they rarely mastered the English language, and while immigrant Jewry rapidly Americanized itself in language and mores, the rabbis remained Yiddish-speaking and their deep and extensive rabbinical knowledge was of little use to the community. They grew more and more out of touch with their congregations and with the community as a whole. They found themselves with a very precarious tenure of office, and often economically stranded in some rundown street which had been a ghetto until their congregants moved away. While the community was constantly adapting itself to American standards, the rabbis and the synagogues of these rabbis stood still.

These orthodox synagogues, originally founded by immigrants at the foot of the economic and social ladder, have in most instances never succeeded in overcoming the handicap of poverty. As the immigrant and his children and grandchildren gain a firmer economic and social hold, they regard the demands of Orthodoxy as burdensome and tend to break away. Those who remain are, as a rule, the financially weak, and upon them rests the heavy burden of maintaining orthodox Judaism in America. The orthodox Jew pays very heavily for his observance of the Sabbath. He pays more for his meat, for the maintenance of his kitchen, for the observance of his Passover. He pays much more than do other Jews for the upkeep of an intensive week-day religious education. He is apt to contribute more for the support of relatives overseas, and he must, in addition, maintain his own orthodox institutions of social welfare.

This comparative financial weakness of orthodox Judaism as contrasted with other types of Judaism in this country is manifest in its institutions. The buildings, as a rule unpretentious, rarely have beauty. They are poorly supported and their religious functionaries even more so. The school is often pitifully unworthy of its great function, and the activities that go on in the typical old generation orthodox synagogues are few beyond the set religious services.

This poverty of the old type of orthodox synagogue has other unfortunate results. It impels some to seek financial support through memorial services. It leads synagogues sometimes to take sensational steps to gather a congregation. It tempts them to cover the walls with the names of contributors. So does poverty tend to degrade a noble institution.

The poverty of the Jewish masses and the difficulty of strict orthodox observance in part account for the fact that there are too few orthodox synagogues in a city like New York. The total number of permanent synagogues in New York City is 1,330. Allow a generous average of 300 seats for each synagogue, and we have 400,000 seats in permanent synagogues in New York City with its community of more than two million Jews. Deduct from that two million the young children under nine years of age (13½ per cent or 270,000), and even those from ten to thirteen

(7½ per cent or 150,000). Allow further, half a million for the sick and aged, the non-religious, the radical, the atheist, the ethical culturists, and other unsynagogued Jews, and there still remain well over a million supposedly synagogued Jews for whom there are only 400,000 seats in synagogues. What happens to these six hundred thousand, and the 150,000 children ten years and older, who have no seats in a synagogue even on *Rosh Hashanah* and *Yom Kippur*? Partial disregard of women and girls has served as one means of meeting this deplorable situation. Another is the commercialized and often harmful "mushroom" synagogues set up in moving picture houses and similar establishments.

If orthodox Jewry had succeeded in achieving a semblance of unity, some of these problems would undoubtedly have been resolved through common action. But organization has proved supremely difficult. The heterogeneity of American orthodox Jewry is one factor of difficulty. It comprises Lithuanian, Galician, Polish, Rumanian, Bessarabian, Hungarian Jews, as well as those of more western type, such as English, Dutch, German, Austrian, etc. Add to these the Syrians, Yemenites, and others, and it becomes clear how superlatively difficult it is to organize a community out of these chaotically disparate elements.

Nor is this all. Every rabbi is in theory the equal of every other rabbi. There is no hierarchy. A rabbi is simply *primus inter pares*. He is the equal in authority of anyone who has authoritative ordination (*semicha*). It is, therefore, inordinately difficult to organize the orthodox rabbinate. All synagogues are likewise equal in rights and authority. No synagogue is dependent on a parish or a cathedral synagogue. Therefore, the community faces great difficulty in organizing its synagogues. The 1936 census of religious bodies listed over 3000 synagogues as orthodox. Yet after forty-three years of work, the Union of Orthodox Jewish Congregations of America has not drawn even one-tenth of this number into its membership. This is due in part to the excessive individuality of the average Jew. The German Jew, accustomed to discipline, is much more amenable to organization than is the East European Jew or the *Sephardic* Jew. Therefore orthodox Judaism in America has barely begun to advance beyond the stage of the highly individualized *landsleute* synagogue which goes its own checkered way without deference to any organization.

More than a half century ago (in 1888), an heroic attempt was made to unite East European orthodox Jewry of New York. A plan was worked out for a federation of orthodox communities to be financed, as similar orthodox communities financed themselves in Eastern Europe, by a *korobka* (a tax on *kosher* meat). The distinguished Rabbi Jacob Joseph of Vilna was brought over and installed as spiritual leader. But three difficulties were overlooked: first, that theoretically any rabbi in a little synagogue was as authoritative as was this great rabbi; second, that the supervision and supply of *kosher* meat could not readily be centralized; and third, the pervasive power of the American principle of the separation of church and state, which made it inordinately difficult to collect a tax on *kosher* meat. When the revenues failed, the attempted organization fell to pieces.

It is disunity and poverty, as well as the exacting nature of the orthodox ritual, which are responsible for the relatively minor role of Orthodoxy in American Jewish life. The management of communal affairs has increasingly come into the hands of those who are not orthodox. It is they who direct the affairs of federations, and who have the determining voice in the government of community chests and welfare funds. Thus the orthodox majority does not have its proportional influence in the organizations which give character and direction to the community as a whole.

There is, however, another side to this gloomy and unhappy picture. True, it has been stupendously difficult to organize orthodox Jewry in America. Nevertheless, progress has been made. The Union of Orthodox Jewish Congregations was founded in

1898. Rabbis also have attempted, and with some success, to unite for common purposes. The Union of Orthodox Rabbis (*Agudath Harabbanim*) has existed for forty years. The Rabbinical Council of America, organized in 1923, is made up of many of the English-speaking American trained younger generation of orthodox rabbis. These are promising attempts to extricate orthodox Jewry from the stultifying chaos of individualism.

In other ways also, American Orthodoxy is making conscious and vigorous attempts to save itself. More and more, one hears of a modern American Orthodoxy, an Orthodoxy which blends with the American scene. Many pulpits, no longer Yiddish, are occupied by English-preaching graduates of the Yeshivah Isaac Elchanan, or of the Hebrew Theological College of Chicago. These seminaries are modern institutions of the highest Jewish learning, which have trained scores of rabbis of unquestioned scholarship, and of authority, ability and influence. More and more are these rabbis helping bring about a rejuvenation and reintegration of Orthodoxy in communities where traditional Jewish life was largely disintegrating.

The status of the orthodox rabbi has been happily raised in the last generation. He no longer belongs to a Jewish social and cultural type that is passing. Increasingly rare is the orthodox rabbi at large, obliged to earn a precarious living through general communal functions. The young orthodox rabbi of today is attached to a synagogue which assures him a livelihood, and enables him, because he has some security, to exercise his authority in American Jewish life.

The modern orthodox synagogue is increasingly manifesting the influence of American standards. Through the country, one finds that small and financially weak communities often erect synagogues which are adequate and sometimes beautiful. Attempts are made to provide orderly and dignified services, and much is done to make them attractive to the young. Male choirs have been introduced and, not infrequently, junior services are held. Activities, like the *Oneg Shabbat* (Sabbath social gathering), lectures, and social gatherings, unknown to the old type orthodox synagogue, are today not uncommon attractions. The little congregation concerned only with religious services is rapidly disappearing from the scene. Its place is being taken by an organic institutionalized synagogue which conducts, besides services, center activities and a religious school.

A characteristic development of American Orthodoxy is the Young Israel movement. This comprises some seventy synagogues with an estimated total membership of about 10,000. The average Young Israel Synagogue is composed of the children of immigrants who, finding themselves uncomfortable in their parents' synagogues, organized modern orthodox congregations of their own. In some of these institutions, the services are conducted by the members themselves, for there is still some Hebrew learning in the laity, and the synagogue gets along without a rabbi, until such time as it becomes financially capable of maintaining one.

Finally, we must touch on the fundamental consideration, the modernizing of orthodox religious education. The first generation of American Orthodoxy knew the *heder* (informal private school) and other woefully inadequate types of religious schools conducted by men who often were quite unqualified as teachers. The country is now dotted with modern orthodox religious schools, which attempt to provide that intensive Jewish religious education without which the survival of Judaism is impossible. These schools are directed by trained educationists and by modern American trained rabbis.

Thus, the struggle is very far from being lost. In some ways, orthodox Judaism is stronger today than it was a generation ago in the United States. Then the community did not recognize how weak it really was, because the constant leakage and loss was counter-balanced by immigration. Now with immigration stopped, the effort is being made to nurture an American Orthodoxy. The environment has not destroyed the orthodox synagogue, but rather is modifying and transforming it into what may truly become an American orthodox synagogue.

REFORM, RECONSTRUCTIONIST AND CONSERVATIVE JUDAISM

Reform Judaism was born in Germany early in the nineteenth century out of an attempt to meet the challenges which appeared to threaten the very existence of the Jewish people. The sudden destruction of the ghetto, and the incorporation of Jews into European society, worked havoc with traditional Jewish beliefs and customs. The rationalistic temper of the age undermined faith. The yearning of the Jews for full citizenship, and their desire to participate fully in the life about them, resulted in impatience with ancestral practices which imposed restraints and interposed barriers between Jew and Gentile. In consequence, there was a widespread flight from Judaism in Germany, and apostasy became rampant.

Religious and lay leaders, distressed by the apparent disintegration of Judaism, sought to preserve what they considered the essentials of their faith, namely, ethical monotheism and prophetic idealism. Other beliefs and ceremonial practices were viewed as of secondary moment, and many were modified in accord with the demands of the time. In the specific innovations, the Christian German environment inevitably exerted its influence.

The *shule* became the synagogue, and eventually the temple. The architectural form of the synagogue tended to become an auditorium, with a platform faced by seats. The men and women were seated together in pews. The ark was spoken of as an altar. The *tallith* (prayer shawl) and *tefillin* (phylacteries) disappeared as did the head covering for men. Prayers were translated into German, and Hebrew was used less and less. The traditional Jewish music of the synagogue came increasingly under the influence of, and eventually was displaced by, German standards of church music, with copious borrowing of hymn melodies and anthems of

Catholic and Protestant composers. The temple introduced the mixed choir and, as a rule, it was open for prayer only at weekends. So the process went on of adapting and adjusting the synagogue and Judaism to what the reformers believed to be the standards of the new age.

The postulate that the Jews were only a religious denomination of Germans without any cultural nationality of their own necessitated the elimination of much that had been characteristic and fundamental in Jewish life. The Hebrew language was minimized and, while references to Zion were not taken out of the Bible, they were removed from the prayer book, or else so denatured as to become purely universal and without recognizable Jewish significance.

In the light of what twentieth century Germany has done to the Jew, this attempted Germanization of Judaism has proved a sterile and pitiful policy. In fact, German reform Jews themselves came to recognize this, in a measure, and reacted against many of their own earlier assumptions. Reform Judaism in Germany, in time, tended to become more conservative.

In the meantime, however, early German reform Judaism was exported to the United States. Here it was developed by the German Jews who immigrated in increasing numbers after the first third of the nineteenth century. In the United States, this transplanted theory of Judaism found a wide open field for development, without the constraints which old-world standards had placed on German reform Judaism. In the open spaces of America, with the American spirit of freedom and innovation, Reform proceeded to go to extremes, and relaxed or abrogated not only incidental customs and rigoristic regulations, but also some of the most fundamental and characteristic of Jewish laws and practices. At times, the "modernization" of the synagogue service came perilously close to the obliteration of its distinctive Jewish character.

German reform Judaism took root in this country and flourished prodigiously. It began as an exact reproduction of German Reform. The earliest reform movement in this country, that of Charleston in 1824, was modeled closely after the Hamburg movement. Later projects of American Reform were also essentially of German transplantation. The very name of the reform synagogue was usually *"Reformverein."* The language used was German, just as the language in the transplanted orthodox synagogues in the 1880's and 1890's was Yiddish.

David Einhorn, one of the nineteenth century rabbinical leaders of reform Judaism in this country, declared the German language essential to American Reform. He said, "Take away from reform Judaism the German spirit, or what is the same thing, the German language, and you have torn away from it the mother soil and it must wither away, the lovely flower. The English sermon can have for its mission nothing else than to utilize the treasures of the German spirit and German literature for our religious life and therewith to enrich it. In a word, where the German sermon is banned, there the reform of Judaism is nothing more than a brilliant gloss, a decorated doll, without heart, without soul, which the proudest temples and the most splendid theories cannot succeed in infusing with life." Naturally such ideas, transplanted to an environment where they had no validity, did not survive. In time, reform Judaism in the United States shed its imported German characteristics and developed an independent American outlook of its own.

During the latter part of the nineteenth century, the reform temple in America became increasingly radical. In the Pittsburgh Program of 1885, the Central Conference of American Rabbis asserted the right to change the religious traditions of Judaism or to abolish them at will. Among the principles enunciated were the following:

> We recognize in the Mosaic legislation a system of training the Jewish people for its mission during its national life in Palestine,

and today we accept as binding only its moral laws, and maintain only such ceremonies as elevate and sanctify our lives, but reject all such as are not adapted to the views and habits of modern civilization.

We hold that all such Mosaic and rabbinical laws as regulate diet, priestly purity, and dress originated in ages and under the influence of ideas entirely foreign to our present mental and spiritual state. . . .

We recognize, in the modern era of universal culture of heart and intellect, the approaching of the realization of Israel's great Messianic hope for the establishment of the kingdom of truth, justice, and peace among all men. We consider ourselves no longer a nation, but a religious community, and therefore expect neither a return to Palestine, nor a sacrificial worship under the sons of Aaron, nor the restoration of any of the laws concerning the Jewish State.*

And practice did not lag far behind theory. For example, Saturday Sabbath services were sometimes entirely supplanted by Sunday morning services. Such minimizing of distinctive Jewish character led Max Nordau, the famous Zionist leader, to refer to the temples as churches without a cross.

However, a reaction soon set in. The Pittsburgh Program, in particular, came as a violent shock not only to the orthodox, but also to the more moderate reform Jews. They saw in it the danger of every man doing that which was right in his own eyes. Once it is granted that there is no divine law too sacred to be tampered with, and that a distinctive religious tradition must be accommodated to the standards of the environment, there is no logical stopping place in the process of adaptation. Many felt that the American reform temple was cutting itself off from the Jewish past, present and future, and from the characteristic religious tradition and feeling of all Israel.

The reaction against radical Reform was strengthened by social factors in American Jewish life. The energetic, efficient and busi-

* See Philipson, David, *The Reform Movement in Judaism*, N. Y., 1907, pp. 491-492.

nesslike German Jew had established himself quickly in the United States and, not infrequently, had achieved wealth. His means had enabled the temple to expand into a grandiose building, with a large budget and heavy upkeep cost. During the nineteenth century, one had to be prosperous to remain in good standing in a temple. Reform Judaism consequently did not attract the poor.

But as the immigration of East European Jews increased and that of German Jews dwindled, the reform temple began to let down its social barriers. Gradually, East European Jews, with memories of orthodox practices, came into the pew and into the pulpit, and the demand arose for more traditional practices in the temple and in the home. Graduates of the Hebrew Union College who had been raised as orthodox Jews and who knew the fervent Jewish life of the East European masses, brought into the reform temple a new type of Jewish knowledge, an increased desire for Hebrew and for Jewish ceremonial, and in the last phase, a sympathy with Zionism. In the early days of Reform in America, it was often the rabbis who had taken the lead in drawing their congregants away from traditional Judaism. But more recently, not a few reform rabbis have been trying to lead their congregations back to more traditional Jewish standards.

The same change has taken place in the attitude of Reform toward Zionism. It had been a cardinal principle of the reform creed that the Jews constituted not a nationality, but only a religious communion. When Zionism emphasized the historic national elements in Judaism, the Central Conference of American Rabbis, in convention after convention, denounced Zionism as an aberration. Today, *Hatikvah* (Zionist hymn) has a place in the Union Hymnal, published by the Central Conference of American Rabbis and used in all reform temples. The attitude toward Zionism is left to the individual leanings of the reform rabbi and his congregation. The majority of the reform rabbinate, especially of the younger generation, is positively sympathetic to Zionism.

There is now a purposive desire and policy on the part of Reform to recapture and restore more and more of the color and life of historic Judaism. Early Reform scorned *Purim* as a nationalistic Jewish festival; today *Purim* is reintroduced with a shortened *megillah* (the Book of Esther), prepared in traditional scroll form. Early reform discountenanced the *shofar* (ram's horn), and substituted for it a cornet or an organ call; today the *shofar* is reappearing, albeit with a wooden mouthpiece.

The tendency of the reform temple to return to tradition should have a salutary effect upon American Jewry as a whole. For, although there are only about 300 reform temples in the entire country, they exercise an influence far out of proportion to their numbers. As East European Orthodoxy yields its rigidity under the impact of American life, and as Reform encompasses more of the cultural and historical aspects of Judaism, there should emerge a more unified Jewry, characterized by greater understanding and co-operation.

Within the last generation, there has been developing a new type of reform of Judaism called Reconstructionism. Like orthodoxy, Reconstructionism denies that Judaism is simply a religion. It terms Judaism a religious civilization and emphasizes, besides the religious elements of worship, ceremonial, faith and ethics, also folkways—its technical term for Jewish customs and mores. It has already been pointed out that these folkways vary from land to land and from generation to generation, and that over the centuries orthodox Judaism has taken on differing aspects reflecting its life in various countries. The fact that there is no uniform Judaism has been used by Reconstructionism to validate its attempt to set up a planned Judaism reconstructed out of its theology and its folkways.

Reconstructionism differs from reform Judaism in holding that

Hebrew is essential, not only as a religious language, but also as a living language. Unlike Reform also, Reconstructionism is by definition Zionist, and it is pledged to the rebuilding of Zion. Finally, Reconstructionism regards Jewish cultural values in literature, music, art, and other branches of Jewish folkways as integral parts of Judaism.

In the view of this writer, Reconstructionism is not an organic growth from within but a deliberate re-forming or re-construction of Judaism. Its vision of God is not the historic conception of the Jewish people, but rather a reconstructed image of sociology. The folkways which it emphasizes are mainly those which help Jewish survival, whereas in orthodox Judaism, folkways (*minhagim*) are less a means to an end than an end in themselves. It is difficult at this time to characterize the reconstructionist synagogue, as it is still in the initial stages of defining itself with liturgical and other experimentation. It has not yet attained definitive character of its own.

Another movement that has been developing in American Jewish life during the last generation is conservative Judaism. Outstanding is its emphasis on the cultural elements of Jewish life. Conservative Judaism, unlike Reform, insists on the traditional observance of the Sabbath and the dietary laws, on the Hebrew language and on the place of Palestine in Jewish life. In all this, it remains close to orthodox Judaism.

Conservative Judaism began to evolve during the first and second decades of the twentieth century, under the leadership of Professor Solomon Schechter, the head of the Jewish Theological Seminary, which was founded and designed as an orthodox institution by Sabato Morais, H. Pereira Mendes, and others. The influence of Schechter still pervades the movement, and conservative Judaism has been limited almost entirely to the Jewish Theological Seminary and its alumni. The Rabbinical Assembly of America, the authoritative voice of conservative Judaism, is composed almost entirely of graduates of the Seminary, and the 350 synagogues which are affiliated with the United Synagogue of America are likewise associated with this rabbinical institution. Conservatism is the lengthened shadow of the Jewish Theological Seminary.

Wherein does conservative Judaism differ from orthodox Judaism? It differs markedly from East European Orthodoxy. But East European Orthodoxy, as we have seen, is not American Orthodoxy. Historic American Orthodoxy is the Judaism of the historic American *Sephardic* synagogues, the Judaism of Isaac Leeser, who emphasized the English sermon, the English translation of the prayer book, and the English translation of the Bible; of Morris Raphall, S. M. Isaacs, H. Pereira Mendes, Sabato Morais, Lewis N. Dembitz, and Cyrus Adler. This American Orthodoxy adapted itself to the American environment, without sacrifice of essential Jewish values. It has an anglicized pulpit, an English-speaking rabbinate, and orderly and aesthetic services. It offers a modern Jewish education, and believes in the freest and fullest secular education.

However, at the end of the nineteenth century, the mass of orthodox Jews in the United States were Yiddish-speaking immigrants who were committed to an uncompromising rigidity of faith and exotic practice. Therefore, those who felt the need of expressing Judaism in more American terms were compelled to assert themselves in an independent movement. The essence of what Schechter did was to emphasize the necessity of meeting certain American conditions more rapidly than the East European Orthodoxy of the immigrant Jew was willing or able to do. Conservatism set out to provide a modern and forward-looking Judaism for the American-born child of the immigrant who no longer felt at home in his father's synagogue.

Today it is growing increasingly difficult to define what is the essential organic difference between Orthodoxy and Conservatism. The main differentiae seem to be that conservative synagogues permit men and women to sit together, and make more use of

English in the services than do most orthodox synagogues. Yet, some orthodox congregations use some English in their services, hold late Friday evening services and seat the sexes, if not together, at least on one floor. No logical or clear line can be drawn today between American Orthodoxy and Conservatism. But it must be remembered that Conservatism has not yet definitely found itself. Lacking either the crusading iconoclasm of early Reform or the fervent certainties of historic Orthodoxy, it is still vacillating between a moderate reform and a flexible Orthodoxy.

THE OUTLOOK

The perils which threatened the survival of Judaism and the synagogue in the early years of American history have not been overcome. Indeed, the powerful secular tendencies of our own day have strengthened the centrifugal forces. In the smallest communities, Judaism finds it extremely difficult to withstand the disintegrating influences of the free assimilation which prevails, and intermarriage with non-Jews results in the abandonment of Judaism by appreciable numbers. For those who remain in the fold, Jewish life is often barren, with few cultural interests and practically no rabbinical leadership.

The disproportionate urbanization of Jewish life in the United States, and the concentration of Jews in metropolitan centers, has, on the whole, likewise proved a source of weakness. True, the large city offers a cultural richness and variety of Jewish life which one cannot find in the smaller centers, but organization is correspondingly more difficult. In ancient days, the man of the countryside was the man who was apt to escape the influence of organized religion. Today, it is the man in the big city who finds it easiest to turn his back on the synagogue. The Jew living in New York City can, if he wishes, evade every Jewish communal responsibility. He does not have to belong to or support a synagogue, or any Jewish organization. In the smaller community, social pressure makes it much more difficult to evade these responsibilities.

To be sure, the Jewish population, particularly in the larger towns, maintains a variety of institutions, but direction and control of these agencies of Jewish communal life have slipped from the hands of the congregational leaders and the synagogues or temples. More and more, the directive power in American Jewry is vested in the hands of the un-synagogued. For example, the community welfare funds and the federations of charity, which have become almost exclusively secular, are conducted in many instances by social workers who happen to be Jews by birth and work for Jews, but who do not work *as* Jews. The character of the Jewish community is being determined in large and increasing measure by individuals and by organizations virtually independent of the synagogue, while the synagogue is playing a subsidiary part in the totality of organized Jewish life.

What of the future? Without assaying the dangerous task of prophecy, it is necessary to appraise current trends in the light of the foregoing analysis and to suggest, in broadest outline, the direction in which Judaism should be guided.

It is a truism that Christianity, like Judaism, has been basically affected by the modern environment. What are some of the currents in American Christian life? Protestantism is barely maintaining itself, but Catholicism is gaining in this country. Does this mean that the religion which makes less demands, and sometimes minimal demands, fares worse than the religion which makes maximal demands? Or does it indicate that the religion with less pomp and pageantry appeals less to the religious emotions of the public than does the religion which impresses with its ceremonial? Or does it mean that a more rationalizing religion appeals less than one that makes demands of a more unquestioning faith? Humanism is not self-reproducing; it has made no momentous gains since the time of Voltaire or Jefferson. Unitarianism is weaker today than it was in the Victorian era.

Ethical Culture remains a still-born movement that is scarcely attracting new membership. Contrast this with the vast gains of a movement such as Christian Science with its appeal for a fervent faith.

The relationship of reform Judaism to Orthodoxy is broadly analogous to the relationship between Protestantism and Catholicism. Reform is more rationalizing, it has less pomp and ceremony, and it makes less demands than the old Orthodoxy out of which it grew in a "reformation." In the light of this, it is interesting to note that reform Judaism in America is either stationary or retrogressing in numbers. In 1930, the families affiliated with the Union of American Hebrew Congregations were 61,609. Ten years later, in 1940, the figure was smaller. In 1940, families affiliated with reform temples in New York City numbered no more than 6,516 out of a Jewish community of two million souls. Manifestly, reform Judaism is not attracting the masses. Is this because it is too precise, too well-mannered and correct, too formally aesthetic? Whatever the reason, reform Judaism has barely maintained itself by replenishments from Conservatism and Orthodoxy. However, the recent trend in Reform to provide more color and more historical continuity to Jewish life through greater emphasis on the Hebrew language, folkways and *Torah* (Jewish tradition—literally, teaching) may enable it to satisfy the spiritual needs of increasing numbers.

It is difficult to speak of the future of Conservatism because it has not yet clarified its position. The positive elements of Conservatism approximate American Orthodoxy. Conservatism is basically traditional in outlook and American in character. It attempts to be consciously self-adapting within the *Torah*, and in identifying itself with Zionism, it has preserved a fundamental tenet of Jewish tradition and, at the same time, satisfied a deep spiritual yearning of the Jewish masses.

What promise is there in Orthodoxy? In so far as it has been identified with the foreign-born, it is passing from the scene. Yesterday's immigrant population which maintained Orthodoxy will be the American population of tomorrow. We can look for no appreciable accessions from abroad to invigorate it. But American Orthodoxy no longer mirrors East European life. It is adapting itself to the American environment. Innovations like the late Friday evening service, or the removal of the women's gallery, or the confirmation of girls or a community *seder* (celebration on Passover eve) would have shocked the worshipers of a generation ago. Today such practices are accepted in numerous congregations. Distinctively American standards of Orthodoxy are emerging. American Orthodoxy may yet succeed in harmonizing unquestioning faith with modern living.

One of the most promising features in American Jewish life is the institutional synagogue. The synagogue center has come to stay, despite fears that Judaism might be diluted by the secular attractions of the gymnasium, the swimming pool and similar extension activities. The house of worship, whether orthodox, conservative or reform, is gradually being transformed into a center of social life in the Jewish community. The week-end synagogue is again assuming the character of the *beth hakneseth* of older times, the seven day a week rallying center of Jewish life. The synagogue center attempts to embrace the totality of Judaism—worship first and foremost, but, along with it, forums and institutes for the study of the Hebrew language, Jewish history and literature, a Jewish library, family celebrations such as *bar mitzvah* or confirmation and weddings within the synagogue. The synagogue is tending to become once more a focus for Jewish needs and causes. In this lies a strong hope of a Jewish life once more reintegrated in and around the synagogue.

However, this process has only begun. The synagogue or temple must think in terms of Jewish life, rather than in the narrow limits of the individual congregation. It must recognize its responsibility for everything that affects the Jew. Defense against defamation must not be left to secular organizations, however devoted these may be. For the non-Jewish world is not so impressed by "racial" attempts to protect the Jew as it is when the synagogue, the parent of the church, and Judaism, the mother of Christianity, speak in condemnation of anti-Jewish movements. In recognition of this need for the synagogue to function not only through isolated units but also as a co-ordinated spiritual force, the Synagogue Council of America has been formed.

The synagogue and temple must become the reservoir of idealism for all Jewish communal agencies. A United Jewish Appeal directed by a group of technical promotion experts may achieve material results. But the synagogue and temple alone can provide the spiritual force necessary to educate the masses in the weal and the woe of world Jewry, the tragedy of the Jewish wanderer, and the thrill and hope of Palestine. The synagogue, and not inchoate districts, should become the center of Zionist education and activity. It was there that the inspiration and idealism of Zionism were kept alive through the centuries. The synagogue must make its influence felt in the community chests, with all that they represent of social idealism. The synagogue and not commercial interests should once more assume the responsibility for *kashruth* and other specifically Jewish functions. Above all, the synagogue should make its own the cause of Jewish education.

Education is the fundamental consideration affecting the future of all aspects of Judaism. This fact is forcing itself upon the consciousness of American Jewry, for local Jewish education committees, boards and bureaus have multiplied throughout the country. But organization, while highly valuable, cannot reach the heart of the problem. If Judaism is to live, we must probe into the method and purpose of Jewish education. We must appraise its accomplishments and courageously face its needs and shortcomings. Not the negative impulse of anti-Semitism, but a Jewish education that is religiously motivated, positive, vital and significant will reclaim to Judaism the children of the perplexed Jews, and give the only unquestionable assurance of the survival of the synagogue as the heart and soul of Jewish life in America.

III

JEWISH EDUCATION—ACHIEVEMENTS AND NEEDS

—

I. B. Berkson

JEWISH EDUCATION, SURVIVAL AND ADJUSTMENT

Meaning and Implications

THE problem of Jewish education is much more than pedagogical —not just a matter of how best to teach the subjects usually included in the Jewish school curriculum, e.g., Bible, Hebrew, History. It is, in a profound sense, related to the whole question of adjustment and survival. An adequate discussion would require an analysis of the various issues and points of view for Jewish education; indeed, the final test of the meaning of any Jewish position might be said to lie in what it signifies for the education of the children and youth. Moreover, it would be necessary to ask what type of Jewish policy and organization is required in order to promote the needed Jewish education. Obviously, such an analysis is the subject for a book, not a chapter, but our discussion would be even more inadequate than it must perforce be, if we did not constantly bear in mind the relation of education to our central problem, which is the perpetuation and enhancement of Jewish life in the United States. Ultimately, Jewish education is the major instrument of Jewish unity and continuity, that is of Jewish "survival," to use the term which has become customary.

However, we must immediately guard ourselves against a possible misinterpretation of the idea that Jewish education is an agency of Jewish survival. Emphatically, we do not mean bare group survival. It is conceivable that the Jews might survive without Jewish education in any real sense of the term. A consciousness of kind enforced by social anti-Semitism might lead Jews to congregate in separate districts, rely on each other for companionship and social intercourse, and depend on each other for various forms of mutual aid. Accordingly, we might find Jews eating "kosher style" foods, marrying within the Jewish group and being buried in a Jewish cemetery, joining with other Jews in philanthropic efforts, even attending synagogue service occasionally; doing all these things and yet remaining quite ignorant of Bible, Hebrew, Jewish history, Jewish literature, Jewish culture and spiritual ideas and aspirations. There would be Jews without Judaism.

Survival which education serves is then the survival of distinct values, conceptions, significant ways of behavior of a community. It is not possible to work out a Jewish educational program without some fairly definite conception of the character of Jewish life, its problems and ideals. Likewise, the term education, as used here, refers not only to the influence of the school, but also to the educational effect of the institutional life, of the home, the synagogue, and of customs and folkways. Where the social life has completely broken down, the school cannot of itself reconstruct it or save a society from disintegration. As in the case of the word "survival," we must think of the values of Jewish life, so in using the term "education," we must bear in mind that the school is part of the many sided influences of society.

These ideas apply to general as well as to Jewish education, and the points made may be clarified by a brief reference to several conceptions formulated by John Dewey—eminent American philosopher and educator—with reference to the relation of education and the school to the community. Speaking of education as the indispensable instrument of social continuity, Dewey points out that all life implies a process of continuity, of reproduction and constant renewal. Among human beings, the continued existence of the race is assured by biological reproduction, which involves a process of transmission of vital energies from one generation of individuals to another. The continued existence and renewal of communities—which are living social organisms—are likewise secured by a process of transmission and reproduction. But there is this crucial and profound difference, namely, social continuity is achieved through education, i.e., through a form of transmission and reproduction that involves mental and spiritual elements. Education in this broad sense means *communication*: i.e., communicating habits of doing, ways of thinking and feeling; conveying ideals, standards and opinions. This communication takes place from one generation to another, and from one segment of society to another.

Dewey underscores the point that people do not become part of a society by living in physical proximity; nor do they become a united community merely by joining together for common defense, the achievement of security, or for any purely material purpose, however necessary and important such objectives are. The process of social communication requires sharing common understandings, common emotions, common dispositions, common values. "There is more than a verbal tie between the words, common, community, and communication. Men live in a community in virtue of the things they have in common; . . . what they must have in common in order to form a community or society are aims, beliefs, aspirations, knowledge—a common understanding—likemindedness, as the sociologists say.* Moreover, the communication of common understanding cannot be achieved only by intellectual processes—by transmission of abstract

* Dewey, John, *Democracy and Education*, N. Y., 1916, p. 5.

ideas, or by the study of books or literature. Real social communication involves common experience, living together, engaging in meaningful common activities. Communication, then, involves *participation in the common life* of the community. In fine, education aims to achieve a *consensus,* i.e., a thinking together; and *cooperation,* i.e., a working together.

What is said here applies to all aspects of education, the incidental education of social life as well as of the school. The school, as the formal educational agency, has an especially important place in the process of social survival, not so much because it deals with literature, history and ideas, but rather because the school aims to be a selected, purified, more ideal form of community life. For this reason, Dewey has proposed that we should think of the school as a "miniature community" which will reflect the various activities of society, but in a better form than is found in adult society. Through this richer and better environment, the child and youth would develop their own personalities and, at the same time, grow into the life of the community. The school thus becomes the deliberate, conscious instrument created by society for the transmission and preservation of the ways of thought and behavior regarded as essential for its preservation and betterment.

The function of the school as the conscious instrument of social continuity becomes of extraordinary importance in times of social change and crisis. When there is special danger of social disintegration, education has the primary function of strengthening continuity and unity by the communication of the common values and common vision. Conservatively minded educators conceive this function mainly in terms of preserving the values of the past; liberal educators hold that the school must reckon with new, emerging values as well. In accordance with Dewey's conception, the school, starting with tradition, should reshape it in the light of contemporary knowledge, of evolving values or, to use a popular term, to "reconstruct" tradition. The school is, therefore, more than a preserver of old values; it attempts the constructive re-interpretation of old values in the light of new conceptions and new needs; and in this way it becomes a factor in building a new and better society. Education thus looks forward as well as backward, and the school becomes mediator between the past and the envisaged future. In this philosophy of education, the school and the teacher occupy a place of leadership in the building of a more unified and better society.

Traditional Jewish Education

The conscious dynamic principle of continuous adjustment is a recent and not as yet widely accepted idea. But the principle that education is a means to the survival of the community is well illustrated in Jewish history, and deeply rooted in Jewish consciousness. Indeed, there is good ground for the conclusion that the development of the chief Jewish educational institutions was stimulated in times of social crisis.* The synagogue, which in the reading and exposition of the *Torah* fulfills the function of popular adult education, arose during or soon after the Babylonian exile. The establishment of schools connected with the name of Simeon ben Shetah (probably for youth) took place in the period following the Maccabean wars, in the course of the struggle with the assimilationist forces of Hellenism. The basis of the Jewish public elementary school system was laid by Joshua ben Gamala about the time of the destruction of the Second Temple. The story of Johanan ben Zakkai, who established the *Yeshivah* at Jabneh after the destruction of the Temple in Jerusalem, is proverbially cited as the wise step which saved Jewish life from disintegration. The sages of the Talmud are tireless in their reiteration of the ideas that a community which neglects to establish schools is bound—and ought—to perish, but that the whole world will not prevail against Israel so long as the voices of the children hum in the schools.

* Morris, Nathan, *The Jewish School*, London, 1937.

In medieval times, throughout the long period of perpetual abnormality and crises, the exaltation of the study of the *Torah* (Jewish law and lore) as the path to life eternal was not, by any means, unrelated to the continuity of Jewish temporal life. It was the study of the *Torah,* and the organization of Jewish life in accordance with the *Torah,* that made the difference between dissolution and continuity. The Hebrew poet, Bialik, has pictured the part that the *beth hamidrash* has played as the reservoir of Jewish courage and idealism, and he has portrayed the *matmid,* the perpetual student, as the hero of the long silent battle for the preservation of the inner spirit of Israel. We know well how much in recent times the teacher and the school have contributed to the renaissance of the Jewish will to live in Eastern Europe, and how much education has done for the upbuilding of Jewish life in Palestine. Considering all this, we may say that the best test of any Jewish movement, or philosophy—whether it leads to negation or whether it aims at a reconstruction of Jewish life—is to be found in the concern it shows for Jewish education.

The history of Jewish education illustrates the correlative idea, that the survival which the school aims to promote is a survival of the ideal and distinct way of life of the community which maintains it. Indeed, the growth and development of the Jewish school is an organic factor in the rise of Judaism itself. From the time of its rise, in the period of the Second Temple, until the nineteenth century, Jewish education had a very definite pattern centered about the study of the *Torah.* The Talmud mentions four institutions as parallel: the *beth din* (court); the *beth haknesseth* (synagogue); the *beth hamidrash* (academy); the *beth hasefer* (elementary school). These are the four pillars of rabbinic Judaism, all resting on the groundwork of the *Torah.* The elementary school had a simple origin: its main aim was to prepare the boys to read the *Torah* when "called up" in the synagogue, and to translate and understand its meaning. The *beth hamidrash,* which later developed into the *yeshivah,* served the function of secondary school and university. It evolved from the ancient school for priests, who were the early custodians of the law, and became an academy for the more intensive study of *Torah* by scholars, and for its application to current life. The synagogue, although primarily a house of prayer, nevertheless also had a central educational function; at the heart of the service were the reading, translation and exposition of the *Torah* to the people at large. The content of Jewish education during the last two thousand years underwent no fundamental change: it was based on *Mikrah* (Bible), *Mishnah*, and *Talmud*. The proportion of time given to each, and the spirit in which they were studied, varied with the period and the country, but its essential character did not change.

New Tendencies in Jewish Education

The change in the traditional *Torah* pattern of Jewish education is traceable to the impact of modern forces, particularly during the nineteenth century. We may note three tendencies, which later come into play in American-Jewish education; viz., the religionist, the Hebraic, and the Yiddishist. The religionist adaptation was characteristic of Germany where, in consequence of the "Enlightenment" and Emancipation, the Jews began, for the most part, to attend state schools, or Jewish schools of the same pattern as state schools. Jewish education was reduced to a form of denominational religious instruction. The study of Talmud was practically eliminated, except for students at theological seminaries. The Hebrew Bible, with translation and some grammar remained central in the course, but the amount of time devoted to its study was greatly reduced. History, as a special subject, was added, but this was generally confined to the Biblical period, and consisted of an ethical interpretation of the Bible stories. The most characteristic innovation was the introduction of a catechism which savored of a doctrinal approach alien to Jewish schools.

In Eastern Europe, where emancipation was long delayed,

where the Jewish population was more thickly settled, where Jewish learning had reached a higher degree of intensity, where social life was generally more self-contained and autonomous, the educational change assumed the character of an inner reform. The *heder* (informal private school) remained the basis of the Jewish educational system, but it was "reconstructed" as the *heder metukan* (modernized *heder*). The schools were greatly influenced by the *Haskalah* (the Hebrew Enlightenment) and the *Lovers of Zion* movement which preceded political Zionism. The Bible rather than Talmud became the central subject, although Talmud was studied in the higher classes. The study of Hebrew as a language, written and spoken, and of modern Hebrew literature became an important part of the curriculum. Jewish history, and, in some schools, Russian and other general subjects were added. Here we see the traditional Jewish school evolving into a modern school with a core of Jewish instruction—Hebrew, classical and modern, Bible and Jewish history.

The third type of school—the Yiddishist—also developed in Eastern Europe. At the close of the nineteenth century, a Jewish working class movement grew up in the factory towns of Poland, and parallel with it a Yiddish cultural movement emerged. Yiddish culture was close to the life of the artisan and working classes, and was characterized by creative effort in the fields of literature, art, and the folk dance. For a part of the Jewish masses, the existing types of Jewish education, the religious and Hebraic emphasis of the old and the new *heder* were too distant from the experience and interests of the common people. Closely connected with organized religion and the synagogue, the schools, it was argued, reflected the life and conceptions of the *baale-batim*, the bourgeoisie, and of the Jewish middle class intelligentsia. Proposals for a new type of non-religious school, based on Yiddish literature, Jewish history, and the folk arts, were made as early as the eighties, but the successful establishment of such institutions did not come until the first decade of the twentieth century.

These three tendencies—the religionist, the Hebraic, and the Yiddishist—have had their influence on Jewish education in the United States. The successive waves of Jewish immigration, and the various sections of immigrants, established types of institutions to which they were accustomed. Until a generation ago, there was no conscious attempt at a reconstruction of the educational program. Both Jewish tradition and American institutions were imitated uncritically and, as a result, the traditional pattern of Jewish education, which had served as the basis of Jewish life for two thousand years, was confused by modifications and adaptations. To this day, no unified reformulation of the Jewish educational program has been worked out.

THE DEVELOPMENT OF JEWISH EDUCATION IN AMERICA

Origins

The Spanish-Portuguese community was small and, as described elsewhere in this volume, it did not bring to America any great fund of learning. Its contribution to Jewish education was, therefore, necessarily limited. Its best known educational effort was the *Yeshivat Minhat Areb* (established in 1731). Despite the appellation of *yeshivah*, it was evidently no more than an elementary school, where instruction was given in Hebrew and Bible. Later it became a "publick school" where, besides "the Hebrew," the usual three R's were taught. Early in the eighteenth century, it was reorganized as the *Polonies Talmud Torah*, so named after a Polish Jew, a member of the congregation who had bequeathed a sum of money for a school. Perhaps it was no accident that the bequest was made by an immigrant from Eastern Europe, where the Jewish educational consciousness was highly developed.

The educational contribution of the German Jews was much larger, if less traditional in character. The Hebrew Union College, designed for the training of rabbis and teachers, was established in 1875; a Sabbath School Union was organized in 1886, for the purpose of developing elementary education. In both these efforts, which emphasize united action for a definitely conceived educational purpose, a communal tendency far beyond the individual congregational interest finds expression. But the local schools established by the German Jews were mostly one-day-a-week, Sunday or Sabbath schools, and the amount of instruction in Hebrew and Bible approached the vanishing point. It was moralistic, theological and catechetical in its approach. Its main subject was Biblical history, which was neither Bible nor history, but Biblical stories retold with a "moral instruction" emphasis.

The East European Jews, who began to arrive in considerable numbers after 1880, brought with them the *heder*, the *talmud torah* and the *yeshivah*, but the transplantation involved a great change. In the old country, all the boys and youths attended school, and the instruction lasted generally from morning till sundown. In the United States, since nearly all the children went to the public schools, the hours of daily instruction were greatly reduced, and the years of instruction even more so. In the East European settlements what the schools had lacked in pedagogical skill was partly counterbalanced by the great amount of time devoted to study; whereas, in America, the amount of time devoted to Jewish studies, as well as the pedagogy, were sadly inadequate.

Little improvement seems to have been made in the first generation. A survey of Jewish education—the first Jewish communal study in the United States—was made in 1910, by a committee of which the young Rabbi M. M. Kaplan was chairman; it was conducted under the auspices of the newly formed *Kehillah* (Jewish community) organized by the young Rabbi J. L. Magnes. The survey revealed that about forty thousand Jewish children— about one out of four or five of all those of school age—were receiving some form of Jewish instruction. About one-third of these were taught individually by teachers of the *melamed* type, or in private *heders*. Another twenty-five per cent were attending *talmud torahs*, that is, public institutions partly supported by fees of the pupils, but mostly by volunteer committees. The instruction in the *talmud torahs* was somewhat better than in the *heders*, but the buildings were poor, the teachers underpaid, and the attendance of the children irregular and sporadic. The average child learned to read the prayers, several of the blessings and a little *humash* (Pentateuch). There were also two *yeshivahs* where the Talmud was studied, but these were not in any sense great centers of learning. The *heder*, *talmud torah* and *yeshivah* were instructional agencies of the immigrant sections of the population, or "the orthodox Jews." The more Americanized part of the population attended reform Sunday schools, or afternoon weekday schools in conservative synagogues. Seven thousand children were receiving instruction in Y.M.H.A.'s, social settlements, and orphan asylums, partly of the Sunday school type, or weekday synagogue school types. In these schools, the externals of organization were better; the teachers had better training, but their Jewish knowledge was inadequate.

Although the survey does not emphasize this, there were, no doubt, some good schools and teachers in each group, and even among the *melamed* type of teacher, there were men of learning and piety who had a profound influence on individual children. Exceptional students could probably learn more than might be thought possible from the general unfavorable description. There were also a number of fairly good private schools, and private instruction in some of the homes was above the average level.

Recent Progress in Jewish Education

During the last thirty years, there has been a great change in the general character of Jewish education. While the proportion of children in regular attendance has not increased, a larger number now attend organized schools. The teachers are better trained, several well-directed teachers' training schools having been developed. The American-born teacher now has a competent knowledge of Hebrew, Jewish literature and history; the foreign-born teachers, who still are superior in Jewish knowledge, include men of excellent general education and pedagogical ability. Textbooks have been greatly improved; in some cases these are as good as those used in the public schools. The courses of study have been broadened to include history, current problems, singing, celebration of holidays and various extra-curricular activities, as well as a much more systematic teaching of Hebrew. Many more girls attend Jewish schools than formerly, and although the high school classes and the youth work are still inadequate, some improvement has been made even in this field. On the average, the schools present a modern appearance, have an organized course of study, and employ trained teachers.

Jewish education in American has developed into a profession with teachers' organizations and a National Council for Jewish Education. Several books have been written on the Jewish educational problem, and a professional periodical of good standard, the "Jewish Teacher," has been continuously published for a score of years. In the larger cities, bureaus of Jewish education, generally affiliated with the local federations of charities, have been established; these help to finance, supervise and improve the school work, without interfering with the educational policies. More recently, the American Association for Jewish Education has been created for the purpose of making communities throughout the country conscious of the importance of Jewish education and its proper organization. The picture is not, as yet, a bright one, but certainly in comparison with the situation of a generation ago, Jewish education has made progress.

Several factors have been responsible for this general improvement. The size of the immigration from Eastern Europe permitted a concentration of settlement requisite for maintaining social traditions and for the establishment of Jewish schools on a neighborhood basis. Furthermore, the East European Jew was conscious of the relation of the school to Jewish life, and he was deeply affected by the Jewish national-cultural renaissance—the revival of the Hebrew language as a spoken tongue, the development of modern Hebrew literature and the movement for the rebuilding of Palestine. The developing Jewish life in Palestine also exerted its influence. Samson Benderly, founder of the Bureau of Jewish education (to be mentioned shortly), came from Safed, and played a leading part in introducing spoken Hebrew, modern songs and the study of Palestine into the Jewish schools. One of the first textbooks used for the teaching of modern Hebrew, the *Lefi Hataf*, was composed by the late David Yellin, for many years the head of the Teachers' Seminary in Jerusalem. It may be added that the introduction of the study of modern Palestine in the schools was of a wholly non-political character; it was stimulated mainly by the cultural movements in Eastern Europe and the practical work in Palestine.

The Bureau of Jewish Education

The most important influence in the improvement of the schools, and in the creation of a Jewish educational profession, emanated from the Bureau of Jewish Education.* The Bureau was founded in 1910; it was the creation of Samson Benderly. With him were associated on the Board of Directors a group of young Jewish leaders who were destined to play distinguished parts in the rebuilding of Jewish life: Israel Friedlaender, expounder of the philosophy of cultural Zionism, met a tragic death in the Ukraine in 1921 while distributing relief funds; Mordecai M. Kaplan, intrepid thinker and founder of the Reconstructionist Movement; Judah L. Magnes, courageous fighter in the cause of peace and understanding and Chancellor of the Hebrew University during the first decade of its upbuilding; and the never-aging Henrietta Szold who, in her integrity and single-mindedness of

---

* The Bureau did not exercise any control over the numerous Jewish schools of New York City. However, its influence, though indirect, was pervasive.

devotion, has never contemned the day of small things, and yet has well understood how "to set the little life in the circle of the greater life." They were all of one fraternity, pervaded by the new creative communal spirit in Jewish life. With them, as the chairman of the Bureau, was the late Louis Marshall, staunch Jew who served as a link between the new forces and the older German-Jewish community. Jacob Schiff, the respected and cultured lay leader of American Israel, provided financial assistance and gave kindly encouragement.

Benderly saw Jewish education in large terms. His primary purpose was to make the community feel responsible for the organization and development of Jewish education. He knew the importance of good organization and modern methods; he laid special emphasis on the education of girls and youths; he recognized the significance of extra-curricular forms of education. He developed the idea of a profession of Jewish education, of teachers who would give all their time to Jewish schools, and of educators who would devote themselves to the scientific study of the theoretical and administrative problems involved in the upbuilding of Jewish education. The greatest source of strength of the Bureau lay in the emphasis on the communal idea and in the vision of renascent Jewish life which pervaded its whole conception. From the very beginning, Benderly has had a profound conviction of the indispensability of Jewish education for the survival and renewal of Jewish life in America. While never elaborated in academic terms, the Bureau had a definite working philosophy. This included a positive attitude toward Jewish tradition, a belief in its cultural and spiritual value, a broad interest in Jewish affairs and problems throughout the world, a sense of unity of the Jewish people, a firm belief in the reconstitution of Palestine as a home for the Jewish people and as a center of spiritual influence throughout the world. And with all this positive belief in Jewish life and values, there was an equal emphasis on the necessity of adjusting and integrating Jewish life with American life, and the conviction that this was possible and would be fruitful.

TYPES OF JEWISH SCHOOLS OF TODAY

The Jewish schools still exhibit a great diversity with reference to organization, point of view, type of program, and quality of work. Schools may be conducted as independent institutions, as in the case of the *yeshivahs* and *talmud torahs*, or they may be associated with congregations. Some receive aid from a central communal source; others must depend entirely on tuition fees and local collections. They vary widely in quality of instruction, and they range from the Sunday school with its one and a half to two hours a week, to the all day program of the *yeshivahs*. For the purposes of a brief description, the schools may be roughly divided into four types: (1) the Hebrew weekday school; (2) the Sunday school; (3) the all day school; (4) the Yiddish culture school. There are several varieties and many individual differences within each type.

The Hebrew Weekday School

This classification is employed to designate the prevalent type of Jewish educational institution, including the *talmud torahs* and congregational schools. The term "Hebrew" indicates that the main emphasis is placed on this subject, but generally the children are taught merely to read the prayer book and to translate from the Pentateuch. In some of the better schools, elements of modern Hebrew are also included. The schools are called "weekday" because, in addition to a session on Sunday mornings (occasionally on Saturday mornings), they meet on weekday afternoons, after public school hours. The schedules vary greatly: classes may meet from three to five times a week, and the total number of hours of attendance varies from five to ten. While there is a definite tendency to reduce the number of sessions per week, in New York City most classes still meet five times per week, averaging from six and a half to seven and a half hours. During 1941,* over 35,000 children were in attendance at these schools in New York City, this number representing more than 60 per cent of the children receiving Jewish instruction, and close to 15 per cent of all of the Jewish children of school age. Besides, a considerable number of children (the estimates vary from 10,000 to 15,000) receive some education in *heders*, private schools or at home. This instruction resembles most closely the type given in the Hebrew weekday schools. It is, therefore, quite proper to say that the Hebrew weekday type of education is the mode or characteristic type of Jewish education in the United States, rather than the Sunday schools, the all day schools, or the Yiddish culture type.

Some of the Hebrew weekday schools are privately organized, but most of them are either "communal" or "congregational." The communal school functions under a local board of trustees, as in the case of the *talmud torahs*, and of some of the schools connected with Y.M.H.A.'s or recreational centers. In the cities where bureaus of education have been organized, some receive financial aid from the federations of charities. The predominating type today in New York City is the congregational school, i.e., a Hebrew school affiliated with a synagogue. One of the definite changes in the last generation has been the increase in the number of congregational schools at the expense of the *talmud torahs*. This is due partly to moving from the thickly settled Jewish neighborhoods to outlying districts, and partly to the development of synagogues into Jewish Centers, giving more attention to education than the old congregational synagogues.

The comparative merits of the two types—"communal" or "congregational"—have been warmly discussed, but the differences are more apparent than real. The courses of study in the better congregational schools tend to follow the Hebraic emphasis of the *talmud torahs*, and they are also becoming more "communal" in

---

* The figures for 1941 have been supplied by the Jewish Education Committee of New York, through the courtesy of Mr. J. M. Horden, head of the department of statistics. All figures are for New York City.

that they admit children from the neighborhood whose parents are not members of the congregation. In Chicago and New York, they have voluntarily affiliated with the bureaus of education, and receive assistance from them. The Hebrew weekday schools, both of the *talmud torah* and congregational types, represent a religious-cultural-communal synthesis.*

The Sunday School

Next in importance, as far as strength of numbers is concerned, is the Sunday school. The Sunday school has frequently been regarded as the symbol of inadequacy in Jewish education, more of a gesture than an adequate means for maintaining Jewish tradition. However, during the last score of years, a notable change has been in evidence. Its pronounced anti-Zionism has been modified to tolerance, and, in not a few cases, to a definite pro-Palestine emphasis. A more favorable consideration of the place of Hebrew in the course of study is noticeable, and this has led to the tendency in some schools to introduce one or two additional weekday sessions for some of the children. Jewish history now tends to be taught as the history of the Jewish people, subject to the same principles that rule the history of other peoples, rather than as a specially divine revelation. In the courses on religion, the practices of the home and the synagogue are emphasized rather than the inculcation of abstract moral or theological doctrines. The discussion of current events deals with all aspects of Jewish life, not only the religious. In a few of the best schools, the following may be expected of graduates: (1) some acquaintance with the literature of the Bible; (2) a fair knowledge of Jewish history from ancient to modern times; (3) an understanding of Jewish current events; (4) an appreciation of the most important customs of the home and synagogue; (5) the ability to read selected Hebrew

---

* For a more detailed description of the Hebrew schools, see Chipkin, I. S., *Twenty-five Years of Jewish Education in the United States,* New York, 1937 (reprinted from the *American Jewish Year Book,* 5697, by the Jewish Education Association of New York City).

prayers of the Union Hebrew Prayer Book. Where there is an additional weekday session, the children will also know some Hebrew excerpts from the Bible, and simple stories and poems from modern Hebrew literature.

As to numbers, the Sunday schools have held their own. The proportion of children attending Sunday schools varies greatly in different cities. For instance, in New York, about 20 per cent of all children attending Jewish schools go to Sunday schools; in Cleveland, where the work is particularly well organized, about 70 per cent of the Jewish children who receive instruction attend Sunday schools. On the whole, the Sunday schools, particularly in middle-sized or smaller cities, are able to keep their children in continuous attendance over a longer period of years. In the case of the average child, therefore, the disparity in total hours of instruction received in the weekday schools and Sunday schools is not as great as might at first appear. In general, it might be said that, while the children who attend Hebrew weekday schools learn more Hebrew, the courses in history in the best Sunday schools are better than in the *talmud torahs*.

The All Day School

At the other extreme from the Sunday school is the all day school, so termed because the pupils receive their Jewish and general education under the same auspices. These schools are sometimes referred to as "parochial schools"; they are, for the most part, of orthodox religious viewpoint, and in some ways analogous to the Catholic parochial schools. However, the all day school now includes three types: the traditional *yeshivah*, the modern type *yeshivah*, and the English type. The traditional *yeshivah* is the characteristic type, strictly orthodox in religious attitude, and largely devoted to the study of the Talmud. In these schools, the Jewish subjects receive primary attention, the morning hours being devoted to them.

In recent years, a new type of all day school has been developing with a shorter school day and more modern pedagogical and educational policies. While these schools are generally conservative and traditional, the emphasis is not so much on orthodox belief and ritual as on an intensive Jewish education. They provide a better balance between Jewish and general subjects, and include modern Hebrew literature as well as the traditional subjects. As a rule, Hebrew is employed as the language of instruction in the Jewish department.

A third type of all day school at present developing is not only modern in its educational conceptions, but sometimes attempts to utilize progressive pedagogical principles. These are essentially private schools for the well-to-do, in which courses in Hebrew and Jewish history are incorporated in the program of general education, thus avoiding the necessity of sending children to a special school in the afternoon for Jewish instruction. These schools are conservative or orthodox in their religious outlook.

In the main, all-day schools are concentrated in New York City, although there are a few *yeshivahs* in other cities. They have grown considerably during the last generation. In 1910, there were only two schools of this type in New York City, with an enrollment of 600 pupils. In 1936, the New York Jewish Education Survey reported sixteen schools with a total enrollment of 4500 pupils, mainly of the elementary grades, but including some high school classes. Today there are twenty-five to thirty such institutions, with a total registration of about 5000. This increase is due both to the dissatisfaction of parents with the amount of Jewish knowledge obtained in the afternoon weekday schools, and to the fact that more girls are attending the modern type all day Hebrew school. The continued growth of these schools undoubtedly reflects a real desire for a more intensive form of Jewish education, but only a small percentage of the Jewish child population is affected, probably no more than two per cent. However, of the children receiving Jewish instruction in New York City at any one time, close to ten per cent are in all-day schools.

The Yiddish Culture School

Yiddish culture schools did not exist at the time of the survey of 1910. They should not be confused with the old *heders* in which Yiddish was used as a language of instruction. The most recent of all Jewish schools, they are the product of the Yiddish cultural movement described above. With the immigration of a working class population during the last generation, Yiddish schools have been opened in South America, Canada, and the United States. In point of organization, they resemble the Hebrew weekday schools, in that sessions are conducted on afternoons, after public school hours, and on Sunday mornings. In terms of content of instruction they are, however, quite different and represent, among themselves, considerable variations. In New York City, the three main groups are the National Workers' Alliance (*Poale Zion*); the Sholem Aleichem Folk Shulen; the Workmen's Circle Schools (*Arbeiter Ring*). The courses common to all the schools generally include Yiddish literature, Jewish history, current events, Yiddish folk songs and folk dances, and Jewish art. The Jewish festivals are celebrated, although not, as a rule, *Rosh Hashonah* and *Yom Kippur*, which are regarded as purely religious holidays. In some schools, a little Hebrew is taught, and in the *Lehrer Seminar*, or Teachers' Training School conducted in New York under the auspices of the *Poale Zion*, Hebrew is a required subject. The schools are generally regarded as secularist. They do not accept supernatural or doctrinal conceptions, nor do they affiliate with synagogues. On the other hand, the Bible is studied as part of Jewish literature, albeit in Yiddish translation. The prophetic ideal of social justice is stressed. Passover is celebrated as a festival of human freedom. The significance of the Sabbath as a day of rest in the development of western civilization is a major theme. Some groups would even go so far as to accept the High Holy days, because they embody the concepts of repentance and spiritual purification. In other words, a social and universal humanistic interpretation is given to Jewish history and tradition, many values usually called religious being included.

Toward Zionism, the attitude of the different groups varies. The *Poale Zion* group represents a vital and creative element in the Zionist movement. Among the other groups, the indifference and even hostility of former years have given way to sympathy and active support. The Workmen's Circle, for instance, while still opposed or indifferent to political Zionism, has rendered constructive assistance to co-operative enterprises of the Labor Zionist movement in Palestine. In their political orientation, the schools are democratic in outlook and broadly sympathetic to trade union and working class interests.*

There are many Yiddish schools throughout the country; over ninety in New York City at the present time. But the schools are very small, in many cases consisting only of a class or two. In 1936, the total registration in New York City represented only seven per cent of the Jewish children receiving Jewish instruction, and it has since fallen from 4500 to the present figure of 3700. The strength of the Yiddish schools appears to be ebbing.

Toward a Common American-Jewish School Program

Viewed broadly, if we combine all types and qualities of Jewish schools, we may say that there are considerable interest and activity in Jewish education. In view of the many difficulties—the necessary reliance on purely voluntary effort, the inadequacy of communal support, very great drawbacks involved in educational work after public school hours, the variety of schools, schedules and courses which impede smooth transfer from school to school as the Jewish population moves from one district to another—

---

* These Yiddish schools are to be sharply distinguished from the schools of the International Workers Order which are partisan in character and, a few years ago at least, appeared to be following the Communist line of propaganda. The schools of the I.W.O. cannot be considered Jewish schools in the sense that the term is used in this discussion.

the achievement of Jewish education in the United States is certainly much better than we have a right to expect. If the general schools were confronted with equal difficulties, their attendance and work would undoubtedly suffer greatly. However, thinking of Jewish education as an instrument of Jewish survival and renewal, we dare not fail to ask ourselves whether Jewish education is fulfilling its major functions; whether it transmits in an adequate degree the heritage of Jewish knowledge; whether it succeeds in associating the individual Jew through participation with the institutions of Jewish life; whether it conveys an understanding and appreciation of Jewish values; whether it develops a sense of Jewish loyalty and responsibility to the Jewish community; and, parallel to this, whether Jewish education is integrated with the general education received in the American public school.

There are, no doubt, schools which succeed, in varying degrees, in achieving such purposes. But thinking in terms of the average child or youth, a favorable answer to our questions can hardly be ventured. The average Jewish child probably does not receive more than two or three years of elementary instruction throughout all the years of childhood and youth. If he has attended a Hebrew weekday school, his major achievement would be the ability to read the prayer book with some facility, a little Bible, a smattering of Hebrew, some stories, some songs, some familiarity with the ceremonies, and a fragmentary knowledge of Jewish history. There would be little understanding of Jewish problems, and probably little serious conviction about Jewish religious conceptions, or about the significance of Jewish cultural life generally. If he has attended a Sunday school, his knowledge of Hebrew would be less; his knowledge of history perhaps better, but rarely adequate. This is the picture of the average; there would be some who would do much better, and many who would do much worse. And there would be a considerable number of Jewish

children who would have had no Jewish education whatsoever.*

As for the youth of postelementary school age, there is almost
complete neglect. Some classes are conducted in the better Sunday
schools, and there are several Hebrew high schools and a number
of post-graduate *talmud torah* classes. In several cities, courses in
Hebrew are offered in the public schools. Club work and youth
groups have been organized in recreational centers and by various
associations. But all together, this touches only a very small part
of the youth. Moreover, the little that is done is mostly in the
nature of instruction in special subjects, in Hebrew, Bible, and
history. Very little of the work deals with the problems of youth,
as felt by the young people themselves, or with the needs of the
community.

Judged from any standpoint, the educational work does not
achieve a satisfactory standard. Regarded from the point of view
of a consciously planned program of American Jewish education,
the inadequacy is far more serious. The various programs now
followed are, to a large degree, transplantations. There have, of
course, been some adjustments, but rarely have these been the
result of a well thought out conception. Consequently, the courses
of study are not well unified or "integrated," as the pedagogical
phrase goes. The central problem of Jewish education is the working out of a program that would give all Jewish children a common grounding of Jewish knowledge and ideas, related to the

---

* It is however not true that only 25 per cent of the Jewish children receive
a Jewish education. This much publicized figure refers to the number of children
attending Jewish schools at *any one time*. 100 per cent attendance would mean
that every single Jewish child attending the public schools would simultaneously be
attending the Jewish schools throughout the course of the elementary school period.
Estimates indicate that at least three-fourths of the Jewish children receive some Jewish
education at some period in their life, and in the more thickly settled Jewish neighborhoods, nearly all the boys do so. With reference to the interest of parents in Jewish
education, therefore, the situation is not as bad as it might look. However, from the
point of view of the quality of Jewish instruction, it is rather worse. A generous estimate
would indicate that not more than five per cent of the Jewish children receive a
minimally adequate Jewish education, corresponding in Jewish life to the education
received in the public school in relation to American life.

needs of the children and youth as they grow up under the influence of American life.

In approaching the task of developing such a common course of study, it is reasonable to take the Hebrew weekday school as the basis. It is the most representative type; it includes both the religious and cultural elements; it is rooted in tradition and yet responds to new trends and conceptions.

The other types—the Sunday school, the parochial school, and the Yiddish school—have a legitimate place in the total scheme of Jewish education, but they fail to fulfill certain essentials. The Sunday school makes no adequate provision for the study of Hebrew, which is to be regarded as an indispensable element. The *yeshivah* type, on the other hand, makes full provision for the *Torah* element in Jewish education. Nevertheless, the all-day type of education cannot be regarded as the one favored by any but a small proportion of the Jewish population, because it fails to fulfill the major need of a common school for all races, denominations and classes. It has, as indicated, a legitimate place in America, and the ill-advised insinuation that it is un-American for Jews to conduct parochial schools is unjustified. Certainly, the Jewish all-day schools have the same right to exist as do other types of private schools. But they cannot serve as the norm of Jewish education.

The Yiddish schools, too, have their values as well as their weaknesses. But they, too, cannot be regarded as a standard. They make inadequate provision for the religious and *Torah* elements. Furthermore, while the emphasis on Yiddish may have a transitional value, it cannot remain the core of Jewish education, since it is not the vernacular of American Jews.

Another major reason for taking the Hebrew weekday school as the basis for the proposed community school is its relative freedom from doctrinal or ideological bias. The communal Jewish educational program cannot, in the view of this writer, be based on a particular ideology. Jewish education should not begin with the theory of nationalism, Reform or Orthodoxy. An educational program may quite properly be colored by views of parents, conditions of the neighborhood and teacher's interpretation. But there is an essential difference of approach between a common program which allows for diversity, and one based primarily on a particularistic ideological conception. Just as the American school aims to avoid the introduction of "isms" in the general education of the child, and to emphasize common American values and aims, so should the Jewish school try, as far as it can, to avoid doctrines and concentrate on the effort of developing a common community life.

Some Jewish educators seem to think that this contravenes the principles of democracy.* But it should be plain that the diversities which democracy encourages imply a consensus on fundamental ideas and values. The ideal of the common public school is to create such a consensus, one of the major requisites of a democracy. On the contrary, if there is anything that contravenes the democratic ideal, it is basing education on doctrinal and ideological platforms. The attempt to build an educational program on ideological bases actually means nourishing the present divisions in American Jewish life which, to no small extent, are grounded in differences and antagonisms developed in the past.

It should be understood that there is no idea in this proposal for a common program of denying to any group or organization the right to conduct schools on the basis of some definite point of view or ideology. But community boards of education should not rest content with financial and pedagogical services rendered to existing schools. The educational director and staff under communal auspices ought to endeavor to work out a program based on common essentials, with due regard to Jewish tradition, American life and educational fundamentals. Such a program should be tested out in an experimental school directly maintained and controlled by the community board. To be sure, the views of parents

---

* See Lapson, Judah, "Proceedings of the Sixteenth Annual Conference of the National Council for Jewish Education," in Jewish Education, January, 1942, pp. 217 ff.

and the needs of the children of the particular locality would be taken into consideration. But it is the view of this writer that the educator could have the necessary freedom only if the laboratory school were conducted under the community board of education; and that the program worked out under community auspices would have a better chance of truly reflecting the common views of the community. Courses of study elaborated in this way would be available to guide other schools, and such guidance would undoubtedly be welcomed. In any case, there is no question of *imposing* a point of view, but of *proposing*. The Jewish educator has no right to impose a program on any schools, and he could not do so if he tried. But he has the duty of proposing one.*

CONCLUSION

A curriculum of common elements (such as is proposed on pp. 88-91) would permit variations of interpretation. Each educational body, or school staff, would need to work out its own conception and emphasis, paying due regard to the views of parents. In the elaboration of such a point of view, a number of basic questions would have to be considered, namely, the relation to American life, to Jewish group life, to religion and to social problems. The following comments on each of these questions suggest the writer's point of view.

Relation to American Life

It is generally agreed that Jewish education should be supplementary to public school education, and that its aim should be to prepare the child for life in an American Jewish community, i.e., a Jewish community properly related to the American community of which it is a part. If genuinely carried out, this means very much more than conducting Jewish education in the afternoon hours, or on Sundays, so that it should not interfere with general education. It implies that the educational principles underlying

---

* The outline of such a proposed course of study is presented on pp. 88-91.

the Jewish school must be in harmony with American education. If care is not taken to keep both systems of education related to each other, there is danger of creating a conflict in the mental life of the child, harmful in itself, and ultimately detrimental to participation in Jewish life.

The conception of a unified Jewish education, well integrated with general education, implies, furthermore, a high evaluation of the cultural and spiritual possibilities of American life. It would not be in accord with the point of view here advanced, to render to American life only such homage as is due a secular society which gives economic and political security, and to seek in Jewish life alone religious and spiritual attributes. Instead, both are to be considered systems of culture which contain spiritual values. The problem is to interrelate the two systems of culture in the life of the growing child, and to produce an enriched and unified personality. The attempt to harmonize the two cultures is fraught with many problems, but the assumption is that a fruitful adjustment can be made. The effort to interrelate the two cultures will lead to focusing attention on the ideal aspects of both. A conception of Americanization is involved in this idea, but by no means a blind conformity to everything called "American." What is suggested is a critical assimilation of the best in American life, along with loyalty to Jewish life.

Relation to Jewish Group Life

Contemporary liberal thought recognizes the principle that the full enjoyment of individual rights implies the right of the development of the group or groups to which the individual belongs. Lewis Mumford, for example, believes that ". . . the individuality of groups of men is as genuine a fact as personality itself. . . . He who uproots nationality kills personality."[*] To be sure, no rights are absolute, and the right of Jewish collective

* Mumford, Lewis, *Faith for Living,* New York, 1940, p. 176.

organization must be defined with due regard to other equally important interests and obligations. But the Jews have collective needs which require recognition and clarification.

A leading American Jewish educator has recently expressed the opinion that too great emphasis has been placed on the importance of the group values inherent in the term "Israel," at the expense of the humanistic and universal values inherent in the two other conceptions of the Jewish "trinity"—"God" and *"Torah."* Apart from the question of the accuracy of the statement—whether there has actually been such an over-emphasis—the idea expressed appears to fall into the fallacy of many cosmopolitan assimilationists, namely, that "group values," particularly Jewish values, and humanistic values stand in opposition to each other. The proponents of such views miss the main point of the conception "God, Israel and *Torah* are one," for the stress is on the last phrase "are one." The essence of any trinitarian conception is that each element is "perfectly equal," and together constitute a true unity. Those who underestimate the significance of the concept "Israel" certainly depart from Jewish tradition in an essential.

The question is not whether to increase or decrease the emphasis on Jewish group values; it is to clarify and define them—to outline a philosophy of Jewish communal life in harmony with the facts of modern life and contemporary trends of liberal thought. In such a philosophy of Jewish adjustment, it should be understood that no special privilege can or ought to be asked for Jews. But we should expect for Jews equal rights of development both as individuals and as a collectivity. Moreover, it is to be understood that any allegiance required of the Jew by the Jewish community can be imposed only on grounds of a sense of responsibility and moral obligation. It is the individual Jew himself who must be the free and final judge of the manner and character of his Jewish responsibility.

Relation to Religion

There is a general recognition of the need of deepening the spiritual note in life. The course of study of the *talmud torahs* and congregational schools, including as it does religious elements, is designed to fill such a need. But it must be admitted that too much of the teaching is directed to the mechanics of the Hebrew language, and to the external aspects of doctrine and ritual. It is necessary to focus attention on the spiritual aspects of Jewish culture to indicate the significance of the traditional heritage for the cultivation of inward experience, and to make clear the pattern of values that Jewish thought and life exemplify. No division can be made between the spiritual and cultural. The need rather is to direct all the teaching to the elucidation of the values, significances, and meanings implicit in every Jewish activity, practice and study.

The problem of particular interpretations and points of view will undoubtedly arise. In such matters, the common school program should allow a wide latitude of interpretation, as wide as prevails in the American Jewish community at large. The teaching staff should, in the first place, be chosen with due regard to the views of parents in any particular locality. Their general orientation assured, however, teachers should be given a wide range of freedom; otherwise, the teaching will not be genuine. It should be understood, also, that any view which the teacher advances must have the support of Jewish scholarship, and that no teacher has the right to force upon his students a purely individual or partisan interpretation. The *Torah* implies a definite way of life and way of thought, but this can be absorbed only through continuous study, and by participation in Jewish life. It is in line with our tradition to trust abundance of knowledge, together with practice in the Jewish way of life, rather than exactness of doctrinal interpretation. Some interpretation and direction will, of course, be unavoidable, but in so far as possible, the *Torah* should be permitted to speak for itself.

Relation to Social Problems

In Jewish thought, as well as in modern thought, spiritual does not mean only inward individual experience, or withdrawal from the affairs of the world. The term "spiritual" has an extension of meaning which applies to the social life. It implies an effort to realize ethical ideals in this world. The vision of the establishment of an era of peace through social justice, the vision of the ancient Hebrew prophets, calls for embodiment "speedily, in our day." It is not enough to glow with pride whenever it is said that the contemporary struggle for a greater measure of social security and economic equality had its origin with the prophets and sages of Israel. We must, along with others, engage in the work of embodying the ancient vision in life.

Everything that is dynamic and vital in modern life is in some way interrelated with "the people's revolution," to use Henry A. Wallace's phrase. It is through contact with the great moving social forces of our day that Jewish teaching can regain needed vitality. This does not mean an artificial introduction of social and economic problems into the Jewish school, or indoctrination in special social "isms"; those have even less place in the school than the theological "isms." Any genuine discussion of Jewish literature, history and current affairs offers occasions for treating the political and economic problems of our day. There are many such opportunities in the teachings of the prophets, in the study of medieval society, in the discussions of the problems of adjustment of Jews in modern times. Best of all, in the presentation of the significance of modern Palestine, particularly in the work of the labor groups and the co-operative colonies, many constructive suggestions will be found for positive teaching of a genuine social democracy.

A common American-Jewish school program is an urgent need, and the formulation of such a program would have to deal explicitly with the problems mentioned—the relation to American life, to Jewish group life, to Jewish religion, and to the general social problems of our era. These aspects would have to be considered as part of an integrated program, as a policy not for one division or fragment of Israel, but for the whole community.

There are schools of thought which hold that a philosophy of education is worked out apart from the school, and that the teacher's function is mainly to inculcate the philosophy determined upon by society. It has also been argued that a common Jewish school program is premature because no "well-digested philosophy" of American Jewish life, applicable to Jewish education, is at present available; that the school must wait on the prior development of an indigenous American-Jewish life. In practical application, the effect of this conception is to minimize the function of conscious leadership of the educator in the formation of educational policy. Determination of educational policy is left to congregational organizations, to lay boards or to some vague working out of the historical processes.

The view which makes of the school a passive agent of society is inadequate to the needs of American Jewish life of today, and it is opposed to contemporary progressive educational philosophy as well. One of the most significant contributions of Dewey lies in his suggestion that the school contributes to philosophical development; indeed, that education is the parent of philosophy. Tracing philosophy back to its origins, Dewey points out that it has its rise in the problems of youth during periods of social change. It is in the educational area that the profoundest issues of life and society are confronted. " 'Philosophy of education' is not an external application of ready-made ideas to a system of practice having a radically different origin and purpose; it is only an explicit formulation of the problems of the formation of right mental and moral habitudes in respect to the difficulties of contemporary social life. The most penetrating definition of philosophy, which can be given is then, that it is the theory of education in its most general phases."*

A "well-digested philosophy" is likely to be a static philosophy, or an obsolete one. A Jewish educational philosophy, in harmony with liberal American conceptions, would be one that looked toward a future, that had vision. To help existing schools in various ways, and to co-operate with them in developing each individual point of view and program is excellent policy, as far as it goes. But the basic problem of working out a community program of Jewish education must not be forgotten. To develop such a program of common ideas, common understanding and common ideals is the major task of the American-Jewish educator in the decades to come. It is only by concentrated devotion to the creation of such a program that there is any hope of fulfilling it, and it is only through the development of such a program that the American-Jewish educator can make his contribution to the promotion of American-Jewish community life.

* Dewey, John, *Democracy and Education,* cited, p. 386.

PROPOSED COURSE OF STUDY FOR A COMMON
AMERICAN-JEWISH SCHOOL

The program which follows attempts to give due consideration to
two interrelated aspects of the Jewish school curriculum: (1) content
and ideas; (2) Hebrew language and literature. The plan is to devote
a two-hour session on Sunday to the content aspect of the curriculum.
The Hebrew program will require additional attendance on weekday
afternoons for two, three or four periods, depending on the character
of the course.

A. *General Course of Study in English*

The course in content and ideas is presented under several general
divisions: (1) Jewish community life and institutions; (2) the Bible
and Jewish classics; (3) Jewish history and social studies; (4) Jewish
ideals, customs, laws and institutions; (5) Jewish songs and chants;
(6) Palestine. These are not to be understood as six separate subjects,
but rather as overlapping areas of interest. These centers of interest,
or "cores," as they are sometimes called in contemporary pedagogical
writings, are to be kept in mind, whether a subject curriculum or
project curriculum is employed. Some of these centers of interest lend
themselves better to project work, and others to subject organization.

1. *Jewish Community Life and Institutions*

The teaching here involves participation in the various aspects of
the institutional life, family, synagogue, festivals, holidays. However,
participation alone is not enough; educationally speaking, participation should always be associated with developing knowledge, understanding and appreciation. Jewish institutions, holidays, and
ritual are replete with ideas, and the "education by participation"
program, if intelligently organized, can become the concrete groundwork for the development of thought and attitudes. In this aspect
of the teaching, there is an attempt to recapture that sort of educational experience which came to the Jew naturally in the past, in the
course of living a Jewish life, with, however, greater emphasis on
proper understanding of the meanings and significance associated
with performance.

2. *The Bible and Jewish Classics*

In the "active participation" as outlined above, elements of story, prayer and literature already are included as part of the educational experience. In addition, the school should provide for the systematic teaching of Bible and Jewish classics. Among Jewish classics, in addition to the Bible, would be included several portions of the traditional prayer book, the Ethics of the Fathers, and at least a few pages from medieval and modern literature, sufficient to indicate that development of Jewish thought has not been static. The Jewish classics should be taught in the English translation wherever the knowledge of Hebrew is not sufficient for full appreciation of the thought content.

3. *Jewish History and Social Studies*

Here, too, we find elements which have already been included partially in the above areas, but definite and systematic attention should also be given to three phases of Jewish social life: (a) the historical development; (b) contemporary Jewish life and basic problems; (c) significant current events. In these courses, the relationship between Jewish history and social life and the non-Jewish life would be a matter of special interest.

4. *Jewish Ideas, Customs, Laws and Institutions*

In addition to the more general study of ideas in courses in the classics, history and social studies, and through participation in Jewish institutional life, there should be a place for the formal teaching of the major Jewish conceptions. However, the doctrinal or catechetical approach should be avoided. Instead, the Jewish conceptions should be taught in their historical, literary, and institutional context, in connection with the prayer book, synagogue and home services, and Jewish literature; and attention should be directed to their historical development and their social implications. In teaching these conceptions, the Hebrew terms by which they are known should always be used.

5. *Jewish Chants and Songs*

Singing should be considered an integral part of the Jewish curriculum, and should include traditional chants, the cantillation, modern folk and art songs. There is also a movement to introduce Jewish crafts and arts into the Jewish school, and this is desirable, but it may be said that the other arts are not, like singing, an indispensable part of the Jewish social heritage.

6. *Palestine*

The establishment of a homeland for the Jewish people in Palestine warrants special emphasis. Zion and Palestine will appear incidentally in every course of study—in the study of the Bible and prayer book, in the discussion of Jewish history and current events, and in the dramatic activities and singing. But in addition, the significance of Palestine for Jewish life today, both as a haven of refuge and as a center of creative Jewish life, is so great and so widely recognized, that it merits inclusion as a distinct subject of study in all types of schools. Even in that minority of schools which do not subscribe to the Zionist interpretation of an autonomous Jewish homeland, the idea should be discussed as an outstanding Jewish conception, and the work in Palestine with its achievements and problems should receive full consideration. In so far as controversial issues arise, the general rules for discussion of controversial questions prevailing in American progressive schools should fe followed in the Jewish schools.

B. *The Hebrew Course of Study*

Hebrew is an essential element in the Jewish course of study for the average child. However, it is not practicable to expect every child to attain to a full knowledge of the language, or to follow an identical program. The course in Hebrew would depend on the number of sessions the child attends, and the probability of continuous attendance over a number of years. This, in no small measure, depends upon the degree of co-operation that parents are ready to give. The course in Hebrew, therefore, must be decided upon in each case on the basis of a full discussion with the parents, as to what it involves. The present course and schedules are of a very great variety, and the first step would be to attempt to reduce the types of Hebrew instruction to several uniform schedules.

1. *For Sunday Schools*

Sunday schools should not attempt to teach the Hebrew language as such. The teaching should rather be along the lines usually referred to as "functional" Hebrew. The course should include a few simple prayers, some Hebrew songs, Hebrew expressions associated with Jewish holidays, Jewish institutional life, and Palestine activities, and, particularly, the basic concepts referred to under (4) above (Jewish Ideas, etc.).

2. *Normal Course*

This would be designed for pupils who are ready to attend at least two afternoon weekday sessions. Its purpose would be to give the child a good "passive" knowledge of Hebrew. This would include ability to understand selected portions of the Bible and of the prayer book, the Ethics of the Fathers, and a few examples from medieval and modern Hebrew literature. The emphasis is on classic Hebrew, i.e., the language of the Bible and the prayer book, not on modern Hebrew; on comprehension and not on active use in speech or writing.

3. *The Full Course*

This would be designed for pupils who are ready to attend three or four afternoons a week over a period of years. The aim would be to gain a full knowledge of classic and modern Hebrew. The emphasis would still be on reading, but a secondary purpose would be Hebrew speaking and composition. Even in this course, Hebrew would not be used to discuss ideas or content.

THE CULTURAL SCENE: LITERARY
EXPRESSION

—

Marie Syrkin

What Is Jewish Literature?

BEFORE one can attempt to describe the Jewish cultural scene, one must first determine how much territory one proposes to encompass under that term, and what figures may legitimately be considered as part of it. This is not a simple task. One is at once beset by questions which are fundamental to this discussion, and which cannot be dismissed by arbitrarily staking out a given area and labeling it as one's preserve. The problem of definition is not merely one of convenient cataloguing and demarcation, but involves the heart of the theme.

Shall we say, for instance, that any artistic or intellectual creation is to be viewed as Jewish solely because it is the work of a Jew? Or shall we insist that the author's Jewish birth be considered irrelevant, and that only a conscious use of Jewish themes warrants the description of a novel or a play or a painting as "Jewish." Such a question does not arise in connection with either Hebrew or Yiddish literature. No one would doubt the validity of viewing *Ecclesiastes* or *Job* or the *Song of Songs* as superlative expressions of the Jewish genius, even though their subjects are the universal themes of man's suffering and man's love, rather than specific Jewish problems. The same holds good for Yiddish literature. Any poem of Yehoash or Leivick, whether it be about the moon or submarines, will be accepted critically as "Jewish," but in other languages the criterion of Jewish authorship ceases to be absolute. We are certain that Heine's *Hebrew Melodies* reflect the creative spirit of a Jewish poet, but what about the *Buch der Lieder* or, for that matter, *Die Lorelei,* which even the Nazis can't bear to part with, though they claim that its authorship is "unknown?" Is the myriad-antennaed sensibility of the half-Jew Marcel Proust in some way racial? Is Franz Werfel only accidentally a "Jewish" writer in his epic narration of the Armenian persecutions in *The Forty Days of Musa Dagh,* and is he more truly "Jewish" in his mediocre drama *The Eternal Road,* which deals with episodes in Jewish history? It is a part of the anomaly of the Jewish situation that such questions can be posed—an anomaly whose paradoxical character becomes most sharply illuminated when we consider that, if *Ecclesiastes* or even *Job* were set before the world as the works of an American Jew, writing in English, we would find ourselves wondering as to their classification. Would they then be viewed as characteristic manifestations of Jewish creativeness at its height or would these supreme plaints on human destiny no longer be considered an integral derivation from the author's racial psyche and background?

If we return to the specific consideration of the Jewish cultural scene in the United States, we encounter the same difficulty. Are we to include dramatists like George S. Kaufman or Lillian Hellman; wits like F. P. A. or Dorothy Parker; journalists like Walter Lippmann or Simeon Strunsky? What about George Gershwin or, for that matter, Irving Berlin?

Non-Jewish writers have been very adept in discovering moral and intellectual niches into which to pigeonhole their Jewish contemporaries. Isolated critics have had little trouble in characterizing the literary output of Jews in the United States as "faintly alien," or as lacking in solidity. One critic has assured us that we need not look for strong and durable character drawing among Jewish writers, but rather for excellent caricature, satire, burlesque, or parody. "Our Jewish novelists and critics are at present the gadflies of American literature." John Cowper Powys, on the other hand,* comes to the rescue with the declaration that it is a poor compliment to the Jewish strain in modern aesthetics to limit its influence to the neurotic, the superficial, and the extravagant. He would lay the chief stress on the life-love, the superabundant "vitalism in the Jewish temper which acts like a sort of cosmopolitan galvanic battery."

Small wonder, if after these characterizations which range from "gadfly" to "galvanic battery," Ludwig Lewisohn should exclaim bitterly, "Satire and irony are the weapons of clever slaves. I wince whenever a new Jewish book or play is acclaimed by other Jews as merciless, mordant, hard, witty," and should add, "A Jewish book is a book written by a man who knows he is a Jew."

A complete evaluation of the Jewish cultural scene would, by rights, take into account both the work of the Jewish artist who "knows he is a Jew" and of the one whose creations, though not deliberately Jewish, may be, nevertheless, intrinsically just as true an expression of the Jewish spirit. But within the confines of one chapter, and for the special purpose of this book, a consideration of the second category would take us too far afield. It would lead us into an attempted evaluation of the qualities that constitute the special Jewish racial genius, not necessarily limiting it to aesthetic manifestations. Even such perennially intriguing speculations as the extent to which the illuminations of a Spinoza, a Marx, a Freud, or an Einstein, in their respective intellectual spheres, derive from their common genus as well as from their uncommon genius, would be pertinent. However, from the point of view of the American Jewish community as a group, only such aesthetic expression which is consciously Jewish can be viewed as relevant. We shall therefore limit ourselves to a discussion of

* "Race and Literature," *Menorah Journal,* October 1923.

those writers who reflect the process of Jewish integration into the American scene, as well as the problems coincident with this process. If the discussion is not to degenerate into a mere catalogue of names, it will not be possible to do more than indicate dominant trends and to consider a few of the chief figures associated with these trends. No brief single essay could begin to do justice to the intellectual ferment of American Jewry as shown by the numbers of the Jews active in every creative sphere and the variety of their contributions. But despite the kaleidoscopic nature of the task, one may allow oneself the luxury of two simple generalizations. The first of these is that Jewish expression in the arts is no isolated phenomenon leading a ghetto life of its own apart from the general American scene, but consistently follows the intellectual and aesthetic currents of our American life. The second of these, however, is that upon these currents, the ballast of a century-old historic tradition and the particular tempests of the present, to which Jewish life is subject, give Jewish aesthetic creation special propulsions whose course can be charted among the many tides of American life, and which can be described as Jewish.

Just as American literature as a whole, from colonial times on, follows the frontier and breaks up into regional segments so that one can see mirrored in novels, poems, and plays the nation's surge from Puritan East to the reaches of the Pacific, and the evolution of local cultural trends which are labeled as "New England" or "the Prairie" or "the South," so one can see the process repeated in the literary creation of the Jewish immigrant. He arrives on the cultural scene later; he has the handicaps of a foreign language, which he shares with other non-English speaking immigrant strains, but his particular saga, which begins with the arrival at Ellis Island and continues with the story of growing into America of several successive native-born generations, of the striking of roots in American soil, of the problems of adjustment with changing historic conditions, finally includes every section of the continent.

The Novel

Though the novel is not the literary field in which the American Jew has achieved greatest distinction, it presents the process of integration most clearly and should therefore be considered first and most extensively. Frequently, it merges into autobiography; therefore the line of demarcation between these two literary forms need not be too strictly maintained.

The American Jewish novel is the product of the twentieth century. Though a few novels by Jews appeared after the Civil War, the size of the Jewish community in the United States before the close of the nineteenth century was not sufficiently large to provide the raw materials of creation in any significant measure. With the first decade of the twentieth century, however, the impact of the Russian Jewish immigration, which had begun pouring into the United States after 1880, commenced to make itself felt. The newcomer, in the land perhaps as little as ten or fifteen years, became articulate. Consequently, there came into being a whole series of chronicles which might be called "Salute to America." They are the immigrant's apostrophe to the new world, mostly the expression of his hope, sometimes the record of his disillusionment. The most interesting as well as popular of these are Mary Antin's autobiography, *The Promised Land,* and Abraham Cahan's *The Rise of David Levinsky*. These merit special consideration because each crystallizes a period of Jewish life in the United States.

The Promised Land was published in 1912, before the author had reached the age of thirty. It is written in a lyric, ecstatic vein which no later immigrant generation was to recapture. It is the rhapsody of the persecuted immigrant child from Polotzk, in the Pale of Settlement, who in little over a decade finds the American dream come true in every particular. The golden land of opportunity has no moment of dross for the eager, gifted girl at whose knock all doors open. "I must not fail to testify that in America a child of the slums owns the land and all that is good in it," she sings, and again, "I am the youngest of America's children, and into my hands is given her priceless heritage." But to this paean is added a significant conclusion. The passion for the new world is accompanied by a desire for divorce from her past. "All the processes of uprooting, transportation, replanting, acclimatization, and development took place in my own soul. . . . I think I have thoroughly assimilated my past. . . . I have done its bidding. . . . I want now to be of today. It is painful to be conscious of two worlds. The Wandering Jew in me seeks forgetfulness." Here is the American counterpart of Zangwill's "Melting Pot" conception of America as the great crucible from which a new race would emerge, with no memory of ancient wounds or triumphs. This particular vision was never to be formulated with such vigorous optimism again. In its exultation it bears only superficial relation to later assimilatory tendencies which sprang from weariness and escapism, rather than from the immense gusto for a new life which one senses in Mary Antin.

The Rise of David Levinsky (1917) is written in a soberer vein. America is not wholly the thornless rose ripe for the plucking. The path to success is steeper, and the goal, once achieved, savors of sour as well as of sweet, but Abe Cahan's account of a Russian Talmud student's evolution into a rich American clothing manufacturer is one of the best of its kind. Levinsky's "rise" is presented without sentimentality, but also without the willful vulgarity which was to distort many later portraits of the Jewish business man in the United States. The character portrayal is clear and honest. The New York East Side is shown neither "quaintly" nor gushily but realistically. And the productive role of the Russian Jew in the development of the cloak and suit industry, which Cahan emphasizes, gives the novel a special sociological importance. Levinsky meditates on the achievements of his generation in positive terms. "Foreigners ourselves, and mostly unable to write English, we had Americanized the system of providing clothes for the American woman of moderate or humble means. ... We had done away with prohibitive prices and greatly improved the popular taste. Indeed, the Russian Jew had made the average American girl a tailor-made girl."

Of the many other writers who turned to the East Side for literary inspiration, it may be enough to mention Anzia Yezierska and Fannie Hurst. Both go in heavily for pathos and sentiment, but each has managed to write live and moving stories. Fannie Hurst, in particular, despite her tendency to tear an emotion to tatters, has genuine vitality as a writer. Fannie Hurst's approach to the ghetto is not that of an original dweller in it—she was born in Hamilton, Ohio—but of a sympathetic outsider who is able to exploit its "picturesque" literary possibilities to the utmost. *Humoresque* is characterized by her on the title pages as "a laugh on life with a tear behind it," and it lives up to the ominous possibilities of this sentiment; but Fannie Hurst, at her best, has a generous warmth and verve which make many of her ghetto portraits tender and memorable.

The sentimental stereotypes of the Jewish East Side mother, the soulful youth, etc., have their humorous counterparts in the work of a writer such as Montague Glass, whose *Potash and Perlmutter* series have become a part of American folklore. Abe Potash and Mauruss Perlmutter, amiably outwitting their rivals in the cloak and suit trade, and being outwitted in turn with equal geniality, are genuine comic types, but as presentations of the American Jew they are nonetheless caricatures. They have the limitations of the comic strip in the daily newspaper, and despite their cheery good nature give as misleading, because one-sided, a conception of the American Jew as the later venomous portraits of a Jerome Weidman. We laugh at Perlmutter's lament, "Real-estaters ain't got no such trouble like we got it, Abe. There ain't no seasons in real-estate. A tenement house this year is like a tenement house last year, Abe, also the year before. They ain't wearing stripes in tenement houses one year, Abe, and solid colors the next," but we know that we are watching a vaudeville show, not a presentation of varied and full-fledged human beings.

One of the first writers to break away from the "quaint" or caricature presentation of Jewish life in the United States is Edna Ferber. Although Edna Ferber's national reputation has been achieved primarily by novels such as *So Big* or *Cimarron,* which are purely American in subject matter, her novel *Fanny Herself* (1917), and her autobiography *A Peculiar Treasure* (1939), give a noteworthy picture of the development of the native-born American Jew. In *Fanny Herself,* we leave the world of the immigrant and the New York East Side. We also leave the "dialect" conception of Jewish life. Edna Ferber describes a Jewish community in Wisconsin. "They were of a type to be found in every small town; prosperous, conservative, constructive citizens, clannish but not so much so as their city cousins, mingling socially with their Gentile neighbors, living well, spending their money freely, taking a vast pride in the education of their children." It is, on the whole, the picture of increasing adaptation to the American scene. Molly Brandeis, the mother, is the ideal American business woman, energetic, resourceful, industrious, honored by her neighbors. Fanny, the daughter, is clearly destined to be the typical heroine of a typical American success story, in which talent and determination find their inevitable rewards. The Brandeis family fits completely into the American pattern. Fanny's Jewishness is something of which she is aware primarily as a spur to ambition, because it is a handicap to be overcome. "She made up her mind that she would admit no handicaps. Race, religion, training, natural impulses—she would discard them all if they stood in her way." But there is a tug which keeps drawing Fanny back.

Fanny Herself is a literary milestone in the integration of the American Jew with his country. Many brilliant Jewish boys and girls over the land, growing up in the years before the first World War, were to find achievement limited only by their capacities, but the proud conviction of Mary Antin is gone. A cloud appears on the apparently unbounded horizon. Hitler is still twenty years in the future, but the realization of a Jewish problem has come. There is as yet no awareness of anti-Semitism, but a rankling consciousness of prejudice, painful rather than tragic in its effects. Fanny meditates on the problem. "Antagonism here isn't religious. It's personal almost. . . . They don't object to us as a sect, or as a race, but as a type." A long road is traveled between this novel and the autobiography written twenty years later. What is merely an angry, puzzled astonishment in *Fanny Herself* becomes a proud affirmation. Jewishness is not only a handicap to be overcome, but "a peculiar treasure" whose riches serve not only as goads but as a reservoir of spiritual sustenance.

As the Jewish community branches out over the United States and begins to take root in various sections of the country, a Jewish regional literature arises which corresponds to the sectional trend in American letters as a whole. The sons and grandsons of immigrants are adding their chapters. The emphasis shifts from the drama of arrival in the new world to the delineation of individual character. Myron Brinig's *Singermann* is the chronicle of a Rumanian Jewish family in Montana. Vera Caspary (*Thicker Than Water*) describes a Portuguese Jewish family living in Chicago. Sidney Meller (*Roots in the Sky*) deals with a Russian Jewish family in California. Meyer Levin (*The Old Bunch*) and Albert Halper (*On the Shore*) have both written of Chicago. Other names could be added, but these suffice to indicate the extent of the geographic scene which American Jewish fiction begins to cover.

Of the writers mentioned, the most significant are Meyer Levin and Albert Halper. Levin's account of a "bunch" of young Jews growing up in Chicago is full of mordant observation. With irony and power he presents the dreary spectacle of an "Americanization" which consists of throwing off Jewish tradition. Albert Halper, who is generally classed as a "Proletarian novelist" because of such novels as *Union Square* and *The Foundry*, is at his best in such sketches as are to be found in *On the Shore*. Despite curious defects of style, he has extraordinary power of character portrayal. There are no types in his stories. Each person is sharply individualized and honestly conceived. His stories, with few exceptions, deal with the pathos of the individual and the pressure of social conditions, rather than with racial or religious problems as such.

Another member of the "social consciousness" school of writers who has written of Jews is Michael Gold. His *Jews Without Money* (1930) merits consideration not so much because of its literary importance, but because of the savage reaction it presents to the romanticization of the East Side and the life of the immigrant, popular a generation earlier. It is the complete antithesis of Mary Antin's passionate tribute. He writes, "The Jews had fled from European pogroms; with prayer, thanksgiving and solemn faith from a new Egypt into a new Promised Land. They found awaiting them the sweatshops, the bawdy houses, and Tammany Hall." Gold's East Side is a world of prostitutes, gangsters, and bed-bugs. America, the land of "opportunity," is castigated furiously: "America is so rich and fat because it has eaten the tragedy of millions of immigrants." Gold drives home his message of social protest with a vengeance. The unrelieved blackness of his picture is, in its way, as lacking in realism as the uncritical enthusiasm of a Mary Antin. It is a romanticism in reverse, whose lyricism finds expression in his outcry, "O, Workers' Revolution, you brought hope to me, a lonely suicidal boy. You are the true Messiah." For Gold, naturally there is no Jewish problem. There is only the class struggle. "Jewish bankers are fascists; Jewish workers are radicals." It's as simple as that.

A much abler "debunking" of the East Side has been achieved by Henry Roth in *Call It Sleep,* a novel which enjoyed an unusual critical success when it appeared in 1934. *Call It Sleep* has been hailed as the most talented novel written by any American Jew. It is an extraordinarily brilliant portrayal of life on the East Side as seen through the eyes of a morbidly sensitive child between the ages of five and eight. Here are no sentimental portraits of pious grandfathers and kerchiefed grandmothers. No quaint Old World atmosphere relieves the drabness of the environment which he describes. But within its color-range, the book has amazing power. Judging solely from *Call It Sleep,* Henry Roth has the literary equipment of a major novelist, which can be said of no other American Jewish writer. However, since no other book by Roth has appeared, it is impossible to tell whether he has reached the stature his first book indicated.

As one considers such novels as those of Roth, Halper, or Gold, one must bear in mind that the Jewish novelist naturally followed the literary traditions and fashions prevalent in his period. His description of Jewish life reflected the style and point of view of his generation. In American letters in general, nineteenth century romanticism, the glow of the frontier, was to make way for a drabber and more analytic realism. With the rise of industrialism, the growth of the metropolis, the simple enchantment with the new soil and the vast vistas of the opening continent was to lose its untroubled freshness. We begin to get the social criticism of a Dreiser, the photographic commentary of a Sinclair Lewis, and finally the fragmentation and dissipation of realism into gross naturalism, cynicism, or emigré escapism. The post-war years of the twenties were to be popularly ticketed as the decade of "disillusionment," of the "Waste Land" mood. With the thirties, with the rise of "social consciousness," the work of the later Hemingway and of John Steinbeck, the era of conscious futility gives way again to a search for new hopes and faiths.

In a narrower compass, one can see the same process repeated by the American Jewish novelist. Ellis Island was the "frontier" of the Jewish immigrant. The whimsy and optimism of O'Henry, the laughter-and-tears twist could be traced on a smaller scale in the work of a Fannie Hurst or Montague Glass. Realistic disenchantment, the novel of "social mores" and the family chronicle finds its counterpart in the works of the younger American Jewish writers. The somber bleak pictures of a Jewish slum in Chicago or New York indicate the same trend as James T. Farrel's portraits of sordid Irish slums, or Erskine Caldwell's presentations of the "poor white" of Georgia. Finally, the debunking mania comes to its grossest and belated climax in the novels of a Jerome Weidman.

I Can Get It for You Wholesale (1937) and *What's in It for Me?* (1938) by Jerome Weidman create still another literary Jewish stereotype—that of the rapacious, Jewish go-getter, without qualm or decency of any kind. The vulgar, vicious Harry Bogen, crooked and cruel in every relationship, is a monster who could have been lifted straight from Goebbel's propaganda sheets. Literary studies of the American businessman on the make have been presented without any roseate trimmings by a host of writers including Dreiser and Lewis, but Weidman's contribution to the gallery is caricature of the Julius Streicher variety. In view of the American Jew's prominence in the clothing industry and the motion picture field, it is natural that fiction should deal with him in these aspects. Harry Bogen, however, bears only the most superficial resemblance to reality of any kind.

Weidman's books are a morbid literary expression of Jewish self-hatred and self-contempt, and for that reason require attention as a phenomenon of our time. To what extent they are unconsciously the result of infection by the epidemic anti-Semitism of our era is a subject of speculation for the psychiatrist.

Weidman is not an isolated figure—Jewish self-criticism is not a new note (vide Ben Hecht in *A Jew in Love*)—but no other Jewish writer gives such a pathological exhibition of masochistic self-flagellation. A much more honest and intelligently conceived picture of a "go-getter" is to be found in Budd Schulberg's *What Makes Sammy Run?* Sammy's febrile rise from office boy to Hollywood magnate is plenty repellent. Sammy has his collection of unlovable traits, which are given a racial rather than individual origin, but he is nevertheless a plausible human being, and a comprehensible part of the fabulous Hollywood scene.

Both Weidman and Schulberg are careful to put in a "nice" Jew as a foil to their creations. The "nice" Jew is idealistic, unpractical, intellectual—the reverse of the chief protagonist. However, what remains in the memory is the furious drive "to advance," whose basis is indicated as the Jewish sense of inferiority and insecurity.

In their ways, even wholly negative portraits like those of Weidman, or character analyses like those of Schulberg, reveal a growing awareness of a Jewish problem in the United States. The awareness is not explicit, but a long distance has been gone from the untroubled assurance of the "Melting Pot" vision at the dawn of the century. American writers as a whole, growing into maturity, became aware of many problems in the huge complex of America and the increasing tension of social forces, but the Jewish writer could not escape the additional challenge of specific Jewish problems. The reactions were varied. The lure of assimilation became apparent in these writers who refused to take cognizance of their Jewish antecedents or their Jewish environment. The "proletarian" writers, like Michael Gold, sought for salvation in the hope of a world revolution which would efface race and class barriers. Even the Weidmans revealed in their misbegotten creations a lack of ease and assurance, a pathological reaction to the fury of Hitler.

The "Wandering Jew" of Mary Antin who expected to find "forgetfulness" begins to realize first that such forgetfulness cannot be achieved, and secondly, that such forgetfulness is not to be desired. The integration with the American scene is perceived to be not merely a painless merging, in which Jewishness is quietly effaced to blend into the richer whole. The shock of resistance encountered by "Fanny Herself," and more sharply by a later generation, gives rise to a group of Jewish writers who begin to affirm their race and cultural tradition in positive terms, instead of merely ignoring or deploring their status.

The eager flight from the past is arrested. The uncritical abandon of the "Melting Pot" intoxication of the first decade, the pained perception of the delusion of assimilation accompanied by a bitter probing of the Jewish organism, is followed by a return to the well of historic continuity. Naturally, the trends overlap. No absolutely neat chronology is possible. But throughout the twenties and thirties, there appears a group of writers that interprets integration with America not as a hasty absorption, not as an apologetic sloughing of a rich tradition, but as an affirmation of a racial personality whose best contribution to America is its proud unwarped self. Of these writers the chief, both in scope of talent and measure of achievement, is Ludwig Lewisohn.

A literary critic of great acumen and distinction, a superb essayist, Lewisohn prefers to think of himself as primarily a novelist, and consequently rejects the major position he has won as a thinker of passion and penetration for the secondary rank he is accorded in the field of American fiction. Yet his novels, good as several are, derive their power chiefly from the intellectual presentation of a thesis—generally, either the adjustment of an individual to the social morality of his period, or of the Jew to his environment. Because the voice of his hero is primarily his own voice, those of his novels which deal with the contemporary scene are stronger than his historical narratives such as the recent *Renegade*.

Lewisohn's literary career has been so fertile, varied and significant for the mental life of the American Jew and the literature of Zionism, that he merits an extensive study. The limitations of space, however, make it impossible to consider more than *Upstream,* the autobiography which is an American classic of its kind, and *The Island Within. Upstream* tells directly the story of the failure of assimilation which Lewisohn was to retell in subsequent novels. The realization that though his "psychical life was Aryan through and through," the fact of Jewish birth was an obstacle to complete acceptance by the American Gentile world, leads him to the poetic formulation: "So long as there is discrimination, there is exile." In *Upstream* Lewisohn already expresses the dominant theme of all his later writing: "The friend of the Republic, the lover of those values which alone make life endurable, must bid the German and the Jew, the Latin and the Slav, preserve his cultural tradition and beware of the encroachments of Neo-Puritan barbarism—beware of becoming merely another dweller on an endless 'Main Street.' "

The Island Within is a remarkably moving and effective fictionalized treatment of the same subject. Some of the most vital writing in English on the perennial Jewish question is to be found in this study of Arthur Levy, the American Jewish intellectual with no apparent Jewish roots, and of his return to his people.

Arthur Levy, after the failure of his marriage to a Gentile, determines to rediscover the treasure of his past which he has lost. He thinks of his child: "He must try to save his son's heritage for him, his incomparable spiritual heritage. His son should not stand before a Gentile friend as he had stood beside Charles Dawson, and wish that he, too, could boast as ancestors tartaned clansmen who had fought at Flodden Field. His son should have too much pride to need to be proud. Too much inner security to be hurt by words or slights. His son should be incapable of feeling excluded; he must possess the knowledge that he stood by birth at the human center of things."

The conscious rediscovery of the Jewish heritage to prevent the warping and impoverishment of the individual, as well as to provide a shield against attack, has been used as a literary theme by such a writer as Irving Fineman in *Hear, Ye Sons* (1933). Through his lyrical description of the orthodox forms and customs of life in a ghetto of Russian-Poland of the nineteenth century, Fineman seeks to show how Jews maintained a way of life rich in beauty and dignity despite oppression and persecution. His parable for our time is clear. Let the American Jew understand his traditional values, the fathers from whom he sprang. Only through such a sense of the ethical nobility of his antecedents, can he find a defense against the resurgent barbarism of a Hitler, and only through such a self-realization can he participate fittingly in the struggle for the redemption of his people, and of mankind,

It is a serious indictment of many Jewish writers that the complete, rather than the one-sided caricature Jew—be the caricature venomous or kindly—is absent from their pages. The easiest way to describe is to exaggerate a contour. A regular profile is harder to capture and to individualize than a hooked nose, consequently the superficial mannerism is frequently exploited at the expense of essential truth. Writers such as Lewisohn and Fineman restore dignity to the presentation of the Jew by virtue of the completeness of their picture. The same is true of certain historical novels which recreate heroic moments of the Jewish past. In this connection, one should mention Milton Steinberg's sensitive and finely written *As A Driven Leaf*, a study of a Jewish skeptic in the second century, and Harry Sackler's vigorous *Festival at Meron*, which also deals with the period of the Rabbi Akiba and the Bar Kochba rebellion. The Nazi persecutions have been directly reflected in American literature in such books as Fineman's *Dr. Addams*, the drama of the cultivated refugee's adjustment in the United States in contrast to the immigrant tales of two decades earlier, and Robert Nathan's *Road of Ages*. Though Nathan's novels reflect the major conflicts of our period, his *forte* is charm of style and whimsy of conception. The essential tragedy of the issues he raises is too often obscured by the sweetness and light of his treatment. However, as the bulk of Robert Nathan's work, like Edna Ferber's, deals with general rather than specifically Jewish themes, he belongs only incidentally to this discussion.

The Essay

The growing concern with Jewish problems which is reflected in fiction comes to even clearer expression in non-fiction. Through the medium of the anthology, the essay, the treatise, even the travel chronicle, the American Jew seeks to orient himself in a world which has seen the beginnings of the reconstruction of Palestine and the rise of Hitler. What begins in the twenties as academic literary discussion develops with the spread of fascism into a passionate and urgent debate. Among the chief figures in this field is Maurice Samuel, who in addition to being a brilliant, polemical writer is a translator, both in verse and prose, of extraordinary gifts. His three main works on the Jewish question *You Gentiles, I, the Jew,* and *The Great Hatred* form a trenchant and vivid analysis of the questions of Jewish nationalism and anti-Semitism. In *The Great Hatred* he advances, with epigrammatic force, the challenging thesis that anti-Semitism is essentially a revolt against Christianity and the Judaeo-Christian tradition. Of this work Thomas Mann has written: "No better analysis has ever been given of anti-Semitism as a phenomenon falling outside the field of normal prejudices and antipathies."

A writer of quite different *genre* is Marvin Lowenthal. If Samuel is at times the unbridled satirist and savage pamphleteer, Marvin Lowenthal is the urbane, sophisticated, gently ironic commentator *par excellence*. His *A World Passed By* (1933), ostensibly a record of a journey to the seats of Jewish civilization in Europe and Africa, manages to evoke forty centuries of Jewish history and the spirit of Jewish survival through ancient, medieval and modern times more poignantly than any other single book. As a stylist of exquisite precision and restraint, as a subtle and refined intelligence, Lowenthal belongs in the front rank of American essayists.

THE DRAMA

It is in the drama that the American Jew has achieved greatest distinction. Whereas it is possible to pick up a serious critical study of the foremost ten or twelve American novelists, and irrespective of the particular handful the particular author may have selected, find not a single Jewish novelist in the list, no discussion of the American drama can disregard the importance of the American Jew to its development. Of the twenty-one Pulitzer Prizes awarded between 1917 and 1938, four were won by Jewish playwrights which, in view of the size of the Jewish population, is a huge percentage. And one need merely mention such names as Elmer Rice, John Howard Lawson, Ben Hecht, George S. Kaufman, Sidney Kingsley, Clifford Odets, Irwin Shaw, Lillian Hellman, S. N. Behrman, to get some notion of the literary caliber and the variety of contribution involved.

Nothing explodes the fallacy of facile generalizations, such as Isabel Paterson's or Burton Rascoe's about the "Judaic strain" in letters, better than a consideration of the work of these dramatists. Ben Hecht and George S. Kaufman are undoubtedly masters of satire and burlesque; they have the sharp wit, the dangerous "cleverness," which enable them to qualify as "gadflies of American literature"—though in view of the derogatory sense in which Isabel Patterson employs the term, it might be well to remember that Socrates also called himself a "gadfly"—but what about the high seriousness of an Elmer Rice, or a Sidney Kingsley, the passionate idealism of Lillian Hellman, the revolutionary ardor of Clifford Odets? If Jews have been prominent in the slick successes of Broadway and Hollywood, they have also been prime movers of such non-commercial experimental theaters as the Washington Square Players, the Neighborhood Playhouse and the Theatre Guild.

The American drama reveals the range and degree of Jewish talent; it does not, however, show the intensification of Jewish consciousness in the United States as clearly as the novel. Vital and dignified Jewish characters appear in any number of the plays as Simon in Elmer Rice's *Counsellor at Law* or Dr. Hochberg in Kingsley's *Men in White,* but Jewish life as such is presented only occasionally. Dreamy Jewish tailors, hilarious Hollywood producers, noble Jewish scientists, smart-alecky Jews and helpless, idealistic souls march across the stage in a considerable number of productions, but rarely is Jewish life or a Jewish problem the dominant explicit theme. Exceptions to this tendency are Arthur Kober, Clifford Odets and Irwin Shaw in his tender and sympathetic *The Gentle People*.

Arthur Kober in *Having a Wonderful Time* and Clifford Odets in *Awake and Sing* both deal with Bronx Jews, but there the resemblance ends. The Bronx has replaced the East Side as a kind of Jewish sociological zoo which provides a happy hunting ground for literary material. In *Having a Wonderful Time* Kober creates the same types that he has popularized in numerous sketches in *The New Yorker*. He has described the type himself as "Fay is the complete apotheosis of that smug and self-sufficient borough of New York, the Bronx. Her features, manners, gestures and sing-song intonation are unmistakably identified." Kober's verisimilitude extends no deeper than a superficial imitation of obvious speech patterns: "Because is all the time more girls in camp than boyess." His characters are second-generation stereotypes, and follow the tradition of the immigrant East Side stereotypes of twenty years earlier; only his Bronx Jews, innocuous and mildly comical as they are, are a grosser and more materialistic lot than their immigrant forebears.

A complete antithesis to the "smug," faintly repellent Bronx of Kober's creation may be seen in Clifford Odets' *Awake and Sing* which, characteristically, takes its title from Isaiah's "Awake and sing, ye that dwell in dust." Odets also captures idiom and speech patterns, but he manages to convey not merely the external cadence and gesture, but the inner rhythm, the conflicts and frustration of his characters' lives. Odets is the leading figure in the drama of social protest, but his plays never degenerate into dogmatic preachments of a revolutionary thesis. He calls *Awake and Sing* "a struggle for life amid petty conditions," but the struggle he presents is not the animal ferocity of a Jerome Weidman or the semi-sordid, semi-genteel "getting on" of a Kober, but a longing for "life" in a more generous sense, a revulsion against the mean and ugly in the social environment. "We don't want life printed on dollar bills," cries out one of his characters. The passion and idealism in Odets' plays, reflect deep aspects of the Jewish spirit more truthfully than the trivial vulgarities of Kober.

POETRY

Jews early made themselves heard in American poetry. In the nineteenth century we come across the recluse figure of Penina Moise (1797-1880), a member of the *Sephardic* Jewish community of Charleston, South Carolina, who composed *Hymns Written for the Use of Hebrew Congregations* and the impetuous Adah Isaacs Menken ("La Belle Menken"—1835-1868) whose brief dramatic career, from her birth in New Orleans to death in Paris, included sensational success as an actress in America and Europe, half-fulfilled literary dreams, friendships with Swinburne and Walt Whitman and a personal tragedy of great intensity. Adah Menken is chiefly memorable because despite her own spectacular successes, she, almost from adolescence, displayed an unflagging awareness of her bond with Jews everywhere. She reacted passionately to the kidnaping of Edgar Mortara by the Holy Inquisition, and to the denial of a seat in Parliament to Baron Rothschild. The poems she wrote on those occasions were notable more for emotion than originality, but they made an impression on a wide public. She seems to have nurtured semi-Messianic delusions, viewing herself as a medium of the restoration. *The New York Sunday Mercury* characterized her in 1860 in the following fashion, "The lady is a Jewess, and almost insane in her eagerness to behold her people restored once more to their ancient power and glory."

A far more significant figure of the same period was Emma Lazarus (1849-1887) whose famous sonnet *The New Colossus* is inscribed on the Statue of Liberty. Born in New York City, in a cultured, middle-class home, Emma Lazarus recapitulates, in her own poetic development, a by now familiar pattern. Her first

literary interests were general. The friend of Emerson, of C.
Stedman, of John Burroughs, the precociously gifted Jewish girl
early won attention through lyrics and poetic dramas on favorite
nineteenth century themes—largely classical in inspiration. A few
titles are self-explanatory—*Admetus, Tannhäuser, Agamemnon's
Tomb,* etc. When Stedman urged upon her the wealth of Jewish
tradition as a source of creation, she is supposed to have replied
that "although proud of her blood and lineage, the Hebrew
ideals did not appeal to her." But the Russian pogroms of 1881
roused her as they roused every sensitive person in the United
States. From this point on she becomes definitely the literary
champion of her people in prose as well as poetry. She dedicates
"Songs of a Semite" to George Eliot. She writes a series of articles
in *The Century Magazine* which attract national attention. In
one of these, refreshingly entitled *The Jewish Problem* (February,
1833) she makes her Zionist declaration of faith: "I am fully
persuaded that all suggested solutions other than this [Zionism]
are but temporary palliatives. . . . The idea formulated by George
Eliot has already sunk into the minds of many Jewish enthusiasts
and it germinates with miraculous rapidity." Subsequently, she
summarizes her objectives in terms which have a curiously modern
ring: The Jews should return to the varied pursuits and broad
system of physical and intellectual education of their forefathers;
they should engage in more fraternal movements for the allevia-
tion of the sufferings of oppressed Jews not as fortunate as those
of the United States. They should study Hebrew literature and
history more widely, and perceive the principles of religion, liberty
and law upon which Judaism is founded.

Her poetic creation began to reflect her new conviction. In addition to numerous able translations of Ibn Gabirol, Halevy, and
Heine, she wrote lyrics and poetic dramas on Jewish themes which
stood comparison with the serious poetic output of her contemporaries. She is derivative in style; she is definitely a minor poet,
but she is by no means a negligible figure within the literary

tradition of her period. Such a work as *The Dance to Death,* a verse drama, set in the fourteenth century, and dealing with the accusation that the Jews were causing the Black Death, deserves to be better known. It is full of a passionate eloquence which begs for quotation. The rabbi calls on his congregation to go festally dancing to the pyre on which they will burn for the sanctification of the name.

> Bring from the Ark the bell-fringed, silken-bound
> Scrolls of the law. Gather the silver vessels,
> Dismantle the rich curtains of the doors,
> Bring the Perpetual Lamp; all these shall burn . . .

And another character offers the eternal Jewish consolation to those about to perish:

> Wherever in the ages shall arise
> Jew-priest, Jew-poet, Jew-singer, or Jew-saint—
> And everywhere I see them star the gloom—
> In each of these, the martyrs are avenged.

Only occasionally were later American Jewish poets to write with so clear and challenging a sense of Jewish dedication.

In the twentieth century, a number of distinguished Jewish names appear among serious American poets. Jewish writers take an active part in the poetic renaissance which begins in the second decade of the century. No Jewish poet reaches the rank of T. S. Eliot, or Robert Frost, or even an Elinor Wylie; but any consideration of American poetry is bound to take cognizance of such figures as Louis Untermeyer, James Oppenheim, Maxwell Bodenheim, Babette Deutsch or Kenneth Fearing—to mention only a few. American Jewish poets reflect the various poetic fads of which the last decades have been so prolific. The imagism of Bodenheim, the "word" fetishism of Gertrude Stein, the "objectivism" of Louis Zukofsky, give one some notion of the variety of styles. Louis Untermeyer writing on "The Jewish Spirit in

Modern American Poetry"* attempts to create a synthesis. He offers three dominant traits as Semitic: the poetry of exaltation, the Messianic note; the poetry of disillusionment and bitter irony; the poetry of exultation and thanksgiving, the old Hebraic impulse to sing and give praise. Such a list is sufficiently general to defeat all attempts at generalization. One is reduced to considering the individual poet as an exponent of a poetic school rather than as a "Jewish" poet unless the core of his interest—as that of Emma Lazarus—makes the characterization justifiable.

The majority of the American Jewish poets turn to Jewish subjects only sporadically. Maxwell Bodenheim, master of the ingenious image bordering on conceit, may write of an "Old Jew." The sensitive intelligence of Babette Deutsch finds expression in an occasional "Jewish" poem. James Oppenheim, using the sweeping rhythms of the Bible and of Whitman, is more consistently Jewish. In a rhapsodic poem *Hebrews,* he exclaims triumphantly:

> Mighty race! mighty race!—my flesh, my flesh
> Is a cup of song,
> Is a well in Asia.

Louis Untermeyer, indefatigable as a poet, anthologist, parodist, translator, and critic, is himself the best illustration of the "troubled energy" he finds characteristic of the Jewish spirit. Without the tortuous imagery of a Maxwell Bodenheim or the delicate music of a Joseph Auslander or Robert Nathan, his verse is direct and forceful as the popular *Caliban in the Coal Mines*. His Jewish verse, at its best, is to be found in *Roast Leviathan,* an exuberant, opulent description of the final banquet that will rejoice God's Chosen People on the Judgment Day.

The Jewish "proletarian" poets, of whom Kenneth Fearing is the most original and most talented, refer to Jewish backgrounds or ghetto scenes primarily as a means of intensifying their social protest. Like Michael Gold in the novel, or Clifton Odets in the

---

* *Menorah Journal,* August, 1931.

drama, their Jewish consciousness is only incidental to their description of the reaction of a particular environment to the economic pressure of capitalist society. Though not strictly speaking in this category, mention of the younger poets should take into account Delmore Schwartz, whose recent *Shenandoah*, a verse play dealing with a circumcision ceremony in the Bronx, has received wide critical acclaim. In its brooding sense of destiny inherent in the trivial circumstance as well as the major catastrophe, it reveals a new, original talent.

Curiously enough, the agony of modern Jewry has found little adequate lyric expression, considering the vastness of the tragedy. There has been no general literary reaction to the Nazi persecutions equaling in scale that aroused by Emma Lazarus after 1881. The specifically Anglo-Jewish poets, who devote themselves energetically to hymning Jewish pain and disaster, are for the most part negligible as literary figures. Two poets that should be separated from the usual run of the mill versifiers that appear in the Anglo-Jewish press are Charles Reznikoff, whom William Rose Benét called "the best of the definitely Jewish poets writing today, since the death of James Oppenheim," and the Canadian, Abraham M. Klein, who has been hailed by Ludwig Lewisohn as "the first contributor of authentic Jewish poetry to the English language." Reznikoff's luminous *Rashi* and his moving *Kaddish* for modern Jewry have been variously reprinted. The body of his work reiterates his faith—as *In Memoriam: 1933*—in the eternal vitality of Israel, despite the fury of the oppressor, be it "the wheel of Rome" or Hitler. Of the recurrent enemy, he writes:

> When they have become a legend
> and Rome a fable,
> that old men will tell of in the city's gate,
> the tellers will be Jews and their speech Hebrew.

Abraham Klein's *Hath Not a Jew* reveals a musical range and versatility of authentic charm. Such poems as his *Design for*

Medieval Tapestry and *Haggadah* show with what skill and whimsical tenderness Klein can use traditional themes.

A poet of slighter scope but significant as one of the few Zionist poets in English is Jessie Sampter. Though lacking great resources of language or imagination, she writes with a sustained clarity of purpose, a simplicity of diction, which preserve her from the banalities and fustian of most minor verse writers. Her *The Emek,* which consist of free verse sketches of the experience of the pioneer in Palestine, is unpretentious and effective. In *The Book of the Nations*, a prose poem modeled on the prophetic books, she formulates her Zionist vision in a more conventionally exalted way:

> My people has found the bread of life growing in a dry land: those that lived by my word shall live also by my wheat.
> For in the clefts of rock, on the rugged heights of Hermon, they have found the mother of wheat, the wild wheat that nurtured man.
> Give, O my people, give to a hungry world the bread of life.
> Give, O my people, give to a dying world the word of life.

One should not conclude the consideration of American Jewish poets without at least mentioning the light verse writers among whom Jews have been superlatively successful. The barbed Dorothy Parker, the deft F. P. A., Newman Levy, Arthur Guiterman, Samuel Hoffenstein, are among the chief of these. Through their light verse, these worthies have managed to deliver many a heavy jab at the "booboisie," and can be viewed in their way, as among the social commentators of the time.

THE PRESS

When we turn to the American press as a whole, we find Jewish journalists and publicists of the first order. It is enough to recall Simeon Strunsky, whose engaging *Topics of the Times* are a daily delight among the otherwise austere editorial columns of the New York *Times*, or Walter Lippmann of the *Herald Tribune*, to make one's point. Every shade of economic or political doctrine has Jewish exponents of first-rate ability, but despite the richness and variety of the Jewish contribution to the general press, the Anglo-Jewish press presents a bleak expanse.

Although more than a hundred Jewish periodicals now appear regularly among sixty-one communities in the United States, reaching approximately 250,000 homes, the general intellectual and literary level of these journals is abysmally low. The reason is not far to seek. Not only do talented Jewish publicists find a ready reception in general American periodicals, but till recent years the average Anglo-Jewish periodical reflected primarily local community interests. Consequently, potboilers and syndicated releases, and editorials on vague sonorous themes, were considered adequate intellectual sustenance for the subscribers.

However, the growing awareness of Jewish issues in the United States and in the world has been accompanied by the establishment of Anglo-Jewish periodicals of a far higher intellectual and stylistic level than had been customary. These periodicals reflect the development of Jewish ideologies in the United States, and the reaction of the American Jew to current problems. Such periodicals as *The Congress Weekly* (published by the American Jewish Congress), the Labor Zionist *Jewish Frontier,* and *Opinion* interpret the political and economic scene in a manner which represents an enormous advance over what had previously been identified as Anglo-Jewish journalism. First-rate articles by first-rate journalists are frequently found in these publications, and though they are associated with definite ideological trends, the influence of these journals extends far beyond the points of view they represent.

The *Menorah Journal*, which at present, unfortunately, appears only as a quarterly, is still the leading literary journal of American Jewry. It has done a genuine pioneer service to American Jewish letters in the course of its history. Many Jewish writers of national reputation first found a hearing in its discerning pages.

Recent years have also seen the establishment of serious scholarly journals like the quarterly *Jewish Social Studies* and the bimonthly, the *Contemporary Jewish Record*. Both these periodicals provide much valuable material for the student of Jewish life. The publication of such journals indicates the need for a Jewish orientation felt among all circles of American Jewry. Even Jews committed to no nationalist or Zionist philosophy of Jewish living seek the firmer background afforded by history to assist them in the confusion of the present.

THE ROLE OF YIDDISH LITERATURE

One cannot leave the Jewish cultural scene in the United States without some reference to Yiddish literature in this country. The subject is so comprehensive that by rights it should be treated at length. Since a perfunctory discussion would be wholly inadequate to the richness of the theme, only a few general comments will be made.

Yiddish literature in the United States is but one branch of a great literature which flourished in Poland, in Lithuania, and, after a fashion, in Soviet Russia. Since the war, with the destruction of the literary centers in Warsaw and Vilna, the center of gravity has shifted to the United States. But even before the outbreak of the war, Yiddish literature, despite numerous gloomy prognostications as to its fate, showed no sign of decline. The number of Yiddish readers may have decreased since the restriction of immigration, but the number of Yiddish writers has constantly been reinforced by fresh talent coming from overseas.

One can get some notion of the nature of the Yiddish literary output in the United States since 1900, if one merely mentions Sholem Aleichem, Sholem Asch, and I. J. Singer in fiction, and Yehoash and Leivick in poetry. Sholem Aleichem has been called the Jewish Mark Twain, but that is an injustice to Sholem Aleichem who is the far greater comic genius and the most considerable Jewish literary figure since Heine. No Jewish novelist writing in English has shown the crude strength and wide sweep of Sholem Asch.

As to Yehoash, even apart from his stature as a poet, he has made a permanent contribution to Jewish letters by his monumental translation of the Bible into Yiddish. Of Leivick, it may be said that he is the most significant Jewish poet in the United States. He has an authentic and individual lyric idiom which displays itself not through eccentricities of form but through a fecund poetic imagination. His poetic drama *The Golem* has been partially translated into English. The whole series of poems that he has written since the Nazi persecutions began, such as *The Yellow Badge*, represents the keenest poetic reaction to the Jewish agony of our era that has as yet been achieved. Leivick has the major poet's capacity to feel, and to translate feeling into images of somber and original power.

The few names mentioned only scratch the surface. Yiddish writing has followed every literary mode in the United States. Realism, expressionism, imagism, free verse, "Proletarian" writing, traditionalism, all have their talented and prolific practitioners. The number of new books, periodicals, anthologies crowding each other off the presses testify to the luxuriant vitality of Yiddish literature.

The Yiddish press in the United States is a phenomenon by itself. The circulation of the Yiddish dailies was recently estimated at 400,000, indicating a decline from the peak of 598,347 which it attained in 1927. The chief Jewish daily is still the socialist *Forward*, edited by Abe Cahan, which boasts a circulation of about 200,000 and is the largest Yiddish daily in the world. The other important dailies are the Zionist *Day*, the conservative *Morning Journal*, and the Communist *Freiheit*.

Though the Yiddish press is curiously uneven in character, often carrying within the same issue sentimental drivel of the most inane quality and a serious political discussion of the first order, its general level is infinitely higher than that of the Anglo-Jewish press. This is due to the fact that it can command the contributions of the ablest Yiddish writers of the period. Consequently, the Yiddish press has served as a forum of intellectual debate in which major economic, philosophical, or literary problems have been threshed out by such superb and many-faceted essayists as Hayim Greenberg, Zhitlowsky, or the recently deceased A. Coralnik. In addition, the daily press is supplemented by weeklies and monthlies which display a similar energy and activity.

The Yiddish theater has something of the unevenness of the Yiddish press. On the one hand, there are the maudlin melodramas of Second Avenue; on the other hand, there has been such an artistic phenomenon as the Yiddish Art Theatre whose influence was reflected far beyond Second Avenue. Even those ignorant of Yiddish, attended such productions as *Yoshe Kalb*. Dramatists of the caliber of Peretz Hirshbein and David Pinski have, in addition to Asch, Singer and Leivick, given the Yiddish theater in America quality and atmosphere.

One cannot escape the conclusion that the literary output of Yiddish writers in the United States has reached greater heights than that attained by American Jewish writers, except possibly in the field of the drama. Whether this is due to a longer cultural tradition, a profounder rooting in Jewish history and Jewish folkways, is a speculation that is worth advancing.

Conclusion

Strictly speaking, the sciences and the arts other than literature belong to the cultural scene, but as we indicated at the outset, many of the chief Jewish figures in those fields do not fall within the limits we have accepted. Albert Michelson in physics, Morris Cohen, Horace Kallen, or Sidney Hook in philosophy, George Jean Nathan and Paul Rosenfeld in criticism, and many others, are indications of the active, productive role played by Jews in the intellectual life of the United States. In contemporary music, painting, sculpture, architecture, or the dance, Jews are creative figures of the first rank. But save for such a musician as Ernest Bloch, who declared, "Racial consciousness is absolutely necessary in music even though nationalism is not. . . . I am a Jew. I aspire to write Jewish music not for the sake of self-advertisement but because it is the only way in which I can create music of ability," they do not belong within the circumscribed province of this discussion.

To resume, Jewish cultural life in the United States reflects the weaving of successive immigrant strains into the many-threaded fabric of the United States. In their intellectual variety and emotional scope, American Jewish writers wholly invalidate attempts to segregate them into pet categories. Our prophets are as vocal as our satirists, our dreamers as articulate as our materialists. Above all, under the impact of the cataclysmic forces shaking the world, American Jewish literature has begun to show a spiritual coming of age, a mature awareness of a Jewish past which carries with it the surest promise of a rich and full American future.

V

HEBREW IN JEWISH CULTURE

—

Abraham S. Halkin

The Background

IN THEIR long history the Jews have learned and forgotten numerous languages. A small and migratory group, they have readily adopted the vernaculars of politically or culturally preeminent peoples. They gave up Hebrew in favor of Aramaic as a medium of expression quite early in their history. Aramaic yielded to Arabic under the driving force of a linguistic mass-conversion which occurred in the territories of the Arab Empire. In Europe, the Jews spoke the languages of the majority in the various countries. And, although in the isolation of the ghetto or Pale of Jewish Settlement Yiddish attained, for a time, undisputed sway, it has of late been retreating rapidly before the tongues of the modern nations.

Yet, loyalty to the Hebrew language has remained a constant throughout the centuries. Economic, social, even cultural forces might induce the Jew to become linguistically part of his environment. But in the intimate spiritual experience of religion, Hebrew reigned supreme. And the less recourse he had to his ancient tongue in his daily speech, the more he clung to it as a symbol. Hebrew became a sacred language—an indispensable element of the Jewish religion.

Moreover, since religion long permeated all aspects of life, the Jew remained in continuous communion with Hebrew. Until very recently, practically all formal prayer was in Hebrew; and that meant at least three daily services. A very important adjunct of the service was the reading from the Pentateuch and the Prophets, which attuned the ear of the worshiper to a considerable amount of Hebrew literature. Similarly, the belief that the education of the male child constituted a religious obligation resulted in a widespread familiarity with Hebrew learning. Practically all Jewish men received at least a minimum amount of instruction in Hebrew and gained a minimum knowledge of Hebrew books, such as the Bible, Mishna and Midrash (homiletic literature). Some became advanced scholars and even wrote books and commentaries. Thus any comparison between Hebrew and Latin as languages of liturgy and ritual would be misleading. Hebrew remained close to the daily life even of the average Jew.

The influence of religion in the preservation of Hebrew has been paramount. But so deep are the roots of the ancestral tongue in the Jewish consciousness, that repeatedly Jews have returned to it and employed it as a medium of literary expression. For example, although completely at home in the cultures and languages of medieval Spain and Italy, numerous men of genius produced a considerable volume of poetry, *belles-lettres,* and philosophic and scientific writings in the Hebrew language. And the employment of Hebrew for secular purposes gained particular impetus during the eighteenth and especially the nineteenth centuries. The impact of the Enlightenment in France and Germany, with its interest in the world of nature and man, and the necessity for modernization which Jewish Emancipation rendered urgent, impelled Hebrew literature to assume new functions and to venture into fields far removed from the traditional confines of religion.

A great deal of this activity was didactic in purpose; the authors preached a message of modernization, and Hebrew was the only literary medium through which a part of the Jewish audience could be reached. Yet most of those who employed the language manifested a deep love for it; a zeal to extend the radius of its influence and to foster its literary creativity. Thus did a modern Hebrew literature come into being—a literature which gave expression to the revolutionary changes which were transforming the East European Jewish communities of the late nineteenth century. The need to express new ideas and conceptions, to clarify novel problems, revitalized the language of the Bible; and it, in its turn, helped awaken the slumbering Jewish towns of Russia, Poland and Galicia.

Haskalah, or Enlightenment, is the name generally applied to this renaissance of Hebrew culture. By the 1880's its influence had become widespread and profound in Eastern Europe. Essayists, novelists, poets and publicists had for half a century battled against conservatism and inertia. With romantic fervor they preached the gospel of physical labor, especially on the soil. They sang the praises of humanism and progress. They beckoned to the masses to leave the isolated and self-contained Jewish community and to share in the glories of European culture and enlightenment. Isaac Baer Levinson and Moses Lillienblum spoke of the nobility of labor. The revolt against conservatism was especially evident in the novels of Smolenskin and Mapu. The poet J. L. Gordon lashed out against the forces which, he thought, impeded progress—against the strictly-regulated religious life, against formalism, against excessive spiritualization of life. Other poets with a romantic strain, like Micah Lebenson and Mordecai Maneh, sang sentimentally of nature and of man's yearning for beauty and for the joy of life—rather new themes in Hebrew literature.

The pogroms of the early 1880's dampened the ardor for "European," that is Russian, civilization, and with startling suddenness, the whole Hebrew cultural movement became impregnated with the ideal of national revival in Palestine. Zionism from its very inception as a movement thus became indissolubly linked with the Hebrew language. And as the Zionist program evolved,

Hebrew assumed a central position similar to that which it occupied in the Jewish religion. To the unconscious recognition of the affinity between Palestine and the Hebrew language was now added a clear realization that Jewish nationhood could find its true expression only through the medium of the ancestral tongue. The profound idea emerged that, if a land was necessary to provide a physically unifying force for a scattered people, a common language was indispensable to transform a linguistically heterogeneous people into a cultural unity.

HEBREW CULTURE IN AMERICA

It was at this stage of its development that a segment of the Hebrew cultural movement was transferred to America with the wave of immigration from Eastern Europe. Not that the two preceding waves had been indifferent to Hebrew. Certainly, the *Sephardic* immigrants had brought a religious heritage, a good deal of it Hebraic. The German settlers, too, among whom there was an admixture of Polish Jews, had been in possession of a rich Hebrew culture. But the seeds which had been sown by these groups had hardly taken root. The number of Jews had been relatively small—too small to provide the atmosphere for cultural creativity. The situation of the new immigrants was different; they came in large numbers, settled in concentrated groups, and maintained contact with the Hebrew movement "back home." With an enthusiasm which bid defiance to insuperable obstacles, attempts were made to organize Hebrew speaking societies and to inaugurate a Hebrew press. The colorful and tragic poet, N. H. Imber, the author of *Hatikvah*, I: D. Eisenstein, editor of the Hebrew Encyclopedia, *Otzar Yisrael*, Reuben Brainin, who edited several of the early Hebrew journals, and others labored, wrote and dreamt of a Hebrew movement in America. But the results of these pioneer efforts were meager. A Hebrew weekly, *Haivri*, founded in 1892, was abandoned after a decade of incessant struggle. A monthly, *Ner Maaravi*, lingered for a little over a year. Unbounded faith and enthusiasm created other publications—some twenty occasional journals—but they could not be kept alive.

Faith and idealism alone could not cope with the circumstances which prevailed among the masses of American Jews during the generation preceding the first World War. Life was hard, the hours of labor in the sweat-shop long and exhausting, and men and women simply could not find the peace of mind to concern themselves with the ideal of a Hebrew renaissance. The religious elements continued to pray in the Hebrew language; they built schools and stubbornly tried to impart the ancient tradition to the young. But social forces worked havoc with their efforts, as it did with the plans of the Hebraists. The struggle for existence absorbed all energies. The masses looked to the labor unions and the radical Yiddish press for leadership, and both were largely anti-religious and anti-Hebraic in the early years. So gloomy was the outlook that the great Hebrew poet, Bialik, exclaimed, "How great, oh, how great is the desolation in the full, widely-open land!"

The profound effects which the first World War had on American Jewry quickened popular interest in the Hebrew movement. Suddenly aware that the Jews of the United States were a distinct religious and cultural group in the making, rather than mere fragments of Old World Jewries, they became more mature, more conscious of their responsibility, more aware of their relationship to fellow-Jews abroad. And particularly stimulating were the remarkable achievements of Zionism. The Balfour Declaration and the Palestine Mandate raised the Zionist movement above the level of party or faction. Distinguished statesmen and powerful governments gave their sanction to Jewish national aspirations, and the Zionist leadership was recognized everywhere as the responsible voice of the Jewish people. The President of the United States and the Congress, without a dissenting voice, commended the efforts to restore Palestine, and the American people cheered and encouraged their Jewish fellow citizens who lent their support to this historic undertaking.

But Zionism was closely linked to the Hebrew cultural movement, and Palestine was conspicuously Hebraic. As the population of Palestine increased and the scope of the *Yishuv* (Palestine Jewish community) expanded, the influence was increasingly felt in America; for the building of Palestine has never been a one-way process. The founding of the Hebrew University in Jerusalem, a wide variety of Hebrew publications, new songs and dances born of the soil of Hebraic Palestine; above all, the miracle of the revival of the Hebrew language as a living vernacular fired the imagination of American Jews.

In this atmosphere, the Hebrew forces began to stir with renewed vigor. New periodicals appeared, notably the monthly *Hatoren,* under the editorship of Brainin, and the *Miklat,* edited by I. D. Berkowitz. The literary standard of the latter journal, a monthly, would warrant comparison with the finest periodical literature in any language. So great was the enthusiasm that an effort was even made, in 1921, to launch a Hebrew daily newspaper, the *Hadoar.* To be sure, that was rather quixotic, and the attempt was abandoned after eight months. But in 1922, the *Hadoar* was converted into a weekly, and it has functioned under the editorship of M. Ribalow to the present day. For two decades the active Hebrew elements have rallied under its standard, and today, it estimates its reading public at approximately 15,000. In 1939, a Hebrew monthly journal, the *Bitzaron,* made its appearance. Under the editorship of Chaim Tchernowitz, it quickly gained a following and, after barely three years of publication, it counts its readers—about 4500—in every state of the Union.

The central agency for the dissemination of Hebrew culture in America is the *Histadruth Ivrith,* or Hebrew Organization. Founded in New York City more than two decades ago, it has provided direction to the local Hebrew committees which function in various cities, and it has initiated or participated in numerous undertakings involving the Hebrew language and literature. Through its weekly organ, the *Hadoar*, readers throughout the United States are brought in spiritual contact with Hebrew literary figures both here and abroad. A bi-weekly children's supplement, *Hadoar Lanoar,* is used widely in Hebrew schools as reading matter. A Hebrew Yearbook (*Sefer Hashanah*) affords an outlet for longer contributions by American authors in the literary and scholarly fields. A publishing company (Ogen), founded by the *Histadruth Ivrith,* has issued more than fifty books and pamphlets, including an anthology of American Hebrew poetry.

The *Histadruth Ivrith* devotes particular attention to Jewish education. It co-operates in the preparation of reading materials for children, in raising the standards of the teaching profession, in providing advanced courses for Jewish teachers, in the publication of a pedagogical quarterly entitled *Shevilei Hahinuch*. All of these efforts are directed to the end that the Hebrew language and literature be recognized as basic elements in American Jewish education.

By means of popular education and propaganda, the *Histadruth Ivrith* reaches a wider audience among Jewish adults. Hebrew circles have been organized in various cities, and lecturers, many of them distinguished writers and scholars, visit the Jewish communities and stimulate their activities. Every opportunity is utilized to arrange public forums and celebrations, so as to keep the Hebrew movement before the public eye. An interesting feature of this propaganda is the celebration of famous anniversaries, such as those of the celebrated medieval Hebrew poet, Judah Halevi, of the medieval philosopher, Saadia Gaon, and of Rashi, the great Bible commentator. Another effective instrument has been the emphasis on the literary values of the Bible. Imitating a similar movement in Palestine, the *Histadruth Ivrith* has helped to popularize daily readings from the Bible. The slogan is, "Read the Bible daily, read it in the original language—in Hebrew."

The most significant achievement of the *Histadruth Ivrith* has been the enlistment of youth in its work. In 1936, a Hebrew youth organization (*Histadruth Hanoar Haivri*) was founded, and young people have been encouraged to take part in the Hebrew movement. Dramatics, the dance and choral work have been encouraged, and a small group of young writers of promise have gathered around a monthly journal dedicated to their own efforts.

The financial support of the *Histadruth Ivrith* is inadequate, for no large sums have been forthcoming from men of means. But this very inadequacy has served to bring the movement closer to the Jewish masses. An annual "Hebrew Week" and a "Hebrew (flower) Day" have been instituted to garner small contributions, and the resulting activity has afforded widespread publicity for Hebrew literary and artistic creations. Recently "Hebrew Week" campaigns have been conducted by local committees in some three hundred communities in the United States and Canada, and the work has elicited the co-operation of no less than 40,000 children who attend more than 800 Jewish schools.

Emphasis has been placed on the *Histadruth Ivrith* as the agency especially dedicated to the furtherance of Hebrew culture in America. But it is by no means alone in this venture. Increasingly, various Jewish groups and individuals who occupy responsible positions in Jewish life have shown an appreciation of the importance of Hebrew. Practically all Zionist bodies are co-operating in the work of extending the influence of Hebrew culture in America. The largest Jewish fraternal order, the B'nai B'rith, makes a financial contribution to the *Histadruth Ivrith*, and its Hillel Foundation includes Hebrew in its program for the colleges. The *Histadruth Ivrith* has also succeeded in gaining the support of over one hundred organized community chests and other Jewish fund-raising agencies which represent hundreds of thousands of American Jews.

The value of Hebrew culture is recognized not only in Jewish circles but also among increasing numbers of non-Jews, especially of the larger cities. This significant fact is evidenced by the introduction of the Hebrew language into the secondary schools and colleges of various American cities. During the past twenty years, Hebrew has been taught in the general high schools of Chicago, St. Louis, Omaha, Chelsea, Mass., and New York City. In the New York metropolis, the Hebrew language was introduced into the high schools as an experiment in the fall of 1929. It quickly won recognition, and today it is offered in sixteen senior, junior and evening high schools which are under the supervision of the Board of Education, and in three of the colleges situated in New York City. About 3000 students are studying Hebrew in New York's high schools at the present time, and a minimum of 14,000 have elected the language since its introduction.*

It is difficult to overemphasize the importance of this development. Considerable numbers of boys and girls have been afforded the opportunity to gain some understanding of the Hebrew spirit and its manifold expressions. And the psychological effect is so far-reaching that its influence is felt in the entire student body of the schools, notably among the Jewish youths. The children of immigrants, Jewish students have often reacted negatively to the customs and values of their foreign-born parents and this psychological disturbance has in numerous cases resulted in maladjustment both to the Jewish group and to American society as a whole. The teaching of Hebrew in the public high schools, however, reassures the disturbed Jewish youth that his father's ideals are worthy of respect. His own adjustment is thus facilitated. As an example, parts of a most significant statement by

---

* Closely related to the teaching of Hebrew in the high schools is the Jewish Culture Council which consists of a federation of clubs in forty of New York's high schools. This movement fosters an interest in Jewish culture and promotes particularly the study of the Hebrew language and literature. It sponsors the annual festival of the Golden "Ayin" ("Ayin" is the first letter of the word *Ivrit*, meaning Hebrew), when the prize students of Hebrew in the public high schools receive awards. The Jewish Culture Council, formerly sponsored by the Bureau of Jewish Education, is today one of the activities of the Jewish Education Committee of New York. The director is Judah Lapson.

John M. Loughran, principal of a New York high school in which Hebrew is taught, and a man who understands his pupils, may be quoted. Convinced that the Jewish heritage has great value and that it can best be transmitted through the study of Hebrew, the educator writes:* "Our American democracy will be enriched and strengthened by the preservation of the cultural legacy.... I believe that, for many of our young people, a knowledge of this inheritance would increase their self-confidence and strengthen their allegiance to ideals, and would make for a continuing spiritual solidarity." Such a statement is of incalculable value in promoting both Americanism and Jewish loyalties.

Conclusion

The Hebrew cultural movement has thus gained a considerable following in the United States, and American Jews in increasing numbers recognize the spiritual and cultural values of ancient and modern Hebrew literature. What effect has the movement had in producing an American Hebrew literature?

Numerous Hebrew writers have made the United States their home, and their works have created in America "an important outpost in the field of Hebrew literature."† Notable contributions have been made especially to Hebrew poetry, and the effects of the American environment are often noteworthy. The late B. N. Silkiner left a quantitatively modest legacy to Hebrew poetry. But his talent is evident in his sad yet serene lyrics, in his wistful nature poems, in his classic characterization of Biblical figures, in an epic which deals with the American Indian. Hillel Bavli's lyrics are rooted in Jewish tradition; yet his sketch of old *Mrs. Woods* depicts the American environment, and Negro poetry has likewise claimed his attention. Israel Efros, with his keen eye for the poetry that is in small, seemingly inconsequential things, and with his

---

* In a letter dated January 22, 1940 and addressed to Judah Lapson, Director of the Jewish Culture Council.

† Bavli, Hillel, in Sampter, Jessie (ed.), *Modern Palestine*, New York, 1933, p. 341.

ability to look beyond the transitory to the permanent, has given us flowing, mostly short lyrics which often ring with a note of optimism. His *Silent Wigwam* and *Gold* (the gold rush of 1848-1849) show the influence of the American scene. Simon Halkin is probably the most metaphysical of the Hebrew poets in America. Extremely sensitive, highly introspective and soulful, he feels keenly man's tragedy in his fruitless struggle to reach what his soul aspires—to ascend to God who is sympathetic but bound by and helpless against a universal order which continues its process of becoming and perishing relentlessly and unconcernedly. He, too, reacts to the American setting, as in the ode, *On the Shore of Santa Barbara.* Among the other noteworthy American poets are A. S. Schwartz, with his gift of description; A. Regelson, with his colorful, philosophic poems; the imagist, keen-eyed and alert Eisig Silberschlag; M. Feinstein, E. Lisitzy, S. Ginsburg and E. Domnitz.

In Hebrew prose, too, American writers such as Shore, Blank, Twersky, Wallenrod, to mention but a few, have made their contributions. In novel and short story, they have dealt with historical themes, with Jewish life in Eastern Europe, and occasionally with the American environment. The essay is likewise well represented in this country, by Ribalow, Epstein, Maximon, and others. But we are here concerned with the broad outlines of Hebrew culture in America. Detailed descriptions of literary works must, therefore, be left for another occasion.

Important Hebrew literary figures thus live and write in the United States. But we can, as yet, hardly speak of an American Hebrew literature, for not one of the important Hebrew writers was born in America. The American Hebrew writer is still basically the product of East European Jewish life which was quickly modified when transplanted to this country. We appear to be living in an era of transition. The Jewish civilization of Eastern Europe which produced a Hebrew literature of a high order does not and cannot exist in America. And, while the American environment has materially affected Jewish living, no distinct American Jewish way of life has as yet emerged. The development of a genuine American Hebrew literature, indigenous to the country and rooted in American soil, must await the crystallization of an American Judaism and an American Jewish culture.

VI

STRUCTURE OF THE JEWISH COMMUNITY

—

Abraham G. Duker

INTRODUCTION

THE American Jewish community of today is a repository of nearly three centuries of historical development. It consists of a great variety of institutions—religious, educational, cultural, recreational, philanthropic. Every layer of Jewish immigration reproduced old-world agencies of group living, and the American environment transformed the old and brought new forms into being.

As a rule, the earliest Jewish communal unit in a new land has been the religious congregation, or the burial society. Hard upon these have usually followed benevolent societies for mutual aid and fraternal associations for recreation and companionship. The pattern of organizational origins has always been woven around the synagogue, the relief of the indigent and newcomer, and social intercourse.*

American Jewry has constituted no exception to the general rule. The earliest form of Jewish organization was the religious congregation, established successively by the *Sephardic*, the Ger-

---

*However, in modern Palestine and in the Soviet Union, variations in communal organization have been in evidence. In Palestine, the "colony" has been the first local unit in many instances, while in the Soviet Union, religious agencies have been deliberately discouraged.

man and the East European settlers. In each case, the earliest synagogues served as the centers of benevolent funds, educational
undertakings and *landsmanschaften*. But increasing numbers
and dispersion in the American hinterland created needs which
the synagogue could not satisfy. Philanthropic and fraternal associations were, therefore, formed independently of the congregations.

Furthermore, the diversity in origin of the Jews who immigrated into the New World occasioned a multiplication of agencies. Thus, the *Sephardim* of New York City organized the Hebrew Benevolent Society, and the Female Hebrew Benevolent
Society, in 1822, but twenty-two years later, the recent arrivals
from Germany established their own German-Hebrew Benevolent
Society. The same tendency was evident in the growth of fraternal
orders. The B'nai B'rith, organized by German Jews in 1843, was
the first Jewish fraternal order in the United States. In 1859, another creation of these Germans, the Free Sons of Israel, appeared;
but the same year saw the establishment of the B'rith Abraham,
which made its appeal mainly to Austrian Jews, and even welcomed East Europeans.

The influx of East European Jews after 1880 added to the complexity in community organization. The *landsmanschaft* synagogue was the first communal institution introduced by this
group, and the early *heder*, or school, was usually attached to the
synagogue. But, like their predecessors, the East European Jews
quickly expanded beyond the synagogue. They established non-
congregational fraternal associations, hospitals, orphan asylums
and similar agencies. Economic needs brought trade unions and
mutual benefit societies into existence.

It should also be noted that the term "East European Jews"
embraces a wide variety of background and orientation, and that
this has been reflected in American Jewish community organization. Natives of the Ukraine, of Lithuania, Poland, Galicia,

Rumania, etc., naturally tended to perpetuate Old-World associations. What is more, European ideological differences, which became acute in Eastern Europe at the turn of the century, were brought over into this country. There were religionists, secularists, Zionists, socialists, and not a few variants within these broad groupings, and each sought to close its ranks and attract new adherents by means of fraternal orders, relief agencies and educational projects.

These diverse influences did not remain static. European factors, themselves in a constant state of change, continued to be imported with every shipload of immigrants. At the same time, the dynamic force of the American environment was increasingly felt. American born or Americanized Jews faced novel problems and needs which necessitated the modification of old institutions or the creation of new ones.

The great variety of parallel and, at times, contradictory interests and needs, which the different layers of the Jewish population have experienced, account for the complexity of the Jewish communal structure of today. We shall first describe the types of Jewish institutions functioning in the United States, and then analyze and appraise the attempts at co-ordination and unity.

THE JEWISH COMMUNITY TODAY

Religious Institutions

The basic unit in Jewish community organization is the synagogue. In the smaller towns, the synagogue or the temple is the most distinctive Jewish institution, and even in the metropolitan centers it plays a significant role in Jewish life.

The last United States Census of Religious Bodies (1936)* listed 3728 congregations. Of these, more than 3000 were identified as orthodox, but this overwhelming number is reflected

---

* See United States Department of Commerce, *Census of Religious Bodies,* 1936, Bulletin No. 72, *Jewish Congregations.*

neither in organizational effectiveness nor in influence in the community. Important orthodox synagogues, with distinguished rabbis who minister to the spiritual needs of a wide membership, and supervise manifold religious and social activities, are found in every large city. But in a great many instances, the orthodox congregation consists only of a handful of members, and its activities often do not go beyond daily worship.

With respect to organization and unity of effort, Orthodoxy has barely passed the incipient stage. A Union of Orthodox Jewish Congregations has been in existence since 1898, but it represents today probably less than 10 per cent of the total number of orthodox congregations in the country. Its Woman's Branch (organized in 1923) and its girls' division, called *Habanoth*, have not yet succeeded either in attracting significant members or in expanding the program of their activities. The rabbis, too, have evidently not found it possible to agree on a common platform, for there are no less than five national associations of orthodox rabbis: the Union of Orthodox Rabbis; the Assembly of Orthodox Rabbis; the Rabbinical Council of America, consisting largely of graduates of the *Yeshivah* College and the Hebrew Theological College of Chicago; the Federation of Orthodox Rabbis; and the *Agudath Haadmorim*, the Hassidic (pietistic) rabbis. Perhaps the best organized orthodox group is the Young Israel,* which embraced in 1940 seventy branches or congregations with a total membership of 10,000.

Its energies dispersed, orthodox Judaism has neither an all-embracing authoritative spokesman nor a publication of high merit and widespread influence. The *Jewish Journal and Daily News,* a Yiddish daily published in New York City, and several periodicals in English, are often spoken of as orthodox organs, but only in the sense that they reflect the orthodox views of their owners or editors. They have no direct relationship to official or representative agencies of Orthodoxy.

* See above, p. 42.

Conservative Judaism has achieved a greater measure of organization. About 350 congregations are affiliated with the United Synagogue of America, which has been in existence for three decades, and the laity are represented in the Federation of Jewish Men's Clubs and the Women's League. The youth, too, has been organized in the Young People's League. *The Synagogue Center,* a quarterly journal inaugurated in 1940, concerns itself with the problems of synagogue center activities. The Rabbinical Assembly of America, whose membership since its organization in 1901 has risen to 301 conservative rabbis, may be regarded as the authoritative voice of conservative Judaism; it meets annually and publishes its proceedings.*

Reform Judaism is the most effectively organized among Jewish religious groups. The authoritative body is the Central Conference of American Rabbis, in existence since 1889, and numbering no less than 475 members. The volumes of its *Year Book* are a record of the ideological and structural development of the movement for more than half a century. The Union of American Hebrew Congregations, organized in 1873, has the active support of 307 congregations and the co-operation of the laity and youth. The National Federation of Temple Sisterhoods embraces 376 societies; the men's counterpart, the National Federation of Temple Brotherhoods, includes 130 groups; and 107 branches containing 10,000 young people are united in the National Federation of Temple Youth. All of these lay associations seek to unite the efforts of individual congregations in spiritual and cultural matters.†

---

* Reconstructionism as a school of thought exerts considerable influence in Jewish life. Recently the Jewish Reconstructionist Foundation was established and it has assumed responsibility for the publication of *The Reconstructionist,* a well-edited and thought-provoking bi-weekly journal. But no well-defined organizational structure of Reconstructionism has as yet emerged. In fact, there is a difference of opinion within the movement whether or not a distinct organization as a religious grouping is desirable.

† The most important rabbinical and lay bodies—orthodox, reform and conservative —are united in the Synagogue Council of America, a consultative body organized in 1925.

Cultural Agencies

Adult education has been for many centuries a Jewish ideal broadly realized in practice. From its very inception in ancient times, the synagogue served as an agency of popular education. Readings from the Bible were introduced at an early date, and interpretation became more extensive and more elaborate with the centuries. The development of the Talmud and of other post-Biblical Jewish literature provided a great variety of subject matter for instruction on various levels.

Adult education was widespread in the Jewish communities of Eastern Europe at the turn of the last century, and at an earlier date, in Western and Central Europe as well. The advanced student spent his leisure time wrestling with the intricacies of the Talmud. The less educated devoted the Sabbath afternoon to more popular works such as the collection of ethical maxims known as the *Ethics of the Fathers*, or to material of a homiletic nature. Itinerant preachers who carried their message from town to town were likewise a potent force in popular Jewish education.

The synagogue and temple have remained important agencies for adult education to this day. Although the nature of the sermon varies widely, it is still a means of imparting Jewish knowledge and of cultivating Jewish attitudes. In addition, the American Jewish house of worship is, in many instances, the center of classes and forums in Bible, Talmud, Jewish History and current events.

However, the seat of Jewish learning in the United States is the theological academy. The most important institutions of this nature, in the order of their establishment, are the Hebrew Union College at Cincinnati (reform), the Jewish Theological Seminary of America (conservative), the Rabbi Isaac Elchanan Theological Seminary and Yeshivah College (orthodox) and the Jewish Institute of Religion (liberal), all in New York City, and the Hebrew Theological College of Chicago (orthodox).* These centers of learning are, of course, the haven of the scholar. But they radiate a wide cultural influence throughout American Jewish life. Their libraries and collections of Jewish art, particularly those of the Jewish Theological Seminary and the Hebrew Union College, are accessible to all who manifest interest. Some of these institutions publish learned journals, and several have experimented with popular courses of lectures, with tracts for the general reader, and with programs and courses of study for the masses.

More directly concerned with adult education are the Jewish teachers' training schools and colleges which have appeared in various parts of the country. Perhaps the best known and most widely influential is the Teachers Institute and Seminary College of Jewish Studies, formally organized in New York City in 1912.† As a rule, instruction in these institutions is in the Hebrew language and the quality of so high a character that various non-Jewish colleges and universities grant credit for courses taken in Jewish subjects. While the primary purpose is to train teachers, considerable numbers of youths and adults utilize these cultural agencies exclusively as a means of extending their Jewish education.

However, considerable knowledge is required to gain admission into teachers' training schools, and their curricula are far too advanced for the general public. Attempts have, therefore, been

---

* Though not a theological school, the Dropsie College of Hebrew and Cognate Learning may be classed with the above institutions. It was organized at Philadelphia in 1905, and has devoted itself to advanced study in Jewish and related subjects.

† Among the other teachers' training schools are the following: Gratz College, established in Philadelphia in 1895; the Teachers Institute of the Rabbi Isaac Elchanan Seminary, originally organized in 1917; the Baltimore Hebrew College and Teachers' Training School, founded in 1919; the Hebrew College of Boston, established in 1920; the Rosenbloom Teachers Training School of the Hebrew Institute of Pittsburgh, organized in 1922; the Herzliah Hebrew Academy of New York City, which commenced instruction in 1923; the College of Jewish Studies of Chicago, and the Hebrew Teachers Seminary of Cleveland, both organized in 1924. The Jewish National Workers' Alliance, a labor-Zionist organization, and the Workmen's Circle likewise maintain academies for the training of teachers for the Yiddish schools.

made to develop courses of study and to establish schools on the level of the intelligent adult with limited Jewish education. A number of such institutions have gained a following. For example, the Israel Friedlander Classes in New York City have in the course of nearly twenty-five years imparted knowledge of Jewish history, literature, religious practices and the Hebrew language to five or six thousand students. But on the whole, it has proved difficult both to finance independent schools and to overcome the problems of time and distance in the large cities.*

These difficulties have been somewhat overcome by centrally located synagogues, temples and community centers, and a considerable number of congregational institutes for adult education have come into being. Their immediate deficiencies, however, have been a lack of sustained and continuous study and ill-digested subject matter. Too often consisting of little more than a series of lectures, the work has satisfied neither the directors of the forums nor the men and women who compose the audiences. But the problem is understood and co-operative efforts are being made to find a solution. For example, the Department of Synagogue and School Extension of the Union of American Hebrew Congregations and the National Academy for Adult Jewish Studies, which functions under the auspices of the United Synagogue of America, are preparing material and elaborating courses of study for the adult groups of their respective congregations.

The cultural efforts of the American Jewish community have not been exhausted by more or less formal schooling. Numerous agencies attempt to reach the American Jew through the printed page. The Jewish Publication Society, a book club in the best sense of the word, has taken as its motto, "more Jewish books in Jewish homes." Functioning for more than half a century, its record of achievement is a notable one. It has encouraged numerous authors to devote their attention to Jewish subjects. It

---

* Experiments of the Menorah Association, and the Labor-Zionist group, with adult schools in New York City have proved unsuccessful.

has published 225 titles, including an English translation o
Bible, and works in history, biography, *belle-lettres,* etc. In
the Society sold 52,844 volumes to numerous persons throug
the country, including its 6357 members. Through its e
three and a half million copies of Jewish books have reache
homes of Jews and Gentiles interested in Jewish knowledge.

The Menorah Association, organized in 1906, has chose
college campus as the field of its activity and thousands o
dents have been affected by its cultural projects. Particularly
found has been the effect of the *Menorah Journal,* the best e
Jewish publication in America, a cultural force among J
intellectuals, and a storehouse of significant reading matte
specting Jews. The American Jewish Historical Society, v
recently celebrated its fiftieth anniversary, has issued thirt
volumes of valuable materials in American Jewish history.
American Academy for Jewish Research with its 300 men
the Conference on Jewish Relations with its 800 member
Yiddish Scientific Institute which has recently establishe
center in New York City, the Jewish Statistical Bureau,
other organizations of similar nature, exert a cultural infl
upon American Jewry by means of meetings, conferences
publications.†

It would be impossible even to list all of the Jewish cu
agencies in the United States.‡ For practically every Jewis
ganization of note, no matter what its primary objective i
be, has its educational or cultural program. Perhaps the
notable is the work of Hadassah, the Women's Zionist Orga
tion, and of the B'nai B'rith Hillel Foundation. A great ma

---

* The National Committee for the Jewish Book Week concerns itself w
popularization of Jewish publications and the Jewish Telegraphic Agency disse
Jewish news.

† Five institutes on peace and post-war problems are likewise making sig
contributions to adult education. The most important are The Research Insti
Peace and Post-War Problems of The American Jewish Committee and the Insti
Jewish Affairs, formerly affiliated with the American Jewish Congress.

‡ Jewish national organizations of all types are listed in The *American Jewis
Book.*

the 843 chapters and groups of Hadassah and its junior affiliate have cultural chairmen who direct the educational work of the membership, and the central education committee in New York City has devoted much time and effort in the preparation of serious material for study and discussion.* The Hillel Foundation serves the cultural, religious and social needs of the Jewish student. Trained leaders are maintained at sixty-two colleges and universities throughout the United States, and many a young Jewish intellectual owes his first introduction to Jewish knowledge and Jewish problems to the Hillel director.

The summer school and summer camp have recently emerged as promising agencies for Jewish cultural activities, especially among youth. Organizations like Menorah and, latterly, Zionist youth groups have experimented successfully with summer seminars, and the movement appears to hold much promise for the future.

Thus, Jewish cultural institutions are numerous and manifold. To say that American Jewry has found the modern equivalent of the Old World synagogue as the center of learning would be a gross exaggeration. Masses of American Jews remain outside the orbit of Jewish influence, and for a good many who are affected the results are hardly significant. Yet it is important to note that the age-old passion for Jewish knowledge has not spent itself, and that efforts are being made to channelize it into forms compatible with modern living in America.

Social and Recreational Establishments

In designating certain institutions as social and recreational, there is no implication that they are exclusively of that character. A great many social agencies include in the program of their activities functions which are clearly educational and cultural, and an indirect cultural influence is often exerted where no such inten-

* See in particular, *Jewish Survival in the World Today*, New York, 1938-1941, prepared by Abraham G. Duker.

tion is evident. However, the emphasis of this category of organizations is definitely social.

It would be hopelessly confusing to undertake a description of the multitude of associations which American Jews have called into being. We shall confine ourselves to an analysis of the three main types, namely, the *landsmanschaft*, the fraternal order and the community center.

1. *The Landsmanschaft*

The *landsmanschaft* is a mutual benefit society of individuals hailing from the same town or region in the Old World. Societies of this character were established in the nineteenth century by Jews of Dutch and German origin, but the full growth of this type of institution was achieved during the period of mass immigration of East European Jews. They may be classified in several categories.*

The first and most numerous is the independent society, which is unaffiliated with any central body. At times, especially during campaigns for funds, a nominal connection may be made with an all-embracing relief agency like the Joint Distribution Committee. But in other respects, the group remains isolated and self-contained. Another type consists of local societies which are federated into units representative of a European country or region, such as the American Federation for Polish Jews, an influential body, in existence since 1908 and claiming a membership of 65,000.† And still another type of *landsmanschaft* is that affiliated with national fraternal orders, many of which have found it useful to incorporate the *landsmanschaft* as a local branch.

The *landsmanschaft* performs a variety of functions. It per-

* For a description of the *landsmanschaft*, see Works Projects Administration, Yiddish Writers Project, *De Yiddishe Landsmanschaft in New York* (in Yiddish), New York, 1938.

† Similar organizations, but with far smaller membership and influence, are the United Rumanian Jews of America, the United Galician Jews of America, the Federation of Lithuanian Jews, the Association of Hungarian Jews of America, and others. Since 1933, refugees from Central and Western Europe have established several additional organizations.

petuates memories of the native town, provides a medium for the continuance of social contacts brought from abroad, affords financial and other forms of assistance to individual members, and collects funds for the relief of the needy in the old home town. The large federations have also co-operated in the struggle to attain civil and political equality for their coreligionists abroad.

The rise and decline of the *landsmanschaft* coincides with the history of Jewish immigration. Along with the synagogue, the first unit of community organization in the life of the immigrant, the *landsmanschaft* filled a real need at the time of mass immigration prior to the first World War. It was the society of his countrymen that first lent a helping hand to the immigrant in times of want, and it was there that he found companionship and understanding.

While the *landsmanschaft* still retains a great deal of vitality, its decline is clearly noticeable. The suspension of immigration has cut off the supply of new members, and the progressive Americanization of the immigrant, and his political and social adjustment, have rendered many of the activities of the *landsmanschaft* superfluous. Sentiment and old associations preserve the loyalty of the older elements, but the American-born new generation does not look to the *landsmanschaft* for the satisfaction of its social and recreational needs.*

2. *The Fraternal Order*

Jewish fraternal orders originated about the middle of the nineteenth century, as has already been indicated. But it was the period of East European mass immigration that witnessed the heyday of their growth. The ceremonial and social attractions impressed the immigrant, while social insurance, perhaps the most important feature of the fraternal order, filled a vital social

* Somewhat akin to the *landsmanschaft*, but with greater appeal to the younger generation, is the family circle. About 500 are estimated to be in existence. See Works Project Administration, *Yiddishe Familien un Familie Kraizn*, New York, 1939.

need. In time, however, the Jew began to show a marked preference for general fraternal orders like the Masons, the Elks, and the Knights of Pythias. This was due partly to the pull of the environment, but the determining factor was undoubtedly the rapid growth of commercial life insurance.

In 1913, probably the peak year of their popularity, Jewish fraternal orders claimed a membership of 520,000; since that year there has been a consistent decline both in the number of orders and in their total membership.* In 1940, there were thirteen Jewish fraternal orders in the United States, claiming among them about 345,000 members. The most important were: the B'nai B'rith, with nearly 150,000 members; the Workmen's Circle—75,000 members; the Independent Order B'rith Abraham—58,000; the Jewish Section of the International Workers Order—36,000; and the Jewish National Workers' Alliance, with 19,00 members, one of the very few orders which has managed to increase its membership.†

The decline of Jewish fraternal orders is likely to be accelerated by the social security program of the United States Government. It should be noted, however, that several organizations have either expanded or transformed the purposes which originally motivated their activities. The B'nai B'rith has completely abandoned insurance benefits, and directs its efforts to educational and cultural projects and to the struggle against anti-Semitism. Similarly, the Jewish National Workers' Alliance is concerned more with the promotion of labor Zionism than with the usual functions of a fraternal order. And significantly enough, it is these organizations

---

* Only two of a minimum of six orders, organized in the decade of the 1890's, are in existence today. Of ten established between 1900-1910, three remain. Only four new orders appeared between 1911-1920; but no less than eleven were disbanded during that period. Between 1920 and 1941, only two new orders were founded.

† Among the smaller orders are the following: the Independent Order B'rith Shalom—15,000; the Independent Order Free Sons of Israel (founded 1849)—9000; the United Hebrew Brothers—6000; the Order Sons of Zion—4000; the Progressive Order of the West—4000; and several others.

which manifest concern for the broader aspects of Jewish life that manage to grow both in membership and in activity.*

3. The Community Center

The Community center is the standard recreational agency in many Jewish communities throughout the United States. An institution native to this country, it is the resultant of many forces and influences. In the years immediately preceding the first World War, it became increasingly evident that the old-type Y.M.H.A., which had been in existence since the last quarter of the nineteenth century, was too limited in outlook to afford a well-rounded program of Jewish activities. The Settlement House of the poorer districts was likewise more concerned with "keeping the children off the streets," than with any purposeful program of youth development. Congregations, too, felt the need of expanding their activities beyond the limited confines of divine worship.

A number of reform temples began to concern themselves with social and recreational functions after 1912. But the first synagogue center with a clearly conceived ideology and a comprehensive program was established in New York City, under the influence of Professor Mordecai M. Kaplan. Its aim was the integration of religious, educational, cultural and recreational activities. However, like the reform temples, the facilities were restricted to members of the congregation.

The real growth of the community center began after the conclusion of the first World War. The intensive campaigns for the

* Notice should also be taken of the Greek letter fraternities. There were in 1941 twelve national fraternities, organized in 265 chapters with a membership of over 48,000, in addition to many units unaffiliated with a national organization. Several of the national fraternities are non-sectarian, but their membership is Jewish. Many of them engage in philanthropic activities. The most up-to-date sources on the fraternal orders and fraternities are the articles on these subjects by Alexander S. Kohanski and Maurice Jacobs in *The Universal Jewish Encyclopedia*, Vol. IV, New York, 1941, pp. 419-423, 423-425.

Among the several Jewish war veterans' organizations, the Jewish War Veterans has broadened its activities to include defense against anti-Semitism and has shown a marked rise in influence.

relief of the Jews in the war zones, the substantial measure of unity achieved in the first American Jewish Congress,* and the solid contribution of American Jewry toward the recognition of Jewish equality in Eastern Europe and the assurance of a Jewish National Homeland in Palestine, heightened the sense of common fate and achievement and enhanced the feeling of community responsibility. General prosperity, too, made ample funds available, and the center movement expanded rapidly. New buildings were erected and old institutions, like the Y.M.H.A.'s, increased their facilities and their professional personnel. The depression ushered in a period of contraction, but the bulk of recreational agencies had been transformed into community centers. Whereas in 1921, there were only 47 community centers with full-time professional workers the number had grown to 234 by 1941. During the same period the membership of these organizations increased from 100,000 to 435,000. At first, the main emphasis was placed on social and athletic activities, but, in time, educational, cultural and communal functions were assumed, until the center became in many communities a genuine *Beth Am*, a people's house.†

It is difficult to generalize about community centers, because differences in local conditions have produced a great variety in structure and function. In some of the smaller communities the center has become the hub of all Jewish activities. It performs all the Jewish social services, from family relief to refugee adjustment. It houses the Hebrew school and provides educational facilities for adults. Frequently, it is the instrument of local and national relief campaigns. It is the common meeting place of the orthodox, reform, conservative, as well as those Jews who have no connection with synagogue or temple. Through the center, the work of the local organizations is co-ordinated, and its mem-

---

* See below, p. 158.

† For a summary of developments in the center field see National Jewish Welfare Board, *Annual Report 1941*, New York, 1942. The best source for more detailed information is *The Jewish Center*, a quarterly.

bership becomes well-nigh synonymous with conscious adherence to the Jewish community.

In many instances, membership is based on the family unit principle, that is, the dues of the head of the family covers every dependent.* The institution is, therefore, obliged to provide facilities for every age level. Naturally, greatest emphasis is placed on the needs of youth and children, and the center has tended to become the major recreational agency for Jewish children and youth. It has been estimated that 55 per cent of those partaking in center activities are persons under twenty-one years of age. For them, the center provides athletic facilities, summer camps, boy scout troops, clubs, as well as classes in Jewish subjects.

Family interest in the center has tended to subject the board of directors to popular control. The center workers, too, feel a sense of professional responsibility. They are organized in the National Association of Jewish Center Workers, and co-operate in the publication of a quarterly journal, entitled *The Jewish Center.*

The National Jewish Welfare Board, situated in New York City, is the servicing organization of the center and kindred social and recreational agencies. Organized in 1917 to promote the religious, cultural and social needs of Jews in the armed forces of the United States, a function it is again fulfilling on a large scale in the second World War, it quickly assumed the responsibility of assisting local centers. It conducts surveys, trains center workers, prepares programs, provides field workers, plans courses, and serves as a clearing house and co-ordinating agency for all center activities.†

This description is undoubtedly too sweeping in its optimism. It is true that the number of centers, especially in the large cities, is woefully inadequate, and that vast numbers of Jews remain unaffected by its activities. In many instances, the program of

---

* The financial support of the center is derived from membership dues and contributions from local federations of charities and welfare funds.

† See Bernheimer, Charles S., "A Review of Studies of the Jewish Welfare Board During the Past Decades," in *The Jewish Center*, Sept. 1940, pp. 2-5.

work is deficient. The Jewish training of a good deal of the personnel is likewise in need of betterment.

However, we are here indicating a tendency, one that augurs well for the future. Especially in the smaller communities, the center is becoming the representative agency of the Jewish group in the eyes of Gentiles and Jews alike. And in many cases, the attractive center building, and its well-conducted activities, have produced a justifiable sense of pride in the local Jewish community. This is of immeasurable psychological importance for the adjustment of the Jew to his environment.

Philanthropic and Welfare Agencies

Charity has become proverbially associated with the Jewish people. A religious injunction of great antiquity, care of the unfortunate became a compelling necessity during centuries of struggle in a hostile world. In all countries and in all periods, Jews have, therefore, provided shelter for the sick and the wanderer, and sustenance for the widow, the orphan and the indigent. In the European small town of the pre-industrial era, local aid contrived to meet the most essential needs. But the immigration of vast numbers of Jews utterly without means, and the insecurity of employment in a planless and chaotic factory age, created a problem of mass poverty for American Jewry.

Naturally under such conditions, planned, co-ordinated and comprehensive welfare work was out of the question. Each problem was tackled as it became acute. To cite but a few examples, the Hebrew Sheltering and Immigrant Aid Society (HIAS) had its beginnings in 1885, when masses of immigrants required temporary assistance and guidance. As the lack of understanding between foreign-born parents and American-bred children weakened family discipline and created the danger of juvenile delinquency, the Settlement House appeared in Jewish neighborhoods, and attempted to facilitate the process of adjustment. And the ever present problems of the sick, the aged, the orphaned and the needy have called into being a great variety of Jewish institutions throughout the United States.

In 1940, sixty-one hospitals and forty-six clinics were maintained under Jewish auspices.* But patients were admitted on a nonsectarian basis; only 57 per cent of the patients in hospitals, and 48 per cent of new admissions to clinics, were Jewish. In the same year, about 5500 aged persons were cared for in fifty institutions, and 11,553 children were supported in foster-homes or orphan asylums. A minimum of eighty-four family welfare agencies rendered aid in 56,286 cases, at a cost of over $2,300,000.

In most instances, charity has remained a local function. The Jews of each city or town have built and maintained their own institutions, which operate as self-contained units, often without reference even to similar agencies in neighboring Jewish communities. A limited number of establishments, however, are independent of local control. They serve a nationwide clientele and seek financial support throughout the country. Among these institutions are the National Jewish Hospital and the National Home for Jewish Children, both at Denver, Colorado; the National Desertion Bureau of New York City, which has assumed the task of tracing missing persons; and the National Braille Institute, which seeks to promote the cultural and religious welfare of the Jewish blind.

The fields of occupational training and job placement have claimed the attention of numerous agencies. Sixteen communities maintain free employment bureaus, several of which attempt to provide vocational guidance. In Chicago, all the major Jewish organizations maintain co-operatively the Bureau of Jewish Employment Problems. And research in the field of employment and vocational guidance has been co-ordinated in the Jewish Occupational Council established in New York City in 1938.†

---

* See Council of Jewish Federations and Welfare Funds, *1940 Year Book of Jewish Social Work*, New York, 1942, pp. 2-3.

† Closely related is the work of the Jewish Agricultural Society, organized in 1900 for the purpose of encouraging farming among the Jews of the United States. It renders advisory services and financial aid to Jewish farmers.

A great number of Jewish charitable organizations still operate independently, and co-ordination on a nationwide scale has not even reached the blueprint stage. Much progress, however, has been made in unifying the work of agencies in individual cities, and the fund-raising efforts have reached an advanced stage of standardization.

The federation of Jewish charities is the standard agency which co-ordinates the efforts—chiefly the local fund-raising efforts—of welfare institutions in individual cities. An early instance was the United Hebrew Charities, which was organized in 1874 to pool the local philanthropic resources of New York City. However, the first effective "Federation" was established in Boston in 1895, and the experiment proved so satisfactory to institutions and donors, that in twenty years the number increased to forty-six. And today, practically every city or town has its federation of Jewish charities.

The success of the federation idea has led to further unity in local communities. Incessant appeals for a great variety of causes created a troublesome problem, because the individual donor had not the means of assessing the value or importance of the multitude of institutions. Community "welfare funds" have, therefore, arisen, and they have spread with great rapidity. The welfare fund combines all fund-raising activities—whether for local, national or overseas needs—of the town or city. Individual organizations and institutions prepare memoranda outlining their activities and needs—some even send "field men" or agents to plead their cause—and the allocation committee of the local welfare fund apportions contributions on a comparative basis. In this work, the local welfare funds are aided by a central agency, called the Council of Jewish Federations and Welfare Funds. This body, organized in New York City in 1932, prepares reports on the activities of various local, regional and nationwide philanthropic organizations, and its conclusions exert a powerful influence on local communities in the distribution of their funds.

The welfare funds, themselves the result of the work of the

federations of charities, have in turn served as the influence in the organization of "community councils" in at least fifty Jewish communities. In many towns, the community council is no more than a name, or an appendage to the local welfare fund, with no significant functions or authority. But in a few notable instances, of which Harrisburg, Pennsylvania, is the model, the community council is the all-embracing, democratically-elected agency of all activities in the Jewish community.*

The problem of German refugees has created, during the past decade, a new claim upon Jewish charity in the United States. A great many of the men, women and children who fled from Germany and from Nazi-occupied territories have required assistance in establishing themselves in the United States. This function might have been performed by the local federations of charities, and indeed, numerous local committees have grappled with the problem. But the leaders in refugee work have found it necessary to establish a special agency for this purpose. The National Refugee Service, organized in New York City, in 1939, has assumed the task of providing the refugee with temporary relief, facilities for retraining, and assistance in establishing a permanent home in the United States.

The whole question of Jewish philanthropy has, of late, been subjected to a great deal of analysis, because many of the most important functions of Jewish charitable institutions have been profoundly affected by recent developments. The suspension of immigration has automatically circumscribed the field of activity. The relief and social security programs of the New Deal have,

---

* In 1941, federations, welfare funds or community councils functioned in 266 urban centers, embracing no less than 97 per cent of the Jewish population of the United States. A directory of federations, welfare funds and community councils and their constituent organizations appears bi-annually in *The American Jewish Year Book*. For reports on their activities see *The Jewish Social Service Quarterly*, *Notes and News*, and *Proceedings* of the General Assemblies of the Council of Jewish Federations and Welfare Funds. A summary of the technical problems involved in the specialized profession of fund-raising is contained in Philip Houtz, "Current Theories and Techniques in Fund-Raising," *The Jewish Social Service Quarterly*, June, 1942, pp. 339-356.

likewise, absorbed many of the services formerly performed by Jewish charity. It is true that a tendency has developed to concentrate attention on family case work involving emotional and social conflicts. But this hardly merits the attention formerly devoted to the economic, social and cultural adjustments of the immigrant to his American environment. Jewish philanthropy will have to enter new fields, and none is more worthy of its attention than the extension of Jewish education and the strengthening of Jewish morale among the masses of American Jews.

Agencies for Overseas Relief and Reconstruction and for the Building of Palestine

Destitution among Old World Jews claimed the attention of their American coreligionists at an early date. During the nineteenth century, in particular, as immigrants established themselves in the United States, individual Jews extended assistance to relatives and friends overseas. The *landsmanschaft*, too, busied itself with the collection and transmission of funds to various towns and districts in Europe. All of this relief work, however, was unorganized and sporadic.

Several events at the turn of the last century sharpened the understanding of American Jews and directed their attention to comprehensive goals in overseas philanthropy. The leadership of Theodor Herzl brought both effective organization and world attention to the Zionist movement, and the settlement of Jews in Palestine at once became a major concern of numerous Jews everywhere, including the United States. The wave of pogroms in Tsarist Russia, particularly the Kishinev massacre, likewise shocked American Jews into a realization that East European Jewish needs could not be met by individuals or small groups.

It was the first World War, however, which brought American Jewish efforts for overseas relief to maturity. The widespread suffering induced by devastation in the war zones, and by deliberate expulsion of Jews from their homes, demanded continuous assistance on a scale so vast as to tax the united energies of American Jewry. American Jews responded with enthusiasm and called into being agencies both for relief in Eastern Europe and for the reconstruction of Palestine. During the past quarter century, these agencies have expanded the scope of their particular efforts, and they have also achieved a considerable measure of unity and cooperation, at least in the raising and allocation of funds.

The most important organizations for overseas relief and reconstruction are the American Jewish Joint Distribution Committee (popularly known as the Joint Distribution Committee, or J.D.C.) and its affiliated organizations, and the United Palestine Appeal. The Joint Distribution Committee was organized in 1914, to meet the exigencies of the first World War. With the coming of peace, its attention was devoted to the reconstruction of the war-torn areas and the rehabilitation of the declassed Jews of the Soviet Union. The savage onslaught on the Jews of Nazi Germany added yet another to its manifold and stupendous tasks. Vast numbers of Jews who have fled for their lives have had to be fed and sheltered in countries adjacent to Germany where temporary asylum was secured; and as the Nazi tentacles reached out to crush neighboring peoples, frantic efforts have been made to transport the refugees to more permanent homes.

The United Palestine Appeal is the culmination of many years of divided efforts to raise funds for the building of the Jewish National Homeland in Palestine. In 1910, the Jewish National Fund of America was organized for the purpose of redeeming the soil of Palestine as the inalienable property of the Jewish people. The establishment of the Mandate for Palestine and the recognition of the Jewish Agency as the supreme Jewish authority in the restoration of Palestine brought into existence another agency—the Palestine Foundation Fund (Keren Hayesod). In 1936, most of the fund-raising activities of these two primary organizations were merged in the United Palestine Appeal.

The Joint Distribution Committee and the United Palestine

Appeal have built up campaign and distribution machinery un-
paralled in Jewish history, and American Jewry has afforded both
organizations unstinted support. The duplication of effort involved
in separate campaigns has, therefore, appeared to large numbers
of American Jews as both unreasonable and wasteful; and pressure from local communities has induced the two primary fund-
raising organizations to come to terms. In 1938, the United Jewish
Appeal was established, embracing the Joint Distribution Committee, the United Palestine Appeal, and a third body, already
mentioned, the National Refugee Service.

The United Jewish Appeal combines the most significant efforts
of American Jewry for overseas aid. However, numerous organizations of lesser compass continue to function, and to appeal for
funds, independently. Only a few can be mentioned by way of illustration.

The American Ort Federation, in existence since 1922, concerns
itself with the promotion of technical trades and agriculture
among the Jews of Europe.*

The American Friends of the Hebrew University, and a number
of related groups, render assistance to specific Palestinian institutions. The American Pro-Falasha Committee has since 1922 engaged in educational work on behalf of the black Jews of Ethio-
pia. The Union of Orthodox Rabbis has recently established an
emergency committee to secure aid for East European rabbis and
Talmudic academies which the war has ravaged or rendered desti-
tute. And similar organizations have been formed by various
Jewish religious, social and labor groups who desire to succor
comrades in the distressed zone of Nazi influence.

Efforts to Achieve a United Jewish Representative Body

The diversity of American Jews in origin, in economic and
social status, and in ideology was bound to produce a multiplicity

---

* The Ort was founded in Russia in 1880, for the purpose of encouraging Jews
to turn from trade to crafts and agriculture. The name is an abbreviation of the
Russian Title for "Society for the Promotion of Crafts and Agriculture Among the
Jews."

of institutions, such as has been indicated. But the need of a central protective and representative body early became evident. American Jews have always been stirred by persecution of their brethren abroad. But protests, to be effective, required an authoritative voice which might be presumed to speak in the name of American Jewry. In the United States, too, local officials have at times committed acts of discrimination, and public charges have been made by irresponsible persons. Charges must be answered with dignity and authority, and discrimination must be fought with vigor and tenacity. No individual or partisan group can undertake such functions.

The first attempt to create a central organization for American Jewry took place in 1859, when the Board of Delegates of American Israelites was founded. Patterned after a similar Jewish body in England, the Board of Delegates devoted much attention to the protection of Jewish rights abroad, to overseas relief, and to the needs of East European immigrants. It labored to secure the removal of relics of legal discrimination against Jews from several of our own State Constitutions. And it concerned itself with the task of systematizing the collection of authentic information concerning the Jews of the United States. It came to an end in 1878, after the Union of American Hebrew Congregations had been formed and had assumed some of its functions.

When it became obvious that an association of reform congregations could not represent American Jewry, the effort to achieve unity was renewed. In 1891, a convention, representing nineteen cities, met at Philadelphia and established the Jewish Alliance of America. The aim of this body was to "unite Israelites in a common bond for the purpose of more effectually coping with the grave problems presented by enforced emigration." Although thirty-one branches were quickly formed throughout the country, the organization quickly fell apart; and public-spirited individuals, like Simon Wolf of the B'nai B'rith, undertook to voice the feelings of American Jewry.

The wave of pogroms in Tsarist Russia early in the twentieth century, and the refusal of the Russian Government to honor the American passport when exhibited by Jews, presented problems requiring concerted efforts. The American Jewish Committee, therefore, came into being in 1906, as a body of representative Jews from all sections of the country. Under the leadership of Jacob H. Schiff and Louis Marshall, it fought the infraction of Jewish rights everywhere, and attempted to alleviate the consequences of persecution. For a decade, the Committee held undisputed sway as a protective organization, a relief agency and a coordinating body. The first World War, however, produced a challenge to its leadership.

The American Jewish Committee was composed chiefly of descendants of the German immigration, and its point of view was in the main non-Zionist and anti-nationalist. But by 1914, the majority of American Jews were East European in origin and actively or passively in favor of a Jewish Palestine. Moreover, many Jews, stirred by the Wilsonian principles of democracy and self-determination, came to regard the leadership of the American Jewish Committee as unrepresentative. The cry was raised for a democratically chosen American Jewish Congress to represent the wishes of American Jewry in the war and the forthcoming peace.

These rumblings of revolt took on the shape of a mass movement when Louis D. Brandeis, Julian W. Mack and Stephen S. Wise assumed leadership of the Congress cause. A severe struggle ensued between the partisans of a congress and the leaders of the American Jewish Commiteee, but in the end an understanding was reached. Louis Marshall himself accepted office in the American Jewish Congress which was held in December, 1918, and he became one of the outstanding leaders of its delegation to the Peace Conference at Versailles.*

The Jewish achievements at the Peace Conference were in no

---

* The American Jewish Committee continued its functions as a central agency for the defense of Jewish rights and for public relations.

small measure due to the efforts of the American Jewish Congress, and it undoubtedly had the support of a great many American Jews. But in accordance with a prior agreement, it was dissolved at the conclusion of its efforts in connection with the peace. When reconstituted in 1922, it no longer voiced the sentiments of a united American Jewry. To this day, it has remained a leading central organization enjoying a wide following among the Jewish masses (nearly 700,000 Jews registered for its elections in 1938), but it is one of several competing central agencies.

In addition to the American Jewish Committee and the American Jewish Congress, two other organizations occupy leading positions on the American Jewish scene, namely the B'nai B'rith and the Jewish Labor Committee. The B'nai B'rith, today the largest Jewish fraternal order, has always wielded much influence, and in recent years it has shown marked qualities of leadership. The work of its Hillel Foundation has already been noted. In 1913, it established the Anti-Defamation League to combat anti-Semitism, and, as intolerance spread in the United States, this organization, and its parent body, gained wide recognition and support among American Jews. The Jewish Labor Committee was organized in 1934, primarily to combat Nazism and Fascism. Representing as it does the large Jewish trade unions and other workmen's organizations, it figures prominently among the Jewish central agencies.

Each of these four organizations has performed useful service. But there has undoubtedly been much duplication of effort, and not a little confusion has resulted from competition and more than occasional wrangling. A considerable body of opinion has therefore developed in favor of co-operation and co-ordination. The rapid spread of anti-Semitism which Nazi propaganda induced even in the United States, finally lead the four agencies to establish the General Jewish Council. This supreme central body was organized in 1938, for the purpose of co-ordinating the activities of the constituent members that "bear specifically on the safeguarding of the equal rights of Jews." It has, however, failed to achieve effectiveness, and its standing as a symbol of unity was further impaired by the withdrawal of the American Jewish Congress in 1941.

For the moment, the prospects for unity, or even for a united Jewish representative body, are not bright, and the American Jewish community remains torn by ideological and organizational rivalries. Yet if viewed in historical perspective, the situation is not entirely discouraging. The Jews of individual towns and cities are progressively unifying their activities by means of community councils and welfare funds. Through the United Jewish Appeal, a substantial measure of co-ordination has been achieved in fund-raising endeavors. And, while over-all unity is still unattained, the desire for co-operation is increasingly evident in local communities. It is to these local communities that we must look for eventual amity and understanding in American Jewish life. It is they who, in all likelihood, will induce the central agencies to forget old antipathies and to discover the means of co-operating in those essentials upon which Jewish life depends.

VII

ECONOMIC TRENDS

Nathan Reich

INTRODUCTION

THE student of the economic trends in American Jewish life is confronted by several difficulties. He is handicapped by a lack of adequate and reliable factual information. As is generally known, the United States census does not classify occupational data on the basis of religious or ethnic allegiance. Whatever factual information bearing on the economic position of American Jewry there is, consists of fragmentary private studies and estimates of limited validity.

Moreover, it should be obvious that there is no independent Jewish economy apart from the general economy of the country; Jews form an integral part of that economy. By and large, the economic position of the Jews, past, present and future, is intimately connected with the fate of the general American economy. A proper understanding of the economics of the Jewish group requires, therefore, an extensive knowledge of the salient trends of American economy in the past; and any evaluation of the economic prospects of the Jewish people presupposes a proper evaluation of the general economic trends in the near future. This is a task of no mean proportions. The subject is still further complicated by the quickened tempo of social and economic change, so characteristic of this dynamic era in our history.

Finally, the war emergency has introduced unpredictable changes which will, without doubt, profoundly affect the immediate future. The extent and effect of these changes will depend upon the duration of the war, the magnitude of effort Americans will be called upon to exert, and the type of peace which will follow upon the termination of hostilities. If, therefore, this discussion will leave the reader with a sense of incompleteness, it is due, not to the writer's indifference to the merits of thoroughness and precision, but simply to the inadequacy of factual material at his disposal, and to the rapidity of change in conditions under which our economic system operates.

Economic Characteristics of American Jewry

The economic structure of the Jews in the United States reveals several leading characteristics which, to some extent, differentiate the economics of the Jewish group from that of any other American group, and also from that of the composite American people. First, Jews are a predominantly urban, perhaps the most urbanized people of the world. In the United States, of a total of about 4,777,000 Jews, over 4,000,000 live in cities of 100,000 and over. New York and Chicago—the two largest cities—claim about one-half of the entire Jewish population in the United States. While Jews form barely 4 per cent of the total population in the United States, they account for 11 per cent of the population of all cities of over 100,000 inhabitants, but comprise only a minor fraction of one per cent of that of the rural areas.*

In New York City, Jews form approximately 30 per cent of the total population. Jews are thus not merely an urban, but to a large extent, a metropolitan people. The economic welfare of a large proportion of the Jews is thus intimately related to the level of welfare of large cities.

A second characteristic of the socio-economic structure of Amer-

* *American Jewish Year Book*, Vol. 43, Philadelphia, 1941, pp. 654-655.

ican Jewry is the generally observed tendency toward occupational concentration in relatively few areas of economic enterprise. It is true that the Jews of today are no longer the people of traders they were at the dawn of our modern era; that during the last 150 years they have established themselves in a variety of economic occupations. Yet, they still tend to gravitate toward a few sources of livelihood.

It is necessary to repeat that we have no precise data on the occupational distribution of American Jews. A number of private studies and estimates, however, give us a roughly adequate picture. In 1937, an inquiry into occupations of Jews in New York City produced the following estimates:

TABLE I

PERCENTAGE DISTRIBUTION OF GAINFUL JEWISH WORKERS, AND ALL GAINFUL WORKERS IN NEW YORK CITY (IN 1937)*

General Divisions of Industry	Jewish Gainful Workers †	All Gainfu Workers
Trade	25.7%	16.9%
Manufacturing industries	25.4	19.8
Domestic and personal service	10.9	14.2
Professional service	7.4	6.6
Construction industries	5.2	9.9
Transportation industries	2.7	5.7
Finance	2.4	5.4
Amusements	2.4	1.7
Public service	2.2	2.9
Public utilities	0.5	3.6
Other	1.7	2.3
Unemployed	13.5	11.0

* Adapted from Committee on Economic Adjustment, *Industrial Classification of Jewish Gainful Workers in New York City*, New York: Conference on Jewish Relations, 1938, 31 pages (Mimeo.).

† The term "workers" includes both employer and employee.

An examination of Table I reveals that Jews form a larger proportion than the composite New York population in trade, manufacturing industries, professional services and amusements, and a smaller proportion in the other industrial divisions. On the whole, the divergence is not too great.*

New York, however, is not typical of the country at large. It certainly is not typical of the economic structure of the Jewish people residing outside of New York City.

TABLE II

OCCUPATIONAL DISTRIBUTION OF JEWISH GAINFUL WORKERS IN SELECTED CITIES *

Divisions of Industry	Dal-las, Texas 1939	De-troit, Mich. 1935	New Lon-don, Conn. 1938	Nor-wich, Conn. 1938	Pas-saic, N.J. 1937	Stam-ford, Conn. 1938	Tren-ton, N.J. 1937
Trade..................	51.9%	54.1%	54.5%	50.8%	43.2%	56.2%	53.7%
Manufacturing and mechan-ical..................	11.4	23.3	16.2	22.7	22.5	16.1	11.7
Professional services......	11.7	9.5	13.7	9.4	12.3	13.5	12.3
Clerical occupations......	20.2	...	4.7	9.2	14.6	...	12.4
Domestic and personal serv-ice....................	1.6	9.6	5.6	3.9	4.6	5.5	5.3
Transportation and Com-munication............	1.3	2.2	2.2	1.6	2.3	...	2.9
Public service............	...	0.9	1.0	1.3	0.4	0.9	0.9

* Adapted from tables in Jewish Occupational Council, *Patterns of Jewish Occupational Distribution in the United States and Canada*, New York, 1940.

Table II shows the distribution of gainfully employed Jews (both employers and employees) in a number of selected cities. The picture reveals a much heavier concentration in commerce, which claims roughly one-half of the Jewish people residing in those cities. The percentage is about twice as large as that of New York City. Also, the proportion of the professional group is considerably higher than that revealed in the New York study. It is, of course, difficult to say with any degree of precision whether the occupational pattern in these cities is representative of all Jews residing outside the New York City area. But considering that the bulk of non-New York Jewry resides in middle-sized

* It should be noted, however, that the totals for "All Gainful Workers" include Jews. If the latter were deducted, the divergence would be somewhat greater.

cities of the type included in Table II, one may be justified in assuming that the occupational distribution of the seven cities is fairly representative of the remainder of the Jewish population. If this assumption is correct, it is possible to arrive at some generalization regarding the occupational distribution of American Jewry as a whole.

New York City includes over 40 per cent of the Jewish population of the United States. If, as we assume, the bulk of the remaining 60 per cent resides in cities of the type analyzed in Table II, we may conclude that of one hundred Jews gainfully employed in the United States, between thirty-five and forty draw their sustenance from commercial occupations; between fifteen and twenty from manufacturing industries; some ten or twelve are in the professions; and the remainder are scattered among personal services, transportation, construction trades and other occupations. The corresponding figures for the American population at large are: in trade 13.8 per cent, in manufacturing industries 26.3 per cent, and in professional services 6.8 per cent. A comparison of the two shows that among Jews the trade group is almost three times as large as among the total population of the United States; in the professions, probably about twice as large as the corresponding groups among Americans as a whole; while the manufacturing group among Jews is below the composite proportion. Agriculture, which claims 17.5 per cent of all gainfully occupied Americans, absorbs perhaps only between 1 per cent and 2 per cent of gainfully employed Jews. The occupational pattern of American Jewry thus reveals marked concentration in a few areas of enterprise.

Moreover, within these occupational areas there is a further concentration within relatively few subdivisions. Thus, of the 236,820 Jews engaged in trade in New York City, 163,500 are in retail trade, and of this latter group, food stores, apparel, furniture, and drug stores claim over three-fourths. In the manufacturing industry, Jews tend to concentrate almost exclusively in the consumers' goods, or so-called light industry. Thus, again taking New York City, for which estimates are available, of 234,378 Jews in manufacturing—20,695 of whom are employers—the clothing and headwear industries absorb 139,058, the fur industry 13,265, the printing industry 18,100, and the food and kindred products industry 10,830; the four combined account for over three-fourths of all engaged in manufacturing. Within the professional group, there is a similar concentration in a few selected branches, such as law, medicine, pharmacy, and dentistry. From general observation, it is fair to assume that conditions in other cities are not unlike those prevailing in New York City.

In the absence of exact data, it is again difficult to form an accurate picture of the distribution of the Jewish people among the various socio-economic classes. Studies made in a number of cities, however, show a fairly consistent pattern of the social composition of American Jewry.

TABLE III

DISTRIBUTION OF GAINFULLY EMPLOYED JEWS BY SOCIO-ECONOMIC CLASS IN SELECTED CITIES*

Socio-Economic Classes	Buffalo 1938	Detroit 1935	San Francisco 1938	Canada 1931
Clerks and kindred workers.......	35.6%	39.1%	40.2%	30.3%
Proprietors, managers and officials .	25.9	26.8	30.6	24.7
Professional persons..............	14.3	7.6	11.4	5.1
Skilled workers..................	16.3	8.9	5.6	13.8
Semi-skilled workers.............	3.0	14.8	9.4	20.4
Unskilled workers................	3.2	2.8	2.0	5.7
Unclassified and others...........	1.7	...	0.8	...

* Adapted from Jewish Occupational Council, *Patterns of Jewish Occupational Distribution in the United States and Canada*, cited.

An examination of the figures in Table III reveals that roughly 60 per cent of Jews are wage and salary earners, with the salaried group much the larger of the two; that between 25-30 per cent fall into the proprietors' group; and that about 10 per cent are in the professional group. New York City would most likely show a higher proportion of wage earners but the figures in Table III are probably fairly representative of American Jewry at large.*

PARTICIPATION OF JEWS IN AMERICAN ECONOMY

The extent of occupational concentration is further revealed when, in addition to occupational distribution amongst Jews, we consider the proportional participation of Jews within the particular branches of economic enterprise. Taking again New York City, we find that while of one hundred gainfully employed New Yorkers, twenty-seven are Jews, the latter form 41 per cent of all New Yorkers engaged in trade, 39 per cent of all engaged in the field of amusement, 35 per cent of all engaged in manufacturing industries; but Jews constitute only 14 per cent of all construction workers, 13 per cent of those in transportation, 12 per cent of all engaged in finance, and only 4 per cent of the personnel of public utilities.

A breakdown of the trade group, in which Jews form 41 per cent, shows that they constitute 80 per cent of the apparel group, about 59 per cent of the furniture and household group, 58 per cent of the food group, 63 per cent of the retail drug group; but they are only 21 per cent of the public drink-dispensing group, 18 per cent of the general merchandise group, and only 12 per cent of the automotive group. In the manufacturing category, in which Jews form 35 per cent of all, the distribution is also highly uneven. They form 82 per cent of the fur industry, 56 per cent of the clothing industry, 39 per cent of the leather goods industry, 38 per cent of the glass industry; but they are only 18 per cent of the metal and metal products group, 5 per cent of the transportation equipment industry, and 4 per cent of the machine and machine shop industry. These percentage figures refer to both

* The exact census figures for Canadian Jewry given in the last column of Table III, on the whole, confirm the fragmentary evidence regarding the social composition of American Jewry. The lower percentage of professionals and clerks, and the higher percentage of wage earners is due to the fact that Canadian Jewry, though similar in origin, is of more recent immigration than American Jews. It is the second generation Jews who move into the white collar class in large numbers.

employers and employees. In terms of Jewish participation as owners and employers, the percentages are uniformly higher. But they too follow the same pattern of concentration, ranging from 94 per cent in the fur and 87 per cent in the clothing industries, to the lows of 13 per cent and 11 per cent in the machine shop and transportation equipment groups, respectively.*

The above figures refer only to New York City, but the national picture is not much different. Some years ago, the editors of *Fortune* magazine pieced together a general picture of the extent of Jewish participation in American economy. In the main, the *Fortune* study confirmed what was already generally known. In agriculture, Jews constitute but a fraction of 1 per cent. They figure hardly at all in the capital goods industries, such as steel (except in the scrap iron division), coal, chemicals, transportation and transportation equipment, electrical goods, oil, rubber, and automobiles (except in the second-hand car market). Jewish ownership amounts to only 5-10 per cent of wool textiles, 5 per cent of cotton textiles, and about 15 per cent of silk and 16 per cent of the rayon yarn industries. Their share in the distribution of textile products is several times higher.

In the insurance field, Jewish participation is limited almost entirely to selling personnel; in New York City, about one-half of the agents are Jews. Jews own three of the four leading cigar manufacturing establishments, and they practically control the tobacco buying business, but they are a decided minority in cigarette manufacturing. They control probably 50 per cent of the distilleries, and 30-40 per cent of the boot and shoe industries. The only industries in which Jews have attained dominant ownership on a national scale are, of course, the garment industries. In this group, Jews operate about 95 per cent of women's dress factories, 85 per cent of the men's garment and 95 per cent of the fur industries, and a large proportion of the millinery industry. Jews also loom

---

* See Committee on Economic Adjustment, *Industrial Classification of Jewish Gainful Workers in New York City*, cited.

large in the moving picture industry. In distribution, Jews figure in considerable strength in independent retail trade, but they are a decided minority of about 5 per cent in the chain store field.

Besides confirming the obvious, the *Fortune* study helped to discredit some widely held notions about Jewish participation in financial institutions. The actual role of Jews in the American financial world is decidedly minor. Thus, of 420 names listed as directors of the nineteen members of the New York Clearing House in 1933, only thirty, or about 7 per cent were Jews. What is more, these represented only minor banking houses; in terms of banking business done, the percentage would be much smaller. In investment banking, the leading houses were, in 1935, J. P. Morgan & Co., National City Co., Dillon, Read & Co., Guaranty Trust Co., and Bancamerica Blair—all non-Jewish institutions. The few establishments in which Jewish ownership was present were in a minority, both in foreign and domestic financing. Of the 1375 members of the New York Stock Exchange, 252 or 18 per cent were Jews; of the 637 brokerage firms, 55 were Jewish, and Jews held part ownership in 63 firms.* It should also be noted that, because of the differences in the size of the individual firms, numerical representation does not coincide with the share of the brokerage business.

Occupational Trends Among American Jews

The dynamics in the Jewish occupational scene are even more significant than the analysis of the existing economic structure. What is the direction of occupational shifts operating within the far-flung Jewish communities? Unfortunately, we have little precise information on this vital subject. General observation, and a few fragmentary studies, suggest a definite shift to professional and clerical work. Thus, in the studies of Jewish occupations in Trenton, N. J., and Stamford, Conn., the foreign-born Jewish group was classified separately from native-born Jews. In Trenton,

* Editors of Fortune, *Jews in America,* New York, 1936, pp. 39 ff.

64.4 per cent of the foreign-born and only 53.6 per cent of the native-born Jews were engaged in trade; likewise, manufacturing absorbed 17.9 per cent of the foreign-born and only 8.9 per cent of the native-born. The professions, however, included 6 per cent of the foreign-born and 18.4 per cent of the native group, and clerical occupations attracted 1.7 per cent of the foreign-born, and 6.6 per cent of the native-born Jews. The figures for Stamford disclose a similar shift.

A study of the economic characteristics of Jewish youth in Baltimore revealed a great divergence between the occupations of fathers and those pursued or desired by their children. While only 4.7 per cent of the fathers were professionals and technicians, 13.4 per cent of the youths were in professions, and 49.2 per cent aspired to such careers; only 6.7 per cent of the parents held clerical and selling positions, but 53 per cent of the youths were so employed. With respect to skilled labor, the trend is in the opposite direction; 32 per cent of the fathers earned their livelihood in skilled labor, but only 7 per cent of the youth had aspirations for such occupations, and even a smaller proportion (2.4 per cent) were actually engaged in skilled labor.* A study of Jewish youth in New York City revealed similar tendencies. The presence of girls in the youth group probably accounts for some of these differences, but alone it cannot explain the full extent of this occupational divergence between the two generations of Jews.

The direction of occupational shift among Jewish youth is also evident in the proportion of Jewish students in American colleges. While the Jews form less than 4 per cent of the total population of the United States, the proportion of Jewish students in the total college enrollment was estimated at over 9 per cent in 1935. Symptomatic, too, is the distribution of Jewish students among the various faculties. Jews formed 26 per cent of all dental students, 25 per cent of those preparing for the law, 23.3 per cent of all

---

* Jewish Occupational Council, *Some Characteristics of 408 Baltimore Jewish Youth,* N. Y., 1940 (mimeo.); *Patterns of Jewish Occupational Distribution,* cited.

aspiring pharmacists, 16.6 per cent of all commerce students, 16.1 per cent of all medical students and down the professional roster to 2.5 per cent of all prospective farm experts.*

Is Jewish Economic Structure Abnormal?

The one-sidedness of Jewish occupational distribution has caused a great deal of discussion, and no little concern, among thoughtful Jews. Anxiety has deepened particularly in the last two decades, which witnessed the economic uprooting of vast masses of Russian Jews in the early years of the Soviet regime, the tragic economic decline of Polish Jewry within the lifetime of the Republic of Poland, and the savage onslaught on the very existence of German Jewry. Those concerned over the "abnormality" of the Jewish economic structure fall roughly into two groups—one inspired primarily by economic consideration, the other by fears of a social and political nature.

Some Jews have expressed the fear that the economic structure of American Jewry is inherently unsound. They argue that many of the favored "Jewish" occupations, economically insecure today, are rapidly becoming obsolete. Unless, therefore, a drastic restratification is effected, American Jewry may soon face a crisis comparable to that experienced by the Jewish communities in the Old World. Others emphasize the political factor inherent in anti-Semitism. They point out that identifiable islands of Jewish enterprise in the midst of American economy provide excellent targets for anti-Semitic attacks. Underlying these fears, there is a vague feeling that some occupations are more, others less socially useful; that, for instance, agriculture is more productive than trade, coal digging more useful than teeth pulling, steel casting more essential than pill dispensing, and ditch digging more desirable than letter filing. It is consequently assumed that Jewish concentration

* Levinger, Lee J., *The Jewish Student in America*, Cincinnati, 1937, p. 72.
  Evidence regarding occupational shifts among American Jews is substantially confirmed by census statistics bearing on professional trends among Canadian Jewry, whose economic life in most respects resembles that of American Jews.

in "less productive" occupations, if not actually a cause of anti-Semitism, adds fuel to the flames of anti-Jewish prejudice.

In appraising the validity of these arguments, it is important to bear in mind that Jews are not alone in exhibiting an "abnormal" occupational structure. A study of the occupational distribution of Americans of non-Jewish origins would reveal "abnormalities" peculiar to each ethnic element. Every immigrant group brought with it certain traditions, skills and industrial arts peculiar to its home country. In arriving on American shores, the obvious tendency of the immigrant was to seek opportunities to utilize skills and experience acquired in the old home. For example, Norwegians turned to seafaring, and Welshmen to mining; Germans attained distinction in beer brewing; Italians became truck farmers and road construction workers; and Slav peasants filled the ranks of semi-skilled and unskilled workers, many of whom gradually filtered into agriculture. In like manner, when Jews arrived in the United States, they naturally gravitated toward occupations in which they were proficient. Most of the Jewish immigrants had resided in towns and cities, and the bulk of them were artisans, petty merchants, semi-professionals, or young people without any special training, but easily adaptable to any number of urban, industrial or commercial occupations. It was quite natural for the Warsaw tailor to become the dressmaker of lower Broadway, or for the Pinsk peddler to blossom forth as the storekeeper of New York, or for the Talmudic scholar of Vilna to make his debut before the American bar.

Fortunately for the economic welfare of the Jewish group, the occupational and social traditions of Jewish immigrants and their descendants coincided with the general trends in American economy during the last hundred years. An examination of occupational distribution between 1870 and the present reveals a continuous shift of population from rural to urban areas, and a persistent trend from agricultural to urban occupations. Thus, while in 1870, approximately 50 per cent of all economically active

Americans were engaged in farming, the percentage has steadily declined and was only 17.5 per cent in 1940. Within urban occupations, too, there has been a marked tendency to concentrate in trade, the professions and the public services. Thus, while the proportion of Americans engaged in manufacturing remained fairly constant during the last few decades, ranging between 26-30 per cent (it was 26.3 per cent in 1940), the percentage of those engaged in trade and transportation rose from 7.5 per cent in 1870 to 23 per cent in 1940, the professions from 2.6 per cent to 6.8 per cent, and clerical occupations from 2.4 per cent to 10.5 per cent. In terms of absolute numbers, the total employed population was quadrupled between 1870 and 1940. But, during this period, the agricultural group increased by little more than one half, far less than the proportionate growth of the population. The manufacturing group increased in the same proportion as the total population, that is, it held its own. Those engaged in trade and transportation, however, increased more than twelvefold, the professional group more than tenfold, the clerical group more than seventeenfold, and the public service group more than twenty-onefold.* With the sole exception of the public service group, the occupations which expanded most rapidly were precisely those to which the Jews flocked in large numbers.

The explanation is simple. American Jews in search of employment obviously tended to congregate in those areas of economic enterprise which were expanding most rapidly. It was a matter of good fortune that the expanding fields of economic activity were those for which Jews were eminently suited by virtue of their age-old urban traditions. The fortunate circumstance that American economy was ready to receive what the Jews had to offer, in the way of skills and services, was responsible, in no small measure, for the solid achievements of the Jewish immigrants in their new American home.

* Anderson, H. D., and Davidson, P. E., *Occupational Trends in the United States*, Stanford University, 1940, pp. 16-17.

However, the successful adjustment of the Jewish immigrants cannot be explained without reference to the remarkable resourcefulness with which hundreds of thousands of Jewish workers faced the grim realities of modern industrial relations. The story of employer-employee relationship, and of trade union organization in the garment trades—the industrial domicile of most Jewish wage earners—is a story of the transformation of an amorphous mass of immigrant industrial fodder into a disciplined group of workers, functioning through trade unions which easily occupy the foremost rank in American labor organization.

The road traveled by the garment workers was not an easy one. Early conditions in the garment industry were deplorable. The sweatshop dominated the scene: wages were low, hours were long and sanitary conditions were of the worst. The industry was, and to some extent it still is, highly decentralized. The ease with which one could enter the field made for keen cut-throat competition. The continuous flow of immigration fed the supply of cheap labor, which further undermined wage standards. In spite, or because of these difficulties, the Jewish immigrant workers tackled the job of union organization with a zeal perhaps unparalleled by any other workers' group.

After years of halting growth, the turning point in needle trade unionism came with the great strike of 1910, which culminated in the conclusion of the famous "Protocol of Peace." This definitely established unionism in the women's garment trades. Other branches of the industry soon followed suit, and before long the needle trades achieved a measure of industrial peace. To be sure, there were temporary setbacks, sporadic flare-ups of intra-union conflicts, and occasional resort to strong arm methods. But the International Ladies Garment Workers Union, the Amalgamated Clothing Workers Union, in the men's garment industry, and the unions in the related trades, which serve the bulk of Jewish wage earners, are today among the strongest, the most orderly and best managed unions in the country.

The International and the Amalgamated never confined themselves merely to the conventional task of raising wages and improving working conditions. From the very beginnings, these organizations differed from the usual variety of unionism. They showed keener interest in the broader aspects of social reform. The history of these unions is replete with social experimentation of the widest variety. It may be said that these unions have been experimental laboratories for many of the principles which are now accepted practices in industrial relations. Arbitration, industrial self-government, scientific shop management, voluntary unemployment insurance, joint sanitary boards, regular educational and recreational programs for the union membership, the maintenance of medical services, health insurance, provision of vacation resorts—all these measures have been tried and most of them retained as established functions of unionism.

The significant role which the needle trades play in American unionism affords proof that the Jewish worker is an organic part of American economic life. In the light of this fact, and of American occupational dynamics which we have discussed, the economic structure of American Jewry can hardly be considered abnormal. The Jews distributed themselves largely in response to the requirements of an expanding economy. The functions fulfilled by Jews were needed in the market. Why then should one assume that these functions will become superfluous in the American economy of the near future? Fear of impending economic doom, which has seized some American Jews in recent years, is without economic justification.

The tragic decline of European Jewry was not primarily due to occupational "abnormalities." The decline of Polish Jewry was partly a reflection of the general poverty of the country, and partly the result of deliberate discrimination by the former Polish Government. With the exception of part of the over-grown merchant group, the functions which Jews performed in Poland did not become obsolete. They were not eliminated, but simply handed over to Poles. The sufferings of Jews in the early years of the Soviet regime were due to the economic collapse of the whole country. When the new Soviet economy was set in motion, the emphasis was on the building of industrial plants, electric power developments and capital goods industries—occupations for which the Jewish artisan and ex-shopkeeper were not trained. As soon, however, as the Soviets began to pay attention to the supply and distribution of consumer's goods and services, the Jews were absorbed without much difficulty into the industrial and administrative life of the country. The savage uprooting of German Jewry was not dictated by the character of German Jewish occupations, but by the logic of an illogical, brutal racial policy. What occupations Jews pursued mattered very little. In fact, among the first victims of Hitler's policy were the few German Jewish families who lived on farms. It was not the economic functions of the German Jews which were not needed; it was the Jews who were not wanted; their functions were avidly swallowed up by worthy "Aryans." Barring the acceptance of Hitler's racial policy in the United States—an extremely unlikely eventuality—the fears of the impending economic doom of American Jewry appear unfounded.

The admonitions that Jews must become farmers, coal miners and steel workers are not only without economic justification, but also highly unrealistic. From the figures quoted above, it is evident that agriculture is a relatively declining source of employment. Until the recent war-induced labor shortage, American farm leaders were concerned about the several million superfluous farm hands. In addition to the obvious difficulties involved in transforming a city worker or trader into a farmer, a Jewish policy of agrarization would have to contend with basic economic trends which have been and still are moving in the opposite direction. It is no occasion for surprise that, except for Palestine where the hardship incident to agrarian resettlement was overcome by the superior force of an intense national idealism, all attempts at diverting Jews into farm occupations met with only minor success. As in the past, individual, enterprising Jews will continue to establish themselves as successful farmers—and there are thousands of them in the United States, Canada, Argentina and Europe—but the possibilities for mass agrarization appear slight. Neither is there any likelihood of diverting large numbers of Jews into capital goods industries. The absorptive capacity of these industries is limited. There is a substantial body of opinion among economists to the effect that the normal long run trend preceding the war emergency did not presage an expansion of the heavy capital goods industries, but rather favored the consumer goods group and the various service trades.*

JEWISH OCCUPATIONAL STRUCTURE AND ANTI-SEMITISM

The argument remains that occupational restratification, while not economically necessary, is desirable as a means of combatting the evils of anti-Semitism. To be sure, anti-Semitism is a grim and painful phenomenon on the American scene, and must be fought with all the resources of, and in close union with, all liberal democratic forces in American society. It is a complex problem. The roots of anti-Semitism are many, but they do not spring from the occupational physiognomy of the Jews. The attempt to justify anti-Semitism in economic terms is merely a rationalization of an existing prejudice. The choice of reasons is incidental. In the religious atmosphere of the Middle Ages, anti-Semitism was justified in religious terms. In the race-intoxicated atmosphere of Germany, the justification is the protection of race purity from Semitic pollution. In the industrial atmosphere of the Western World, the argument is couched in economic phraseology. There is no reason to assume that economic restratification even if feasible and desirable would have any effect on the preachers of hatred. To assume that, where the sight of a Jewish dentist or tailor

* See the testimony of Professor Alvin Hansen and others before the Temporary National Economic Committee, *Hearings . . . Savings and Investment*, Part 9, Washington, 1940.

arouses hostility and friction, the appearance of a Jewish coal miner or hod-carrier will promptly generate admiration and love is, mildly put, unrealistic. The Negro certainly performs some of the hardest physical labor at the lowest level of remuneration. Yet, the sweat of his brow and the badge of poverty have not earned him the privilege of full equality. Were all the Jews to don workmen's overalls, anti-Semites would still continue to ply their trade, this time, to be sure, under some different pretext. In a free democratic world, major occupational restratification is economically unwarranted. In a Hitlerized world, it would make no difference.

Conclusion

There are certain developments in American economy which create new problems for the Jew. The foremost of these is the growth of concentration of economic power. This "collectivization" of American economy proceeds in two forms. One is the gradual extension of public control over economic activities, ranging from regulation of industry and trade to direct government operation of business enterprises (e.g. Tennessee Valley Authority). The second form is the increasing control of private enterprise by larger but fewer private corporations. The causes and extent of this two-pronged trend toward collective control are too well known to require detailed discussion. Suffice it to say that, as far as present indications go, the trend will continue to operate in the near future with perhaps accelerated tempo.

Concentration of economic control in the hands of public agencies and private corporations affects the economic prospects of Jews in two ways. First, it narrows the range of individual enterprise, and consequently forces an increasing number of people to seek employment in government and large scale corporate enterprise. An economic world, consisting predominantly of a multitude of independent, competing individual operators, is gradually being replaced by huge corporate units comprising thousands of individuals working under the co-ordinated direction of centralized management, fitted like so many cogs into a highly co-ordinated machine.

The narrowing range of independent individual small scale enterprise, while affecting millions of Americans of all origins, probably affects the Jewish groups to a greater extent. For reasons into which we cannot enter here, the Jew has displayed remarkable gifts for this form of enterprise. Centuries of struggle for survival in an unfriendly environment developed in him qualities of ingenuity, commercial resourcefulness and a keen sense of economic independence—qualities which helped him immensely in the era of economic individualism. But these qualities may not prove indispensable in an era of corporate economy.

Even more important is the danger of employment discrimination under a system of corporate economy. It is a fact that even the United States, with its humane, liberal and democratic institutions and traditions, was never entirely free from prejudice against religious and racial groups. Under a system of decentralized free enterprise, anti-Semitism was largely confined within the limits of social relations. Humiliating though such experiences may have been to the Jew who tried to make "the grade," it did not, on the whole, affect the "bread earning" opportunities of the Jewish masses. Enterprise was free and accessible to all men with some means. The possession of the proper ancestry counted for little in the "rough" world of competitive enterprise. But the growth of large scale economy, and the consequent diminution of small scale enterprise intensifies the danger of discrimination. At a time when ever increasing numbers of young Jews will have to seek employment in large corporations or government agencies; when the opinion of the personnel managers may decide the fate of thousands of job seekers, the "social" prejudice of those in charge of employment policy acquires a new and menacing significance.

Fortunately, the extent of discrimination in public employment has thus far been kept at a minimum. Thanks to the deep-seated democratic traditions of American society, and to the effective civil service safeguards against the intrusion of religious prejudice in the selection of applicants, Jews have little cause for complaint in the matter of public employment. In Jewish historical experience, this is a rather unique development. While throughout the centuries Jews were, for the most part, barred from public employment and compelled to seek an outlet in private trade, today, in the United States, young Jews are frequently refused work in private institutions, and must perforce seek an outlet in public employment. Assuming a democratic victory, there is no reason to fear a reversal of the employment policies pursued by our government agencies.

But public employment is obviously limited in scope. The bulk of industry will probably remain in private hands, and discrimination in private business is thus one of the most serious problems facing American Jewry. The extent of discrimination cannot be statistically measured, but tens of thousands who have experienced it can testify to its existence. The problem is complicated by the fact that it is very difficult to enforce fairness in employment through legislation. The constitution assures legal equality, and some states have passed statutes outlawing economic discrimination on the ground of color or religion. More recently the federal government initiated an energetic policy of preventing religious and racial discrimination in industries producing for national defense. Through the President's Committee on Fair Employment Practices, a special agency has been established in Washington to enforce equality of opportunity in employment. How effective such public measures will be is an open question.

Because of the difficulties inherent in legislative or administrative attempts to prevent discrimination, voluntary co-operation assumes paramount importance. The American Jewish Congress has for several years been engaged in an effort to break down employment bars in many of our large business organizations. From the reports of its officers, it appears that, in many instances, such efforts were crowned with success. The growth of trade unions opens new avenues to the problem of discrimination. Many unions already control job placement, and many more will probably acquire such control. Important, too, is the fact that the union movement is being extended to white collar groups, which include Jews in considerable numbers. The safeguarding of complete equality of opportunity in the placement policies of unions is an important step in minimizing discrimination. The essentially democratic spirit of the overwhelming majority of labor leaders, and the liberal orientation of the labor movement in this country, are favorable factors in the situation. The success of the struggle against discrimination will depend on the effective mobilization of public opinion in the interest of fair play in employment. Recent events abroad have deepened the appreciation of the meaning and value of religious and racial equality. It should not be difficult to point out that such freedoms would be meaningless without equality of opportunity. The atmosphere is thus favorable for a determined effort to win the support of public opinion in preserving one of the most basic tenets of a free, democratic society.

Finally, the combating of external discrimination alone is not sufficient. Young Jews must be psychologically and vocationally prepared for a broader occupational distribution. The point has been made that Jews have gravitated toward economic activities for which they were best suited by previous training; and that, on the whole, these activities were and still are the expanding sectors of American economy. However, within these major fields, Jews tend to concentrate within too few selected subdivisions. Such concentration is unsound, not because they may become grist in the anti-Semitic mill, but because they simply offer poor opportunity for making a living.

It is generally known that hundreds or perhaps thousands of young Jewish lawyers do not earn a living income; that hundreds of teachers cannot secure appointments. Our economy is a highly dynamic one. Old professions become crowded and new ones expand. Old skills become obsolete, but new trades make their appearance. Traditional forms of business organization decline, but new forms become established. Thus, while the teaching profession is on the whole overcrowded, there is a shortage of teachers of trade subjects. The legal profession is oversupplied, but the profession of the social and public welfare worker is in the ascendancy. Medicine is overcrowded in large centers, but there is a shortage of medical facilities in rural areas; and there is a growing field of public health administration. New technological inventions displace labor, but workers are needed both to make and operate the machines.

The problem of vocational adjustment of young people to changing economic conditions is, of course, not a Jewish, but a general problem. The interest in vocational guidance has recently attracted wide public attention. Long before the war emergency, the United States Office of Education launched a comprehensive study of the changing occupational trends in the United States, in order to determine which occupations were contracting and which expanding. School systems in various parts of the country have instituted special departments to provide vocational guidance to young people. The information gathered in connection with the administration of the social security program and the national defense requirements will without doubt provide a more comprehensive picture of occupational dynamics in the United States. This should serve as the basis for a systematic policy of vocational orientation.

The growing importance of vocational guidance opens new perspectives for Jewish communal work. Jewish social organizations are, to an increasing extent, incorporating vocational guidance as a regular part of their functional scope. They can utilize the mass of information which comes from public and private agencies to good advantage, by making the facts known among the Jews who require aid and guidance in vocational choice. Jews are a highly adaptable people. There is no reason to assume that, having survived so many vicissitudes, they will fail to adapt themselves to changes in the current economic scene. The paramount problem facing American Jews is the preservation of the free opportunity to make the desired vocational adjustment.

VIII

ANTI-SEMITISM

——

Jacob J. Weinstein

No STUDY of contemporary Jewish life can ignore the problem of anti-Semitism. It is, of course, basic to any analysis of the relationship between the Jews and the larger American society of which they form an integral part. It has its place, too, where, as in this volume, the emphasis is not primarily on such relationships but mainly on the complex of social and cultural factors which are uniquely Jewish. For so pervasive has been the influence of anti-Jewish prejudice, that even "internal" Jewish life, that is, specifically Jewish institutions and conceptions, has been seriously affected.

ITS PATTERN

If anti-Semitism has been a constant theme in Jewish history for two thousand years, the forms it has assumed have varied from country to country and from century to century. To understand anti-Semitism in any particular period or area, we must examine not only the overt act but also the social conditions out of which it emerged and which shaped its expression. Thus, the development of anti-Jewish prejudice in this country can be adequately understood only against the background of America's origins; the dynamic and expanding nature of its economy; the successive waves of immigration that came to its shores; the impact of two world wars and economic depression.

One fact stands out clearly—the people of the United States have never been infected with the violent forms of European anti-Semitism. The very first settlers, it is true, were not wholly free of anti-Jewish prejudice. But even this milder form of intolerance generally remained dormant in the liberalizing atmosphere of the New World.

The Pilgrim Fathers were driven by a double hunger—a hunger for free land and a hunger for free worship. A generation after they had landed at Plymouth, they were confronted with Jewish refugees from persecution in South America. Drawing so much of their moral inspiration from the Old Testament, the Puritans might have been expected to transfer their regard for the ancient Hebrews to the latter's Jewish descendants in the New World. But the Puritans, eager to establish some form of theocratic society, were impatient of dissent. They did not relate the contemporary Jew to Biblical ancestors such as Samuel, Saul and David who were greatly admired, but were rather reminded of his stiff-necked obduracy in refusing the Saviour. The Jews of colonial days were, therefore, subjected to discrimination in many ways similar to that visited on the Quakers, the Seekers, the Catholics and members of other dissident religious sects. And, in the case of the Jews, there were added to the religious prejudices, deeply-rooted myths and stereotypes that the early settlers brought with them from the Old World.

But the number of Jews in the Colonies was small. The need for manpower, particularly for traders, was great. The frontier was exercising its magnetic pull. And these factors tended to nullify ancient bigotries. The Jews who came to America from its colonial beginnings until the middle of the nineteenth century readily adjusted themselves to the major patterns of American existence. Thus, for example, the letters of Rebecca Gratz, covering the span between 1808 and 1866, reflect a genuine intercultural assimilation between Jew and Gentile of the upper strata—an assimilation that in some cases, such as the Clays and Gratzes of Kentucky, was marked by a mutual observance of each other's religious forms.*

The bulk of the Jews who were in America during the early decades of the nineteenth century would, in time, probably have been absorbed into the pattern of life of the majority with a minimum of friction. That might equally be said of the 200,000 Jews who came from Germany, or were born to German immigrants, prior to 1880. They came as part of a larger tide of non-Jewish German immigrants and settled in the same cities and towns. One of the most heart-warming phenomena of American life was the sudden sterilization of the virus of religious bigotry, once it was transferred to American soil. German peasants and townsfolk, brought up on the hoary myths of Jewish Christ-killers and well-poisoners, were able to live most amicably with Jews in Philadelphia, Cincinnati, Milwaukee and St. Louis.† Expanding America, occupied with the myriad tasks of building and peopling a continent, had little time for religious prejudice. The natives saw in the immigrants a supply of cheap labor and welcome consumers. For the farmer and his family, the Jewish peddler who brought them much-needed consumers' items and in turn purchased their farm products, performed a valuable economic function. The German Jew's thrift, his sense of organization and his commercial ability appealed to the Yankee mentality. Then, too, the issue of slavery dominated American politics and offered a safety valve for latent prejudices and subconscious frustrations.

Thus, anti-Semitism did not enter the consciousness of the average American very deeply. There were, it is true, some anti-Semitic undertones during the Civil War. But it is interesting

* See Philipson, David (ed.), *Letters of Rebecca Gratz*, Philadelphia, 1929.
† Even the literature concerning the Jew among the German settlers in America, while it retains some of the old-world caricatures, is often mellow and complimentary. See Glanz, Rudolf, "Jews in Early German-American Literature," *Jewish Social Studies*, April, 1942.

to note that the leading role played by Judah P. Benjamin in the Confederacy aroused no perceptible resentment toward the Jews in the North or South during the worst days of the Civil War and Reconstruction animosities.

By 1890, however, the Civil War had been sublimated in the conquest of the western frontier. The sons of the pioneers were settling down to enjoy the great fortunes of their hardy sires. In the place of the aristocracy of birth that had characterized the Old World, America had already developed its aristocracy of wealth. And with the growth of that aristocracy, there emerged a certain social snobbery and exclusiveness which barred Jews from elite social circles, from summer resorts, from private schools, from a few colleges. Nor did the aristocracy find it necessary to justify their prejudices. They were, as Thorstein Veblen, America's great social thinker, later saw, part of the invidious distinctions by means of which the leisure class maintained a sense of its superior status.*

These pin-pricks of social discrimination apart, there cannot be said to have been any important anti-Semitic movement during the nineteenth century. The three serious movements of organized intolerance—the Know-Nothing, the early version of the Ku Klux Klan, and the American Protective Association—were, it is true, directed against foreigners and everything "alien." They were exclusively "white Protestant" organizations. But the Jews, as yet, did not claim their special or direct attention; for they were too insignificant and inconspicuous an element in the structure of American life.

Between 1880 and 1914, however, almost two million Jews came to the United States from Eastern Europe. They made one of the most difficult transitions ever recorded of a migratory group. Leaping across several centuries in time as well as thousands of miles in space, they left a seventeenth-century, pre-industrial, *Torah*-regulated society for the twentieth-century machine culture

---

* See Veblen, Thorstein, *The Theory of the Leisure Class*, New York, 1899.

of America. The wonder is not that there was some friction in the process of adjustment, but that there was so little. By settling for the most part in the congested quarters of the larger cities, they increased the visibility of the Jew. Non-Jews saw Yiddish signs, *kosher* markets, bearded and gabardined Jews; and all these externals served to sharpen the sense of difference between the Jewish and Gentile communities.

If this sense of difference did not develop into violent hostility, the more subtle forms of anti-Semitism were already taking root in American soil. The forms of social discrimination established by the upper classes were spreading, and their repercussions were beginning to be felt in the professions. Jewish lawyers were barred from the leading law firms. Jewish doctors were refused places on hospital staffs. Jewish instructors were denied promotion on college faculties long after less able Gentile colleagues had gained recognition. Certain bank and bond houses were difficult of access to Jews, for success depended on social mixing after business hours. The man who could not cultivate a customer over a dinner table, or on the golf course, was simply not eligible for the job.

These handicaps, however irritating and portentous, were by no means serious. The middle class Jews organized their own clubs and fraternities and established their own forms of wasteful and conspicuous consumption. They organized their own hospitals, law firms, bank and brokerage concerns. Denied executive positions in large concerns, they opened their own small businesses. And they found compensation by aspiring to leadership in Jewish communal institutions.

Frequently, the Jews moved to smaller towns where the forms of social discrimination had not yet fully crystallized. But as the Jew came closer to the heart of rural America, he discovered a widespread, if vague, suspicion of the city man. Those suspicions were an important factor in the strong tide of sentiment William Jennings Bryan had been able to arouse against Wall Street with his "Cross of Gold" speech in 1896. As yet, there was neither the need nor the inclination to channelize sectional and economic discontent into anti-Semitism. But the spread of anti-Jewish discrimination in the cities and the identification of the Jews with urban and financial America in the rural areas were ominous developments. Already, some astute observers were beginning to realize that an acute social crisis might turn latent prejudice into overt and serious hatred.

That crisis came with the World War. The hysteria and passions aroused by the war created an atmosphere in which dormant prejudice was transformed into active hostility. Blind hatred of the enemy led masses of people to suspect anyone associated even remotely with Germany or things German; and persons of German origin, including Jews, as well as those who had been known to admire German culture, were, therefore, regarded with considerable suspicion. The hostility to the Tsarist regime of those American Jews who had fled from Russian persecution served to heighten those suspicions. For reactionary Russia was an ally of the democracies. War passions do not allow for careful observation and logical reasoning; people leap to conclusions. If American Jews were so bitterly opposed to Russia, an ally, they might perhaps not be altogether unfriendly to Germany, the enemy not only of Russia but of the United States as well.

Anti-Semitism was given even greater impetus by the disillusionment of the post-war era and the fears of Bolshevism that the Russian Revolution had aroused. The American people were sorely disappointed with the outcome of the war. Convinced that their own participation constituted a crusade for democracy, they were shocked to find the victorious Allies scrambling for booty and power. The heavy cost of intervention, likewise, fostered a spirit of resentment which was exploited by isolationists and made the basis for a bristling distrust of all European entanglements. And some reckless men did not hesitate to point to the Jews, who manifested concern for fellow-Jews across the sea, as the symbol of all this hated internationalism. Bolshevism, too, engendered deep uneasiness among Americans, because it struck at the heart of the cherished sentiments of religion, political democracy and rugged individualism. The masses of Russian Jews suffered more acutely from the effects of the Revolution than perhaps any other group. Their deep religious sentiments were outraged, and their means of livelihood were destroyed. Hundreds of thousands of Jews were declassed and despised as bourgeois and "clerical" reactionaries. But the Bolshevists discountenanced and suppressed anti-Semitism. What is more, a number of individual Jews figured prominently among the leaders of the communist hierarchy. This seemed to lend plausibility to the identification of Jews with communists.

It is doubtful that Americans unaided would have made this association. It was Russian emigres who became the spearhead of anti-Semitism during the confused post-war years. Large numbers of Tsarist bureaucrats and aristocrats fled from the Revolution for their lives and found asylum in Western and Central Europe and in the United States. Never seriously concerned with the troubles of the Russian masses, they failed to understand the temper of the Revolution, and clung to the belief that the new regime had been foisted upon their country by a willful minority and could be overthrown with foreign aid. To gain support, they resorted to a technique which Tsarism had found useful in the past. They sought to convince the world that the Jews and not the Russian people had made the Revolution and employed the words "Bolshevists" and "Jews" as synonymous terms.

To support this fantastic claim, the Russian emigres adduced the notorious *Protocols of the Elders of Zion.* Today, every intelligent person knows that the *Protocols* was a fabrication of Tsarist days, employed by the bureaucracy to discredit its opponents by labeling them Jewish.* In the early 1920's, however, this spurious concoction startled some Americans, who were innocent of

---

* See Curtis, John S., *An Appraisal of the Protocols of Zion,* N. Y., 1942; Bernstein, H., *The Truth About the Protocols of Zion,* N. Y., 1935.

European affairs, and a few inclined willing ears to the charming aristocrats who spoke mysteriously of a "Jewish conspiracy." Thus, for example, Henry Ford gave the massive weight of his name and fortune to these libelous forgeries. In May 1920, his newspaper, the *Dearborn Independent,* began a series of articles which attributed the world's unrest to what it called the "International Jew." Not until 1927, on threat of a suit for libel, did Ford publicly confess his error and agree to the withdrawal of all anti-Semitic utterances in his publications, a retraction reiterated in 1942. Ford's attitude, a compound of hatred for Wall Street, fear of Bolshevism, and plain ignorance of Jewish and world history, was symptomatic of the forms anti-Semitism was beginning to assume. The articles of the *Dearborn Independent* constituted the most consistent and widespread anti-Semitic agitation that America had yet known. It touched off other movements and gave aid and comfort to lesser demagogues.

Among those movements, particular mention should be made of the revived Ku Klux Klan, an expression of the same forces that had produced the Know-Nothing movement in an earlier period. By the 1920's, however, the Jews had become a significant and visible element in American life; and they were added to the Negroes and the Catholics as the special objects of the Klan's efforts. The Klan represented the first serious attempt in the United States to exploit anti-Semitism—and racial and religious hatred generally—for reactionary political ends; for it was primarily the instrument of some of the most reactionary political elements in the country in their effort to arrest social progress. For several years until its disintegration through internal corruption in the late 1920's, the Klan struck terror into the hearts of racial and religious minorities throughout the land.

Nor were other manifestations of that current of intolerance lacking. In the early 1920's there were occasional disparaging references to Jews, particularly those from eastern Europe, as a special menace to American democracy. A. L. Lowell, the President of Harvard University, stirred a hornet's nest by suggesting a *numerus clausus* for Jews at Harvard. In 1928, enlightened America was stunned by the action of a state trooper in Massena, New York, who, in questioning a rabbi about the disappearance of a four-year-old child, implied that Jews made use of the blood of Christian children in their religious rites.*

The agitation to restrict immigration, which culminated in the Immigration Act of 1924 (the Johnson Bill), sharpened hostility to the foreign born, especially the more recent arrivals from Southern and Eastern Europe. The desire to limit immigration derived from a variety of causes. The disappearance of the frontier and the abundance of cheap labor alarmed many, notably organized labor, who feared unemployment and a reduction in the American standard of living. It was argued that the ravages of the first World War would induce multitudes to seek refuge in the United States and the country would be flooded with masses of broken and pauperized humanity.

Still another factor entered into that hostility. The earlier immigration had consisted chiefly of North and West Europeans of the Protestant faith, whereas the immigrants of the twentieth century were in the main Catholics—Italians, Poles, etc.—and Jews. To the conservative element, this trend foreshadowed material changes in the religious, social and cultural complexion of the country. And these fears inspired considerable propaganda about the undesirable qualities of non-Nordic peoples, including the Jews. A number of writers, drawing upon selected ethnic data, advanced pseudo-scientific rationalizations of Nordic superiority.†

The Jews, however, did not lack ardent defenders. John Spargo, S. W. McCall, Ada Sterling, among others, wrote passionately on their behalf. And groups such as the American Jewish Committee,

---

* The revival of the blood libel in twentieth century America shows that prejudice like war cuts a quick path through the outposts of civilization to the jungle of the primitive.

† See, for example, Grant, Madison, *The Passing of the Great Race*, New York, 1916, and Stoddard, Lothrop, *The Rising Tide of Color*, New York, 1920.

the Federal Council of the Churches of Christ in America, the Anti-Defamation League, published documented refutations of the charges against the Jews.

After 1925, when America swung into the dizzy period of Coolidge-Hoover prosperity, the belief was widely held that a population, busily and successfully engaged in the pursuit of material goods, would have no use for the substitute stimulus of race-prejudice. The attacks of the *Dearborn Independent,* the activities of the Ku Klux Klan, the utterances of a President Lowell or a Burton Hendrick could be regarded as irritating but isolated events, and by no means representative of any significant current in American life and thought.

The depression, however, brought all the latent and slumbering prejudices to the fore, and created new ones as well. The collapse of the stock market in 1929, and bank failures wiped out the life-time savings of innumerable American families; the shut-down of factories resulted in mass unemployment on an unprecedented scale. And as government measures proved ineffective, panic gripped the American people. Fears and anxieties were rapidly intensified; and the need to project those fears and anxieties became acute. Unable to understand the complicated processes of economics, masses of people were searching for a scapegoat on whom to fix the responsibility for their plight. Wall Street and international bankers had already begun to play that role; and the bridge was soon built in the popular mind between international finance and the Jews.

The Roosevelt Administration which assumed office in 1933 was determined to provide food and work for the unemployed regardless of the cost. It inaugurated extensive social reforms which set limits to unbridled individualism and threatened the power of vested interests. However salutary their economic effects may have been, the situation remained confused and uncertain. And in that atmosphere, anti-Semitism thrived and grew apace. To the normal ravages of the depression, there were added the special discriminations visited on the Jews. Large numbers were employed in the distributive trades where economies could most easily be made; and Jews became the favored victims of those economies. In many business enterprises, Jews were the first whose services were dispensed with.

Much more serious, however, was the deliberate and organized attempt to use the Jew as a scapegoat for economic distress and political tension. The depression was attributed to "Jewish bankers" and the New Deal to "Jewish radicals." Numerous anti-Semitic organizations made their appearance. Some of them, it is true, were led by self-seeking cranks. Others, however, had the support of men of means and influence.

The crisis in American life, and the intensification of anti-Semitism which it produced, coincided with the accession to power of the Nazis in Germany and the spread of fascism in Europe. With malevolent genius, Hitler realized that he could use anti-Semitism as the Trojan Horse, in whose cavernous belly he could hide the shock troops of Nazism. This issue had confused and weakened the democratic forces in Germany, and had enabled Hitler to pick them off one by one. He was confident that he could use the same strategy in any country where there were Jews, or where the picture of *the* Jew could be created in the public mind. This tactic was worth a flotilla of battleships. Therefore, under Goebbel's direction, lavish sums were expended on agents abroad whose chief function was to spread anti-Semitic propaganda; and their tactics were emulated by native fascists and reactionaries in America who admired both Hitler's purposes and methods.

As early as the fall of 1933, detectives employed by "Information and Service Association," an organization which tracked down and publicized the work of the "Friends of New Germany" and other fascist groups, revealed that native anti-Semites, like William Dudley Pelley and Robert E. Edmondson, were being aided by Nazi funds. By 1940, there were 121 organizations in this country whose chief stock-in-trade was anti-Semitism.* They bore such names as "American Aryan Folk Association," "American Gentile Protective Association," "Pro-Christian American Society," "White Shirts," "World Alliance Against Jewish Aggressiveness," etc. More than half of those organizations were still active in 1942, though not more than ten were of any considerable size and effectiveness. An analysis of these groups reveals that they were most numerous in the Middle Atlantic and North Central states, the Pacific Coast and the South Atlantic states. Twenty-six had their headquarters in New York City, eighteen in Chicago, seven in Los Angeles, and six in Washington. The peak years for these organizations seem to have been 1934, when nineteen were founded; 1937, which witnessed the birth of twenty-two; and 1938, when twenty-four put out their letterheads.

The organizations which, early in 1942, appeared to have the most efficient staffs, and the most ample resources, were the German-American Bund, the Silver Shirts, the National Union for Social Justice, the Christian Front, the Defenders of the Christian Faith, the Edmondson Economic Service, the American Vigilant Intelligence Federation, the Industrial Defense Association and the Paul Reveres.† Donald S. Strong summarizes his study of 121 anti-Semitic organizations in the following significant paragraph:

> Apparently almost all the organizations were formed since 1933. The obvious deduction which follows is that the Nazis' rise to power in Germany in 1933 and the long severe economic depression of the 1930's in the United States violently spurred the formation of anti-Semitic groups. Save for minor American twists, the ideology of these groups is identical with that of the Nazis. Since 1933, the annual number of new groups has, by and large, increased. This significant fact should be noted in any attempt to predict the future

* Strong, Donald S., *Organized Anti-Semitism in America,* Washington, 1941, pp. 139 ff.

† See *Life,* magazine, April 13, 1942, for the most up-to-date review of these and similar organizations.

of the anti-Semitic movement in America, for it suggests that an intransient anti-Semitic ideology has taken root . . . the curve of the anti-Semitic movement can be drawn verbally. The curve rockets from virtually zero in 1933 to a high point in the summer of 1934. Falling steadily until the autumn of 1935, it rises again, reaching, just before the 1936 presidential election, almost the level of its highest point. After the election, the curve descends abruptly, and only in the late spring of 1937 does it slowly begin to ascend again. In the autumn of 1938, its ascent increases in rapidity, and by 1940 it is above the high level of 1934. The rapid rise in 1933 and 1934 is, to a large extent, a result of the increased organizing activities of the German-American Bund and the Silver Shirts. The valley between the summer of 1934 and the autumn of 1935 represents an aftermath of the McCormack Committee hearings, which gave unfavorable publicity to the Bund and the Silver Shirts and temporarily discredited the entire anti-Semite movement. From the autumn of 1935 until the 1936 elections, most of the anti-Semitic groups campaigned actively with the anti-New Deal forces. They presented the New Deal as a part of the "Jewish-revolution-ary" conspiracy and worked themselves into a high pitch of activity. After the New Deal's victory at the polls, their activity decreased very pronouncedly. Many groups permanently suspended operations, others did so temporarily. For three months virtually no activity was evident. Then came the proposal to enlarge the Supreme Court and the wave of strikes in 1937—events that increased the insecurity of the middle classes and made them again receptive to anti-Semitic propaganda. The business recession of late 1937 and 1938 further revitalized the Pelleys and the Winrods. In the autumn of 1938, after Father Coughlin adopted anti-Semitism, he quickly proselyted a very large Catholic group to his new creed. The anti-Semitic movement soon exceeded all previous proportions.*

The impact of the second World War on anti-Semitism has

---

* Strong, cited, pp. 146-147. See *The Universal Jewish Encyclopedia*, Vol. I, pp. 398 ff., for a more detailed treatment of both the native fascist organizations and those inspired and subsidized from abroad.

been a mixed one. On the one hand, it has placed the Jewish problem in its proper context as an aspect of the world struggle against totalitarianism. More and more Gentiles have come to recognize anti-Semitism as one of the most important Nazi techniques of war and aggression; they have begun to appreciate its function as one of the most potent anti-democratic weapons in the arsenal of world reaction. And whatever their personal like or dislike of Jews, they are rallying to the defense of the Jews. On the other hand, the war has given rise to certain unfavorable tendencies. There persists the impression that the great majority of refugees from European oppression are Jewish; and some consider these people a threat to the native job holder and job seeker. Other confused or fascist-minded Americans, unwilling or unable to blame the war on the dictators and their aggressive ambitions, are happy to repeat the slogan of the demagogues: "This is a Jewish war." Some Americans, more than ever disillusioned with Europe, and convinced that it is responsible for the world chaos, have become even more set against any form of international co-operation. And they are, therefore, prepared to accept the explanation that Jewish international financiers are bent on keeping the country at war.

The America First movement was an interesting example of the complex of motives and factors that make up anti-Semitism. Many of its leaders were undoubtedly sincere and convinced isolationists. But the movement attracted many appeasers who desired not only that we should come to terms with Hitler, but that we should adapt some of his techniques to the American scene. This element in the movement shrewdly tolerated anti-Semitism as a means of adding German sympathizers and Jew-haters to their ranks. Another significant section of the America First leadership was concerned with the old struggle of the country against the city. These men resented the growth of federal authority with its attendant supervision of state and county governmental organization. Farmers were becoming increasingly dependent on federal aid. It is probably more than a coincidence that many of those who were most outspokenly anti-Semitic were representatives of rural areas.

Rural and provincial America has tended to resist the growing power of the Federal Government, a development which economic progress has rendered inevitable. And, because historical circumstances have identified the Jew with the city, that resentment is being projected onto the Jew. Which of these many tendencies will be strengthened by the war and its aftermath, it is too early to predict. But this much is clear: the survival of the Jew and the weakening of anti-Semitism are intimately bound up with the victory of the forces of democracy and progress throughout the world.

Its Roots

Why has anti-Semitism been endemic in so many parts of Europe? Why has it taken root in the United States? What are the mainsprings of this phenomenon? To those questions there can be no single nor simple answer. For anti-Semitism is the product of a vast complex of forces which we can here do no more than enumerate.*

There is, first of all, the primitive fear of the unlike. The folklore of all peoples reflects suspicion and mistrust of neighbors and strangers. The Jews have adjusted themselves to the life of the societies in which they have settled—and that has been particularly true of America—yet, they have remained an identifiable group. Jews have largely maintained their religious identity. They are heirs to a distinct cultural tradition. They have preserved a sense of their religious or cultural unity. Their long history of expulsion and migration, their feelings of kinship with their fellow-Jews in other lands, have generally imparted to them a cosmopolitan rather than a provincial outlook. Thus, while the Jews of America

* For a fuller discussion of the problem, see Valentin, Hugo, *Anti-Semitism*, New York, 1936; Graeber, I., and Britt, S. H. (eds.), *Jews in a Gentile World*, New York, 1942.

have become an integral part of the larger community, they have also maintained a definite pattern of Jewish life.

Fear and suspicion of the unlike is hardly enough to account for anti-Semitism; nor need difference make for hatred and discrimination. This is particularly true of America, settled as it has been by groups of such diverse national, religious and cultural origins, and where the traditions of freedom and liberty have been so dominant. But the religious traditions of Europe—and in religious matters, the United States is an extension of Europe—have been an important factor in the persistence of anti-Semitism. They have taught that the Jews rejected and killed the Savior of Christianity and were themselves, therefore, rejected by God and doomed to suffering. The legend of the Christ-killing has persisted in Christian thinking. Children, taught the legend at an early and pliant age, carry that prejudice through life; and crises fan it into active hatred.

The Nazi campaign against Christianity—and religion generally —has focused attention on another fundamental aspect of anti-Semitism. The Nazi leadership has idealized force and hatred; it has rejected the ideal of the sanctity of the individual personality. In that rejection, it is in revolt against the entire Judeo-Christian tradition of love, justice, human brotherhood and individual dignity. That revolt against Christianity has found its most violent expression in the attack against Judaism as the progenitor of Christianity. Basically, such anti-Semitism is an inverted form of Christ-hatred directed against the Christ-giver, the Jew.*

There are, however, many other factors that enter into anti-Semitism. Direct economic competition breeds jealousy and envy. Particularly, in times of economic contraction, Jewish economic activity excites the hostility of the non-Jew; and the elimination of Jews from business and labor comes to be regarded as the panacea for unemployment and economic distress.

* For an elaborate exposition of this thesis, see Samuel, Maurice, *The Great Hatred*, New York, 1940.

Important sources of anti-Semitic prejudice have been revealed by modern psychology. Psychological analysis has fairly clearly established that aggression and hatred are, in one form or another, fundamental human impulses, either innate or acquired at an early age. Social convention and the demands of organized living force people to repress those impulses. Repression produces frustrations and those frustrations must find expression. Anti-Semitism has become a convenient outlet for the expression of repressed and frustrated impulses. It is, of course, clear that other means would serve those psychological functions as well as anti-Semitism. But Jews, as an identifiable group, constitute an accessible object. The world has been conditioned for centuries to anti-Semitism as a socially acceptable form of prejudice. And the factors of difference provide an easy rationalization for hatreds that really have profound psychological roots.

The psychological elements in anti-Semitism become all the more apparent, when one studies the type of leadership that generally comes to the fore in prejudice movements. Coughlin, Pelley, Winrod, Dilling, Edmondson, like Hitler and Mussolini, are persons whose inner frustrations require violent expression. They strike a responsive chord when economic and political dislocations throw masses of people into a disturbed, fear-stricken state of insecurity. The neurotic leaders symbolize the frustrated groups. Their incoherent ravings reflect the confused, impotent rage of the average man who cannot see the cause of his troubles, nor even verbalize them adequately. There is a deep craving for unusual emotional outlets and satisfactions. People are prepared to accept uncritically attractive panaceas, and they readily project their anxieties and fears onto others.

It is in this setting that anti-Semitic prejudice becomes violent and aggressive. It becomes comparatively easy to project all one's insecurities onto the Jews, to vent one's frustrations on them through discrimination or actual physical attack, to blame them for all one's personal dilemmas or for the world's chaos, to regard their destruction as a social panacea. That psychological atmosphere, too, renders anti-Semitic propaganda so effective a device, whatever its falsity or irrationality. For in times of crisis, people believe not those things that are true or logical, but the things they want to believe, the things that respond to their psychological and emotional needs. And, in such circumstances, truth and logic become largely ineffective weapons in combatting anti-Semitism.

The functions anti-Semitism serves have been considerably increased in recent years. The technique of using anti-Semitism for political purposes is by no means a new one; and history abounds with instances of its deliberate manipulation. That technique, however, has been refined and perfected in modern times. The new insights psychology has contributed, the centralization of political control, the development of the means of communication, the elevation of propaganda to the status of a science, have given unscrupulous and power-seeking groups vastly increased opportunities for the employment of anti-Semitism on a mass scale. It has enabled demagogues to climb to power by preaching a false doctrine of national unity—a unity induced through artificially stimulated fears of a universal Jewish plot. It has enabled governments to escape the consequences of their ineptitude and failures by transferring the blame to the Jews. It has won to the support of fascist movements considerable numbers of people by playing on their fears of competition or anti-Jewish prejudices, and by promising them prosperity through the liquidation of Jewish business and professional activity.

Anti-Semitism has played an important role in the fascist preparation for war and aggression. Anti-Semitic agitation in countries regarded as potential enemies has helped to destroy social cohesion by sowing suspicion and distrust in their midst. It has won for the fascists considerable support in non-fascist countries, either by enlisting the active aid of native anti-Semites, or by neutralizing non-fascists with anti-Jewish propensities.

Nor have those tactics been limited to fascist regimes. The success with which they have been employed in Germany has led reactionary groups everywhere to attempt their use. In every land, anti-Semitism has become an integral part of the strategy of those movements and forces that would overthrow democratic institutions and traditions.

What Can Be Done?

It is obvious that no simple, unilateral solution will be adequate for so complex a problem as anti-Semitism. Nor is it a problem exclusively for Jews; for in its modern form, it is directed ultimately against non-Jews and the democratic way of life as much as against the Jews. Moreover, Jews constitute so small a portion of the population of this country that the removal of the larger causes of anti-Semitism is more dependent on the Gentile than the Jew. Certainly, the destruction of Hitlerism is a prime condition for any amelioration of the problem of anti-Semitism. But that will not in itself eliminate Jew hatred. The effects of intensive indoctrination will take years to counteract. The adjustment of a war-torn, exhausted world to a new democratic world order will involve stresses and strains out of which anti-Semitism may once again emerge.

Fundamental to a solution of the problem will be the co-operation of all groups in the creation of a new social order in which the factor of economic competition will be removed as an element making for prejudice. A social order in which recurrent economic crises will have been eliminated, which will raise living standards, which will provide greater cultural opportunities and facilities for normal psychological adjustment will do much to eliminate the atmosphere in which anti-Semitism thrives. In such an order, many of the impulses today making for active anti-Semitism will disappear.

Jews, too, must actively aid in the vast educational enterprise of developing not merely a tolerance of difference, but an active appreciation of the creative potentialities of cultural diversity. The ideal must be not the artificial standardization of culture, but the creative development and harmonization of cultural differences.*

It is important that the task of countering anti-Semitic libels and falsehoods be diligently continued; for prejudice is frequently born of and feeds on ignorance. But it would be naïve to hope that the dissemination of the true facts of Jewish life can prove a major factor in lessening anti-Semitism of the more virulent sort. For, as has already been suggested, the periods in which anti-Semitism flourishes are those eras of crisis and instability in which reason loses its hold over men's acts, and in which logic becomes less potent a force in human affairs than emotion.

There is, however, one area in which specifically Jewish effort can play a very effective role, and that is in the development of the Jewish National Homeland in Palestine. It is clear that the establishment of a Jewish Homeland will eliminate that permanent status of homelessness and minority existence that has been an important factor in the attitudes non-Jews have held toward the Jews. The absorptive capacity of Palestine, already proven in the settlement of close to a half million Jews, will enable it, in the post-war world, to relieve the pressure of Jewish poverty and destitution in many lands of Eastern and Central Europe, and to lessen the specter of Jewish competition.

* In America, this movement, known as Cultural Pluralism, calls for a federated integration of the cultural strains of American society. Under a common constitution and within the framework of a common social order, each cultural, religious, racial, and nationality group would be encouraged to contribute its native and unique insights, art-forms, folkways, and idealisms to the larger American civilization. The theory of acculturation differs from the melting-pot theory in rejecting any particular set of values and traditions as the norm. It recognizes the priority of indigenous American forms and symbols, but favors free cultural trade in an open market so that the best might win its way into the majority of American hearts. Louis Adamic has written extensively on this theme. See especially his *From Many Lands*, New York, 1940, and *Two Way Passage*, New York, 1941.

The theory of Cultural Pluralism was earlier adumbrated by Randolph Bourne, Horace Kallen, I. B. Berkson, and John Dewey. Certain groups, like the Progressive Education Association and the Bureau of Intercultural Education, have been developing curricular material embodying this point of view. For an admirable presentation of a twofold approach to the problem, cultural pluralism and a Jewish National Home, see Niebuhr, Reinhold, "Jews After the War," *The Nation*, February 21 and 28, 1942.

A Jewish Homeland in Palestine would, of course, impose no special political obligations on Jews in other lands. But it would normalize Jewish life, by giving Jews everywhere equal status with peoples of other national origins, who have settled in lands other than their ancestral homes. That normalization of Jewish status would have favorable and positive repercussions both on the reactions of non-Jews to the Jews in their midst, and to Jewish attitudes as well. It would save Jews from the demoralization and self-hatred that are the inevitable by-products of anti-Semitism. It would restore Jewish self-respect. It would dissipate the necessity for apologetics in which many Jews feel impelled to indulge. It would prove an inspiring source of Jewish cultural creativity, capable not only of strengthening Jewish life everywhere, but also of enriching Jewish contributions to their various homelands. Palestine, too, can make a significant contribution to the solution of the general social problem which is so closely related to anti-Semitism. During the past few decades, the Jewish National Homeland has become a laboratory of social experimentation. Its ventures in co-operative enterprise, in communal organization, in social progress hold lessons of significance for the rest of the world.

The deepening of the self-respect and self-confidence of the Jew will guard him against despair. The normalization of the status of the Jewish people, the enrichment of Jewish culture, the social inspiration of the Jewish National Homeland will all be important factors in mitigating the evils of anti-Semitism. But they will not destroy it. Complex and intricate as anti-Semitism is, it will have to be attacked by a variety of weapons. It will, of course, have to be combated wherever it rears its ugly head. Both Jews and non-Jews will have to co-operate in educating people to the facts of Jewish life; in revealing the threat to democracy that anti-Semitism constitutes; in developing the idea of cultural pluralism. Above all else, they will have to join, as they are now doing, to exterminate the roots of totalitarianism. Together they will have to build a new democratic order in which men can live in peace and plenty, in which the dismal story of man's inhumanity to man will be brought to a close. As long as poverty and insecurity continue to torment human beings, they will yield to the temptations of prejudice and intolerance. Only where freedom from want and insecurity have become living realities, can men hope to live in brotherhood and decency. Only in a world of security and peace can men be free from envy, hatred, and intolerance.

CURRENT PHILOSOPHIES OF JEWISH LIFE
IN AMERICA

———

Milton Steinberg

———

CONCEPTIONS of Judaism are essential to any discussion of the American Jew. To undertake a description and evaluation of theories of Jewish living at a time when Jewry and the world at large are beset by critical practical problems may seem unrealistic. It is to invite the charge of toying with academic trifles while the world burns.

Yet theories are more than the playthings of scholars. They too are matters of large practical import. They constitute a precondition for ease of mind. If nature abhors a vacuum, human nature cannot long tolerate intellectual confusion. What is more, as blueprints are necessary to guide builders, philosophies are indispensable in all areas of interest if activity is to be orderly, sustained and purposeful.

Among American Jews, there exists at the present time a wide divergence of opinion, or lack of opinion, concerning the nature of Judaism and of Jewish identity, the relationship of Jewish loyalties to the American, the purposes which Judaism is to fulfill, the form in which it is to be carried on; indeed whether it is to be carried on at all. Such conflict and uncertainty represent a relatively recent development among Jews.

Until the Emancipation, there was no question in the mind of any Jew either as to the nature of his Jewishness, or as to those distinctive and differential qualities in it which made its preservation a prime moral obligation. To Christian, to Moslem and to Jew alike, before the French Revolution, the Jews constituted a nation, a nation in exile, to be sure, but a nation nonetheless. On this issue there was no dissent. What is more, all Jews were convinced that the Jewish nation was chosen of God, elected by Him out of the peoples of the world to a central role in the divine scheme for human salvation. To the Jewish people, He had revealed His Law through which alone the individual Jew could achieve the good life on earth and salvation in the world to come, and the nation, if it remained steadfast, an ultimate redemption. Simple, concise, and comprehensible, this ideology of Jewish life enabled the Jew to live at ease with his Judaism, to see it clearly in relationship to other interests, and to answer for himself the question as to why he ought continue to be a Jew in the teeth of the hardships and adversities to which his Jewish identity exposed him.

It was only with the Emancipation that this philosophy ceased to be universal. But once it began to disintegrate among Jews, it disintegrated very rapidly. The Emancipation affected this classic rationale in two fashions. In the first place, under the Emancipation the Jew either became a citizen of the land in which he lived, or he was encouraged to look forward to achieving that status. But Jews could not, many felt, accept the benefits of citizenship in one nation and still regard themselves as members of another nationality. Some other definition of Jewishness had to be evolved. Again, the world in which the emancipated Jew found himself, challenged the religious notions in the light of which heretofore he had found special purposes for his group life. The belief that the Jewish tradition represented an especial revelation of divine will was shaken. The faith in other worldly salvation, and in the ultimate redemption of Israel, was dislocated. In other words, the

Emancipation not only threw the Jewish mind into confusion as to the nature of Judaism, it raised doubts as to the utility and necessity of the continuance of Jewish group life.

So the ideological problem in its modern guise was born. In essence it consists of two questions—first, what are Judaism and Jewishness, and what are their relations to other social affiliations; and second, what is there of a differential or special character in Judaism to justify to the individual Jew, the Jewish community and the world the extraordinary efforts required for Jewish survival.

These questions have been hotly debated in Jewish circles. Various answers to them have been formulated. It shall be our purpose both to state these answers and to examine them critically. But throughout our discussion, the reader should bear in mind the fact that the attitudes with which we are treating reflect the opinions of limited segments of American Jewry, of its Jewishly sophisticated elements. The mass of American Jews, while not unaffected by current philosophies, is both largely uninformed concerning them, and uncommitted to any one of them in particular. Indeed, many otherwise literate American Jews are altogether innocent of the very existence of an ideological problem, let alone of the diverse solutions which have been offered for it. Thus, the great bulk of American Jews has no clear-cut definition of Judaism. Witness the confused fashion in which Jews speak of it, the looseness with which they use the words, "religion," "nationality," "race," or "culture," in referring to it, as though these words all connoted the same thing. Nor have they thought out the issue of the relationship of their Jewishness to their Americanism. And since they have no theory for Judaism, they are in consequence incapable of formulating programs on its behalf.

The results are a widespread confusion of mind, which in itself is no slight influence in alienating Jews from Jewish life, and a vast indecision and waste motion in action. The individual Jew tends, because he does not know where he wants to go, to be forever riding off in various directions at the same time, and constantly colliding with other Jews as aimless as he. The Jewish community is a tumult of divided counsels and of no counsels at all.

It is perhaps too much to hope, indeed it might be undesirable, that all Jews should agree on one ideology for American Jewry. But certainly every Jew could be considerably benefited in mind, and in the efficiency of his action, were he to win through to some tenable philosophy. And the Jewish community as a whole would be much better off were differences of viewpoint to be clarified and mutually understood. To say that theories can save Judaism in America would be an exaggeration. It is altogether sober to assert that it cannot be saved without them.

The Philosophy of Assimilation

There is a touch of paradox involved in describing assimilationism, which aims at the extinction of Jewish life, as a philosophy of it. Yet, if a definition and program constitute a philosophy, then the assimilationist approach must logically be included among rationales of Judaism.

Assimilationism derives in part from the accidents of circumstance, rather than from any particular doctrine. There are persons who are unconscious assimilationists, who, having lost interest in Judaism, are drifting out of it unwittingly. In other instances, that drift is accelerated by a desire, recognized or unrecognized, to escape the penalties of a minority identity. And in still other instances impetus is lent to the movement by those emotions of inferiority, self-contempt and self-hatred which have infected the personalities of many American Jews.

On the other hand, there are assimilationist attitudes which do represent deliberate programs. The protagonist of assimilation exhibits certain special attitudes toward the Jewish tradition. However it be conceived, he rejects it. If Judaism be a matter of religion, he is either of the opinion that all religion is obsolete, or else that the values of the Jewish religion are available for Jews in the larger religious communions. If the essence of Judaism be cultural, then his position is either that its cultural equipment is so outdated as to be without significance for modern Jews, or so remote from them as to represent merely another alien culture. And if the Jewish identity be defined in nationalist terms, then he responds that such an identification involves a hyphenization of American citizenship.

Rejecting Judaism, however it be conceived, the conscious assimilationist argues further that nothing is to be gained and much lost by the continuance of any type of Jewish distinctiveness. To preserve the Jewish group, he insists, is to preserve a surface of friction between Jew and non-Jew. It is to expose the Jew to social penalties and to encourage a splitting of interest within Jews between Judaism and Americanism.

The assimilationist therefore draws what appears to him to be an inevitable inference—namely, that the Jewish group ought to abandon its special traditions, dissolve itself as an identifiable group, and seek to lose itself in the enveloping populace.

Some Jews prize assimilation as a means of advancing human brotherhood. They feel that all lines of demarcation among men on the basis of culture, tradition, or religion have proved unfortunate; that such schisms have been, in the main, productive of antagonisms, hatreds, and strife. These persons look hopefully to a future in which all group distinctions shall have been eliminated from society, in which an undifferentiated mankind shall at last achieve peace and harmony. To this end, all groups, including the Jewish, must surrender their identities. The abandonment of Judaism then becomes an act of service to humanity. Not all Jewish assimilationists advance such utopian arguments for their program. And of those who do, some, at least, are probably more than a little disingenuous. But it would be an underestimation of assimilationism not to admit that it is often inspired by idealism.

Assimilationism has then a case to argue on its own behalf. It is, however, a case which even to casual examination reveals itself to be totally untenable. In the first place, it is hopelessly unrealistic. Let every individual Jew, let the Jewish group as a whole, resolve to abandon Judaism, and Jews will still be Jews, the Jewish group still an identifiable group. For the fact is that the Gentile world, taken as a whole, is at present of such temper that it will not allow Jews to cease to be Jews. The only effect then of an effort at assimilation is to make the Jew less Jewish in sentiment and practice, without achieving for him the purposed oblivion.

Again there are psychic hazards involved in the assimilationist enterprise. It implies that the Jew, as he is, is less desirable than if he were made into a Gentile. Such a doctrine cannot but foster attitudes of self-reproach, self-contempt, self-repudiation; in brief, an aggravation of an already widespread sense of Jewish inferiority. Nor are the opponents of assimilationism prepared to agree that Judaism is either obsolete or replaceable. On the contrary, they insist that it possesses significant differential qualities, and that by very virtue of them it has large contributions to offer to the Jewish individual and to the society of which he is a part. As for the contention that mankind will best be served by the expunging of all distinctive traditions, the anti-assimilationist contends rather that differences among groups as among individuals are both natural and desirable, that they enrich life, that they make possible progress and cross-stimulation, person to person, tradition to tradition. What is wrong with human variation is not difference itself but man's reluctance to tolerate it and use it creatively. The good society, if and when it is attained, will be not a perfect homogeneity but a diversity of elements operating peacefully and co-operatively with one another.

To the proponent of Jewish group survival, nothing in the assimilationist philosophy is more nonsensical than the notion that loyalty to Judaism is somehow incompatible with a wholehearted and devoted American patriotism. In the framework of American liberties, the right of the Jews to maintain their religion is certainly beyond question. The fostering of a second culture, over and above the shared American civilization, is not only thoroughly consistent with the law and spirit of the American democracy, but demonstrably a contribution to it. And as for the Zionist program, Zionists have made it abundantly clear that their interest in Palestine does not in the slightest impugn their loyalty to America, or imply the assumption of a second political allegiance. In the light of all this, the contention that a patriotic devotion to America requires assimilation, or a repudiation of Zionism, is entirely baseless.

The communist approach to Judaism represents a second pattern of assimilationism. The communist rejects the Jewish religion as he repudiates all religions. With regard to Jewish national and cultural individuality, his position depends on geography. He agrees that in Eastern Europe the Jews constitute both a minority culture and a minority nationality, and as such, are entitled, if they desire it, to the same status which the Soviet Union allows to all analogous groups within its borders. For the American scene, the communist line is by no means so clear. The over-all tendency is to regard Jewish cultural and national life as reactionary, and to treat the Jewish heritage as something which, the sooner done for, the better. Nor does the use of the Yiddish language and the establishment of special Jewish organizations by communists indicate the contrary. Such devices are for communists not ends in themselves, but instruments whereby they hope to win Jews to their doctrine. Of the whole gamut of Jewish interests and concerns, the communist then addresses himself seriously only to the issue of anti-Semitism. This he regards as an expression of a decadent capitalism, destined to disappear with the coming of the classless society.

Those who are committed to programs of Jewish survival reject the communist ideology in general and, in addition, are profoundly skeptical of its promise to liquidate anti-Semitism. To them, it appears that communists oversimplify the whole issue of group tensions, when they insist that economics is the sole, signifi-

cant cause. Moreover, since the Jewish survivalist feels that there
is worth to the Jewish tradition, he naturally fails to see a program
which seeks to liquidate Judaism as a solution to the Jewish problem.

Withdrawal from the Jewish group has of late become extremely difficult, if not impossible, of realization. But this does
not mean that the internal problems of Jewish life have thereby
been favorably affected, or that assimilationism has been repudiated by its adherents. Men need not be capable of attaining an
ambition in order to yearn after it. Jews in considerable numbers
desire to be quits with Judaism. Their inability to achieve their
goal serves often not to impel them toward Jewish life, but only
to engender hostilities toward it. This mood presents a major
obstacle in the way of the successful realization of all positive programs for Judaism in America.

PHILOSOPHIES OF SURVIVAL

The philosophies which envisage the continuance of the Jewish
group on the American scene fall naturally into two types: those
on the one hand which see religion as the essence of Judaism, and
those on the other which define Judaism in national-cultural
terms, as basically secular. It is of the religiously centered ideologies for Jewish life that we shall treat first, proceeding as it were
from right to left, from the most traditionalist to the least.

Orthodoxy

Orthodox Judaism may well be characterized as Jewish traditionalism made self-conscious on the American scene by the
diverse challenges of assimilationism, secularism and Reform. It
is the ancestral pattern of life and thought striving to maintain
itself in the contemporary world. The difficulties which confront
Orthodoxy and the adjustments which it has been obliged to
make have been surveyed in another chapter.* Here, we shall

* See Chapter II.

concern ourselves solely with Orthodoxy as a theory of Jewish living.

As a philosophy of Judaism, Orthodoxy rests on faith in revelation. In its view, Judaism represents a divinely revealed truth concerning God, the universe and man; a divinely revealed ethic; and a divinely revealed regimen of personal and collective behavior—all of which are manifest in Scripture and in the rabbinic tradition which clothes it. From this basic premise follow two large implications. The first is that, except within the narrow limits allowed by the Law itself, the Law is immutable. The second is that the fulfillment of God's will is obligatory on all Jews, regardless of the sacrifices involved. The temper of Orthodoxy, then, is one of intransigence. It will not countenance tampering with the tradition, nor will it, save under conditions of special crisis and then only for the moment, exempt Jews from the performance of the *mitzvoth* (religious injunctions). This refusal to compromise flows naturally from its theory of Judaism, and it has been strengthened by observation. Far too often have procedures of compromise led to the abandonment of Judaism.

Orthodox Judaism experiences no difficulties in defining its relationship to the larger life of America. In his adjustment to America, the typical orthodox Jew is not perplexed by the national and cultural aspects of Judaism. These he accepts naturally, since they are explicit in Scripture and in the rabbinic tradition. They are for him based so completely on religious concepts, and so shot through with them, that they too are transmuted into religious expressions.

The orthodox position has the advantage of clarity. So lucid is the theory that it can be caught in one or two propositions. It possesses further the strength of a faith rooted in revelation— one which, in theory at least, knows neither hesitations of the mind nor indecisions of the hand. It is invested, too, with the romance of the continuance of an ancient tradition.

Nevertheless, Orthodoxy has its problems. It must preserve

among Jews faith in the truth of its central postulate, a task extraordinarily difficult at a time when the main currents of thought in the modern world run in a counter direction. Again, the comparative inelasticity of orthodox Judaism on matters of ritual procedures, advantage though it be from one point of view, is from another a very serious disability. Life changes constantly. Orthodoxy is, by its premises, precluded from deliberate adaptations to meet such changes.

Conservatism

Conservative Judaism had its origin stimultaneously in America and Western Europe among those Jews who either in theory or practice could no longer be orthodox, and who yet refused to accept what they regarded as the extreme non-traditionalism of Reform. Conservative Judaism therefore antedated the great East European migration to this country. And yet, it was from among these Jews that it recruited the overwhelming mass of its present adherents. As with all movements, the drift from Orthodoxy to Conservatism was variously motivated. In many instances, the transfer of allegiance was a matter of reasoned decision; in others, it was so gradual as never to be recognized as a transfer of loyalties at all; and in still others, it represented no more than the unconscious course of least resistance.

There is as yet no authoritative formulation of the conservative rationale for Judaism in America, but from the pronouncements of some of its principal spokesmen, the following provisional description may be derived. Two motifs dominate conservative Judaism. The first is the assertion of the centrality of religion in Jewish life. While Conservatism speaks of Judaism as a way of life and admits the legitimacy within it of cultural and nationalistic elements, it views the Jewish religion, more particularly the God-faith and the *Torah* (the Law and tradition) as its essence. The second theme, heavily underscored, is the sense of tradition, of history, of the continuity of Jewish life both through time and in space. It is this feeling of the organic unity of present with past and of one Jewry with other Jewries which Professor Solomon Schechter, the leading figure in American Conservatism, caught in the phrase "Catholic Israel." This phrase is more than a description. It is intended to serve as a norm for the guidance of behavior. That shall be done by Jews, it implies, which is normal to Catholic Israel. The concept of revelation, so pivotal to Orthodoxy, plays something of a role in Conservatism. But in the main, it is the sense of history which serves as judge of what in Jewish thought and practice is to be maintained, and what modified. In effect, the notion of Catholic Israel, of historical precedent, serves to impel conservative Jews to hold on to the traditional, to sanction modifications slowly, reluctantly and, if at all possible, within the framework of Jewish law.

The program of conservative Judaism can then be summarized in a phrase—it is the preservation of the historic Jewish religion, plus the historic cultural and nationalistic overtones, with only such modifications as circumstances compel and as the standard of Catholic Israel permits.

Toward Zionism conservative Judaism takes a positive attitude. It sees in Zionism both the fulfillment of a traditional hope and the opportunity for a revival of Jewish cultural life. But like orthodoxy it is discontented with certain secularistic tendencies which have manifested themselves in Palestine. It insists on the centrality of religion in the life of Jewish Palestine, even as it hopes to preserve and emphasize the primacy of religion within Judaism in America.

Envisaging Judaism as in essence a religion, conservative Jews claim for it a place upon the American scene analogous to that of other communions. In so far as it embraces also national-cultural elements, they contend that it is altogether compatible with American life, first because of its religious associations, and second because they believe that cultural diversity, operating over and beyond shared American interests, is desirable, not only for the minority group itself, but also for the general welfare of America as a whole.

The goals of conservative Judaism tend in the main to be practical in character: the quest for an adaptation of Jewish traditional religious beliefs and practices to the tone, temper and exigencies of contemporary living, the striving after a balance between historic Judaism and the modern world.

Its major weakness lies in its failure to achieve an articulate, authoritative description of its own nature and purposes. Conservative Jews, in consequence, are always somewhat uncertain as to what they represent. What is more, for want of a clear-cut program, they must always be more or less indecisive as to what their commitments require of them on any specific issue of practice.

Reform Judaism

The origins of reform Judaism in Germany and its transplantation to the United States have already been described.* In nineteenth century America, a land of novelty and experimentation, with a Jewish population of youthful and precedent-shattering immigrants, Reform evolved its distinctive theory and practice of Judaism. It has also been noted† that in recent years a growing discontent with both the theory and program of reform Judaism has manifested itself among reform Jews themselves. This discontent has crystallized in the formulation of a new rationale and prospectus for Judaism. It is apparent then, that there are at present *two* reform philosophies. The older, that expressed in the Pittsburgh Platform of 1885, with which we shall treat first, we shall call classical Reform. The newer will, for the sake of clarity, be denominated as neo-Reform.

Classical Reform conceives Judaism as a religion, the Jewish group as a communion of human beings who share a faith and ethic. The religion which is Judaism is, moreover, an evolving

* See above, pp. 43 ff.
† See above, pp. 46-48.

religion. In its long history it has recurrently cast off beliefs, values and practices which had outlived their utility, and taken on new attitudes and forms. So it must continue to do in the present and future. But through all the changes imposed by time, one element remains constant—the doctrine of ethical monotheism, the belief in one universal God, and the corollaries of that belief for behavior, personal and social.

To the question as to why, when other religions share that belief and that ethic, Judaism should continue its distinctive existence, the answer given by Reform is the doctrine of the mission. The Jewish people exists to communicate the faith in one God to the peoples of the world, and both to exhibit and to teach the good life. To fulfill its purpose, Israel must live among the peoples of the world, so that they may have before them a visible embodiment, individual and collective, of religious faith and of the morality inherent in it.

This definition of Judaism in terms of a credal communion has inescapable implications which the early leaders of classic Reform drew rigorously. Thus, by their very presuppositions, they were led to adopt a free hand with traditional Jewish rituals. Since the purpose of Judaism is to communicate the God-faith, rituals may be dispensed with, if they are not necessary to effect that end; new rituals may be instituted, should they function more effectively than traditional forms.

Similarly with the Hebrew language. If the purpose of Judaism be to induce within its communicants a specific religious outlook and particular ethical commitments, then the language of Jewish worship becomes of secondary importance. Classical Reform has therefore tended to employ the vernacular primarily and to relegate Hebrew to a secondary position.

Again, from its very inception, classical Reform has rejected the hope of a reconstitution of Jewish life in Palestine. Nor could it have done otherwise. In the light of its theory of Judaism as a religious communion, the locale of Jewish life must be regarded

as unessential. Man can worship God anywhere. And in view of
the doctrine of the mission, the diaspora, far from being a disad-
vantage, enlarges the opportunity for the fulfillment of the ultimate purpose of Jewish existence.

On the issue of the relationship of Judaism to America, the
reformist doctrine offers a ready answer. Since the Jew is a Jew in
religion only, he is in all other respects an American. He stands
in the same relationship to America as a Methodist or an Episco-
palian.

The opponents of classical Reform reject its definition of Judaism, as well as the program which flows from it. They argue that
both in the past and at present, the Jewish group has constituted
more than a religious communion. Contained in the Jewish
heritage there have always been national-cultural along with
religious elements, and the Jewishness of the contemporary Jew
does not depend on his attitude toward the Jewish religion. Even
if he be agnostic, he may regard himself as a Jew, and be so regarded by other Jews and by the world. The definition, therefore,
is not adequate to the phenomenon which it seeks to describe.

The "mission theory," too, has been subjected to adverse scru-
tiny. Opponents of it contend that modern Jews possess no special
aptitudes to serve as religious teachers to others, that the whole
notion smacks of self-righteousness, and that even reformist Jews
have never attempted seriously to implement it. The doctrine has
been termed by its critics a rationalization for the survival of
Jewish life on the part of persons who, by their theory of Judaism,
have left no real basis for the continued existence of the Jewish
people.

As a program for Judaism, classical Reform is rejected by its
critics on the score of inadequacy. A Judaism without Jewish law,
without Palestine, without the Hebrew tongue, without music,
art, literature, and social institutions except such as are demonstrably religious in purport, is, it is contended, too thin to elicit

loyalties and enthusiasms, and too tenuous for hardihood, let alone for creativity.

Neo-Reform, which has for some time been evolving out of classical Reform, derives from the criticisms which we have adduced, and from the influence of East European Jews in the reform pulpit and pew. The painful experiences of world Jewry during recent years have hastened the crystallization of this tendency. In 1937, the Central Conference of American Rabbis, meeting at Columbus, Ohio, described Judaism as "the historical religious experience of the Jewish people."* By placing alongside of the word "religious" the words "historical," "experience," and the phrase, "of the Jewish people," an attempt was obviously being made to recast the conception of Judaism, so as to make it larger than religion alone. This would give sanction to the Hebrew language, Palestine, folkways and such cultural manifestations as were not of a specifically religious character. It seems then that under this new formulation reform Judaism is moving in the direction of a reassertion of Jewish culture, perhaps even of nationality, and toward traditional values and forms which the older Reform had repudiated.

It is still too early to discern the significance with which this new formulation will be invested, to appraise the program which is to be the consequence of it, or the success with which it will be executed.

Religious Ideologies—A General Criticism

To all theories which envisage Judaism exclusively in religious terms certain general criticisms are applicable. In the first place, any such definition must be untrue to the historical character of Judaism, and unrepresentative of the actualities of contemporary Jewish living. Again, all such theories must ultimately make the identification of the individual with Judaism contingent on his

* See *Yearbook of the Central Conference of American Rabbis*, XLVII, Columbus, Ohio, 1937, pp. 97 ff.

acceptance of a religious viewpoint. But what then shall be done with the Jew who is genuinely devoted to some aspects of Judaism, but is nonetheless incapable of a religious affirmation? Finally, religions do not exist disembodied; they are always expressions of cultures, representing, as it were, those facets which are self-conscious and cosmically oriented. To equate Jewish life with religion becomes in effect an attempt to excise the head or heart of the body and to seek to preserve it alive, yet isolated from the rest of the organism.

Nor do such theories fare better as sources of program. They must undervalue, they may even declare illegitimate, all cultural and social interests which are not directly motivated by religion. Much that is most significant in contemporary Jewish living would, if the protagonists of these doctrines were thoroughly consistent, have to be ruled out as inappropriate. Such a verdict of illegitimacy would have to be leveled, for example, against the typical Jewish community center which is not in any immediate sense a religious institution, against the new folk song of Palestine, against the Jewish paintings of modern Jewish artists.

These theories retard a realistic approach to the organization of the Jewish community. The Jews of America, religious, non-religious and anti-religious, face problems together. The Jewish community should then be organized so as to reflect the will of all groupings. But Judaism conceived as religion can recognize only the synagogue as the focal point of communal organization, and must exclude the irreligious Jew who in all conscience cannot associate himself with a house of worship. And so between the contention, "it must be the synagogue and naught else," and the cry, "let it be anything but not the synagogue," the effort to achieve a democratic, integrated communal structure is sometimes defeated before it has been begun.

It should be observed finally, that to deny that religion is the whole of Judaism is not necessarily to deny that it is a part, even an indispensable part. There are, of course, Jews whose outlook is completely secular and who repudiate religion in all its forms. But there are, on the other hand, Jews devotedly committed to the Jewish religion, who feel nonetheless that a theory of Jewish life predicated on religion only is unrepresentative of the historic character of Judaism, untrue to its contemporary nature, and unequal to the large challenges confronting Jewish life.

Secularist Philosophies

In direct antithesis to the ideologies with which we have just treated are those theories and programs for Jewish life which envisage Judaism essentially in the secular terms of *culture* and *nationality*. The proponents of such doctrines may themselves be sympathetic, neutral or antagonistic toward the Jewish religion. In any case, they discern the core of Jewishness to lie elsewhere. Religion has been so much a dominant motif in Jewish history that the very existence of such sentiments requires a word of explanation. All secularist theories of Judaism have emerged since the Emancipation, and their appearance may be explained by the continuing loyalty to Judaism of those who have rejected religion, or relegated it to a secondary position. Such Jews place greatest emphasis upon the non-theological elements which have always been a factor in Jewish life, and their Jewishness expresses itself primarily in social identity, in national-cultural affiliations, in philanthropy, and in defense against anti-Semitism.

Zionism

Zionism constitutes a secularist philosophy not because it is anti-religious but because it takes, as it were, an attitude of benevolent neutrality toward religion. In actuality, the Zionistic movement embraces both religious and non-religious Jews—more perhaps of the former than the latter. Much of the dynamism and fervor of Zionism has derived from the synagogue. Zionism then is charged with religious connotations and associations. Yet it takes no official stand on doctrinal issues. These it leaves to the individual for determination. Of even greater moment is the fact that it considers nationality and culture, rather than theological affirmation, as the core elements of Judaism. In the light of these considerations, Zionism is generally, and with justice, characterized as a secularist philosophy of Jewish life.

The points of departure from which the Zionist theory and program proceed are the social status of the Jews, and the needs of their cultural tradition. To Zionism, the Jews constitute a people, but one which exists in dispersion. It is by virtue of their anomalous position, the Zionist insists, that Jews are victimized by anti-Semitism. The character of the individual Jew, too, is adversely affected. Subjected to the stresses and strains of a minority identity, he tends almost irresistibly to slip into moods of inferiority, self-contempt and escapism—moods which are both destructive of personality and inhibitive of creativity. The cultural heritage of Jews suffers also. For under diaspora conditions, Judaism naturally becomes the second, and secondary civilization of Jews. The first of their time and energy flows inevitably into the majority culture of their adopted homeland; their most gifted creative personalities are forever being diverted from Jewish to general interests.

The answer, in whole or in part, to all these impasses is to be found, according to Zionism, in Palestine, and in the reconstitution there of the Jewish people in a commonwealth as populous and as fully autonomous as may be possible. The Jews who come to compose that Jewish community will, in the first instance, be free from anti-Semitic pressures and persecutions. Living the life of a normal people resident on its own soil, the Jews of Palestine will be permanently emancipated from the psychic stresses of a minority status. And Jewish culture, under the favorable circumstances of being the primary civilization of Palestinian Jewry, will take on a new lease of life for that Jewry and for all the Jewries of the world.

Both the diagnosis and prospectus of Zionism have been broadly validated by events of the past decades. The savage recrudescence of anti-Semitism in Europe has confirmed the judgment that its Jews require a land of their own. At the same time, Palestine has demonstrated its unparalleled, indeed its unique, capacity to serve as that land. The spirit of Palestinian Jews, their self-reliance, courage and creativity, have revealed that the Zionist program is indeed a cure for sick Jewish souls. And the rebirth of Jewish culture in Palestine has justified the confidence of Zionists that their program would guarantee not only the survival of Judaism but its regeneration.

It has never been suggested by the proponents of the Zionist position that all the Jews of the world should migrate to Palestine. The general Zionist expectation is that the Jews of countries where they are free will continue permanently as citizens of these lands, maintaining the loyalties and discharging the obligations involved in their status. But even for them, a Jewish Palestine will have great significance. Anti-Semitism is likely to bear on them less heavily as they cease to be sociological freaks and become like so many other Americans, individuals of diverse national origins who live, and have assumed citizenships, outside their people's land. The very effort toward rebuilding Palestine, let alone its achievements, will serve to strengthen their self-respect and psychic ease. And they will have a fountainhead of Jewish creativity on which to draw for the invigoration of their Jewish lives.

In the light of the clarity of the Zionist position concerning the status of Jews outside of Palestine, it is more than a little difficult to comprehend the misgivings expressed by anti-Zionists. Persons of that persuasion insist that Zionism involves a political disloyalty to America. The charge is so fantastic as to constitute misrepresentation. The American Zionist acknowledges only one political allegiance and one citizenship—the American. He is, however, the heir of, and concerned over, two cultures—both the American and the Jewish. His desire to see Palestine rebuilt as a Jewish homeland, and to draw upon it for infusions of Jewish culture to replenish his Jewish life, has no bearing whatsoever on the integrity of his political and social devotion to America.*

Diaspora Nationalism

Diaspora nationalism regards the Jews as a nationality, not in exile but in dispersion. As the bearers of a distinct culture—of a language, literature, history, folkways, values, institutions and aspirations—the Jews, it contends, exhibit all the traits which make up any nationality or culture, except the possession of a territory of their own. Diaspora nationalism envisages the permanent continuance of this condition. It opposes the notion that a national homeland is indispensable. It recommends rather that Jews seek to be recognized in the lands of their residence as a minority nationality, partaking of citizenship but enjoying, in addition to civil and political also cultural equality. The theory is secularistic in that it holds religion not as essential to Judaism, but as a matter for personal determination.

The very statement of this ideology makes it apparent that it was conceived in Eastern Europe where numerous nationalities claimed and, after the first World War, actually achieved the status of national minorities. The theory is clearly inapplicable to Jews of western democratic lands, and its protagonists have

---

* A small number of Zionists who are concerned with the ultimate future tend to despair of any solution of the Jewish social problem outside of Palestine, and to abandon all hope for Jewish cultural survival in the diaspora. They see a future only for those Jews who migrate to Palestine. The others, they prophesy, will, at the worst, eventually be crushed by anti-Jewish pressure; at the best, their Jewishness will fade out into a final assimilation.

This highly pessimistic forecast has been ignored by the overwhelming majority of Zionists, and even those who view it as a probability have not acted in accord with their convictions. Logically, they should regard the efforts now devoted to the maintenance of Judaism outside of Palestine as ultimately wasted. Yet, they, along with all other Zionists, seek to strengthen Jewish life in the diaspora. At all events, the prevailing Zionist view is not disposed to prejudge the issue of the perseverance of Jewish culture in the diaspora. Given the Jewish institutions and movements now in existence and dedicated to Jewish ends, given also the influence of Palestine which is already palpable and which will grow in potency, there appears to be no reason to believe that non-Palestinian Jewry must, of necessity, disappear.

been both very few and practically without any following among American Jews.

Within each of the secularist philosophies—Zionism and diaspora nationalism—there are subordinate variations of doctrine and program. These derive from differences on the function of religion in Jewish life, on the role and priority of the Hebrew and Yiddish languages, and on social philosophy. Within Zionism, for example, there are several sub-parties distinguishable from each other and from general Zionism by economic doctrine or religious complexion.*

Secularist Philosophies—A General Criticism

The major objection to all secularist theories of Judaism derives from their common attitude toward religion, from their attempt to assign to it either a subordinate role in Jewish life or, in some instances, to deny it any role whatsoever. Historically the Jewish religion has been the central motif and the climactic expression of the whole complex of Jewish living. Can that motif be eliminated without disjointing the entire organism and losing the very point of its existence? Again, must not the secularist Jew remain a victim of embarrassments? Since religion pervades the whole Jewish tradition, must he not be forever disquieted, as he approaches the Jewish tradition, by the presence of elements with which he is not in sympathy. Finally, those who are convinced that religion is a necessity in the life of every individual and group must adjudge

---

* Two variants to the general Zionist position merit special comment by virtue of their large significance. Mizrachi Zionism accepts the general Zionist program but expresses the will of Orthodox Jews, who are also Zionists, that the Jewish society which is in process of establishment in Palestine shall be constituted in conformity with the beliefs and practices of the Jewish tradition. It represents, in brief, a synthesis of Orthodoxy and Zionism. Labor Zionism, a second significant variant of Zionism, represents Zionism in association with socialism. The Labor Zionist is dedicated to the creation in Palestine, not only of a Jewish commonwealth, but of a Jewish commonwealth organized along the lines of economic collectivism. It is Labor Zionism, therefore, which has been responsible for many of the advanced co-operative enterprises in the Palestinian Jewish economy. For the diaspora scene, the Labor Zionist strives simultaneously for the survival of Jewish cultural values, for the preservation of political democracy, and for the achievement, along evolutionary lines, of economic democracy as well.

the effort after a secularist Judaism as a wanton disregard of historic Jewish resources, and a tragic blunder in the ordering of the lives of Jews.

RECONSTRUCTIONISM

Reconstructionism is, in a sense, unique among current philosophies of American Jewish life in that it is indigenous to America, and hence altogether an expression of Jewish thought and experience on the American scene. Its theory and program have been elaborated by a group of Conservative Jews whose outstanding leader is Professor Mordecai M. Kaplan of the Jewish Theological Seminary of America. Their primary purpose has been to arrive at a satisfactory theory of Jewish life, one which would avoid defining Judaism in terms of either religion or culture exclusively, one which, at the same time, would escape the intransigencies of Orthodoxy and the anti-traditional tendencies of Reform. The second goal has been to evolve a program for the recasting of Jewish life in conformity both with Jewish tradition and with the ideas and exigencies of American living.

Originating among Conservative Jews, Reconstructionism has won adherents from among other groupings. Since it regards itself as a "school of thought," it does not require from its followers the severance of their particular associations. It asks only that they seek to diffuse its doctrine and implement its program wherever they may find themselves. In terms of numbers, the advocates of Reconstructionism total no more than a handful, nor are there any signs that the movement is likely to grow to mass proportions. The very nature of the doctrine tends to limit its appeal to Jewish intellectuals, rabbis, educators, social workers and to laymen of considerable Jewish literacy and concern. Yet, its significance is much larger than pure arithmetic would lead one to infer. Its ideas and objectives have penetrated far and, often anonymously, have exerted a powerful influence in modifying the thought and program of the American Jewish community.

Reconstructionism begins with a definition of Judaism as a religious civilization. By this definition it asserts, against the secularist, that the Jewish religion is an integral part of Jewish life, and, against the religionist, that Judaism is more than a creedal communion. It holds that in addition to religion, Judaism contains within itself all the elements normally associated with the concepts "culture" and "civilization." Among these elements are social identity, language, literature, music, art, folkways, institutions, ethical values, folklore and a homeland.

Judaism is further characterized by the fact that, like other civilizations, it represents an organic unity. Its parts interpenetrate one another. Given the organic character of Judaism, it becomes virtually impossible to isolate any single aspect from the whole, without distorting that aspect and the whole alike.

Jewish civilization is characterized, moreover, by the fact that it is an evolutionary phenomenon. In its present form, it represents the results of a long process of constant change. It is then to be expected, and it is desirable, that it continue to modify itself in the future. The task which confronts the individual Jew is not to resist change but to direct it consciously and deliberately toward desired ends. It is on this issue that Reconstructionism and Orthodoxy part company.

What, in the light of this position, is the relationship of Jewishness to Americanism? Reconstructionism holds that on the American scene the Jew has only one political allegiance, and that is to America. He has only one religion, the Jewish religion. But he has two cultures, the American culture of his homeland, and the Jewish culture of his ancestry. This dualism of civilization, the Reconstructionist contends, both enhances the life of the individual Jew and renders him a richer and more creative personality for American life as a whole.

On the basis of this definition of Judaism as an organic, evolving religious civilization, Reconstructionism proposes its program for American Jewish life as follows:

1. The reinterpretation of Jewish theological and ethical concepts, so as to indicate their relevance to modern life and to current social problems.

2. The preservation of traditional ceremonial practices with such modifications as conditions render necessary. Reconstructionism regards ceremonial usage as both ritual (that is, symbolical expression of religious attitudes and values) and as folkway (that is, a pattern of Jewish behavior). In either capacity, ceremonials are indispensable, for no religion can live without rituals, and no civilization, especially a minority civilization, without folkway. The traditional character of the ceremonial should be maintained, so as to preserve continuity with historic Judaism. But modification is equally necessary, for every living civilization undergoes change and acquires new forms.

3. The encouragement of Jewish culture. Since Judaism is culture as well as religion, music, art and literature are integral parts of it. Therefore, the stimulation of these interests among Jews is as vital as ritual practices.

4. The reconstitution of the American Jewish community. Judaism as a religious civilization can best be reflected in public life through an integrated Jewish community. Jewish communal councils, representing all elements who manifest interest in any aspect of the Jewish religion or culture, should, therefore, be constituted and charged with the direction of Jewish institutions.

5. The rebuilding of Palestine. Zionism is a logical consequence of the reconstructionist position. To Reconstructionism Palestine is indispensable for Jewish culture. Everywhere, Judaism as a civilization tends to be auxiliary to the majority culture, whereas Palestine is the one place in the world to which Jews can look with high expectations—expectations which have already justified themselves—for the spontaneous appearance of new Jewish civilizational forms and values. From Palestine the Jews of the diaspora are already deriving, and will increasingly derive, that music, art, literature and folkway which they require but which,

given their circumstances, they are incapable of fashioning for themselves.

It should be observed that the Reconstructionist emphasis in Zionism is unique. The usual Zionist approach tends to make the Zionist program and its actualization the core of Jewish enterprise. Reconstructionism tends to see Judaism as a world-wide phenomenon, and Zionism as a logical and necessary expression of it.

Reconstructionism—Critique

The very attempt of Reconstructionism to resolve the impasse between the secular and religious points of view has evoked sharp criticism of its entire doctrine. The secularist tends naturally to regard the reconstructionist insistence on the centrality of religion as unfortunate. Those, on the other hand, who consider religion the essence of Judaism accuse reconstructionists of diluting Judaism and of distorting its true meaning and significance.

The program of the reconstructionist philosophy has also been subjected to sharp criticism. While stressing the need of a rethinking of Jewish theology, Reconstructionism has refused to propound any particular religious doctrine, contending that such matters must be left for individual determination. Indeed, at times it comes dangerously near saying that it does not matter what a person believes about God, so long as he believes something which for him functions effectively.

Ritual, too, has been something of a storm center. The readiness of reconstructionists to modify traditional forms and to supplement them with new patterns and materials has aroused deep misgivings. Can traditional practices be tampered with, without inviting their ultimate disintegration? Will not the reconstructionist technique lead even at best to innumerable variations in Jewish usage, which can only result in confusion and disunity? To which the reconstructionist replies that disintegration and confusion are a present condition, that Jewish observance cannot be saved, unless it is systematically, boldly, yet reverently, recast.

Only the future can determine whether the reconstructionist approach will be help or hindrance to the survival and revival of Judaism.

Conclusion

To some observers, the number and variety of philosophies extant among American Jews must seem most distressing. Considering how sharply Jews differ among themselves as to the nature of their Judaism, and what ought to be done about it, the unreflecting person may be strongly tempted to despair over the possibilities of a successful Jewish life. Against such a misreading of the Jewish situation, two thoughts ought to be advanced by way of conclusion.

First, the danger to Judaism does not lie in differences of conviction among Jews. It resides rather in the fact that so many Jews have no opinions at all. The committed person, whatever be his commitment, possesses what to him is both a clear understanding of his Jewishness and a fruitful procedure for expressing it. He can therefore be mentally at ease with Judaism and positive and creative in his disposition of it. Such strengths and virtues are absent from confused Jews who, for want of comprehension, must be mentally unhappy in their Jewishness and hesitant, if not impotent, in their practice of it.

Again, difference of opinion among the members of any group is both natural and desirable. Ideas clarify and sharpen themselves under challenge. They cross-pollinate and fertilize one another. It may be that in the future American Judaism may develop one normative philosophy. But even if that end should be attained, it would not be desirable that all differences of outlook be eliminated or obscured. Judaism is now the richer for variety.

ZIONISM IN AMERICAN JEWISH LIFE

—

Sulamith Schwartz

A DISTINGUISHED American Jewish writer, newly returned to Judaism, wrote on a visit to the Palestine of 1925: "Palestine, it must never be forgotten, does not exist for itself alone . . . it exists for the Jewish people everywhere in the world . . . Palestine has healed thousands of souls, it has spread the sense of national and human dignity in the remotest regions of the dispersion . . . It is self-recovery; it is salvation."*

This sense of the Jewish people's need for its center in Palestine has been one of the underlying themes of Jewish history throughout the dispersion. It has sprung to life even in prosperous and well-adjusted Jewish communities, and it has always been a basic element necessary to integrated and creative Jewish living anywhere. The history of American Jewry is no exception. Even in the days when the Jewish community was very small and isolated from the problems and griefs of world Jewry, prophetic individuals arose who urged and demonstrated the need for the rebuilding of the home in Palestine. Their influence merged with and stimulated the Zionist urge which was brought from the East European Jewish centers by the immigrants who came in great waves after 1880. The Zionist hope, retained at first by

* Lewisohn, Ludwig, *Israel*, New York, 1925, pp. 158, 220.

only the most sensitive of the new immigrants, was inevitably to conquer sector after sector of the developing American Jewish community till it became the powerful and all-pervasive influence it is today. Zionism has given new strength and dignity, new spiritual and cultural content to the life of American Jewry. The story of its growth, told in the pages to follow, is the story of the awakening to self-consciousness of American Jewry.

Beginnings of American Zionism

There were hardly 5000 Jews in the United States of 1818. Distance and their share in the new freedom of young America might well have made them forget the universal Jewish problem. Yet here was one of them writing of the seven million Jews of the world: "The signal for breaking the Turkish scepter in Europe will be their emancipation; . . . they will march in triumphant numbers and possess themselves once more of Syria, and take their rank among the governments of the earth." To Major Mordecai Manuel Noah, descendant of *Sephardic* Jews who had settled in America in the early eighteenth century, it was clear that the return to Zion was the goal of Jewish history. Even when in a grand, melodramatic and ineffectual gesture he dedicated Ararat, "a city of refuge for the Jews" on Grand Island in the Niagara River, and invited the Jews of the world to come there in their multitudes, he made sure to add: "The Jews never should and never will relinquish the just hope of regaining possession of their ancient heritage, and events in the neighborhood of Palestine indicate an extraordinary change of affairs."* Indeed, it was this ex-consul of the United States to Tunis, this sheriff of New York City and orator of the Tammany Society, who may be said to have initiated the idea of the Jewish state in modern times, preceding Theodore Herzl by half a century.

There was much that was eccentric about the first American Zionist, but the very fact of his appearance is deeply significant.

* Goldberg, Isaac, *Major Noah*, Phila., 1936, pp. 140, 194.

The second great figure in American Zionism was, like Noah, a product of a family rooted in America for many generations, and she, like Noah, saw the Zionist idea in its full scope as the only permanent solution of the Jewish problem. Emma Lazarus (1849-1887) was a gifted young writer whose interest in Jews and Judaism was first aroused by the Russian pogroms of 1881, and then intensified by contact with the masses of Jewish immigrants who began to pour into the United States after the pogroms. The pogrom wave of the 1880's constituted a turning point in Jewish history and Jewish thought: it made clear the fact that emigration from Eastern Europe was the most pressing problem of an entire generation and it accordingly started not only the influx into the United States but also modern Zionist settlement in Palestine. Indeed, 1881 served as the starting-point of political Zionism. Practically all the ideas later to be proclaimed by Herzl were set forth in *Auto-Emancipation,* that extraordinary and prophetic brochure on the world Jewish situation by Leon Pinsker, who became president of the Russian *Hovevei Zion* (the "Lovers of Zion" who sponsored agricultural settlements in Palestine).

Emma Lazarus read and agreed with Pinsker, but she had reached her Zionist conclusions independently, before she read *Auto-Emancipation.* Europe was becoming a place where Jews could no longer live, and America, she argued, would surely accept masses of European Jews, but there would be so many millions to resettle that America would—as it did—eventually shut its gates. The re-establishment in Palestine of "an independent Jewish nationality" was the only remedy which was not a "temporary palliative." And at a time when the 250,000 American Jews were just beginning to be augmented by the large new influx, Emma Lazarus forecast accurately the relationship which would develop between the great American Jewish community of the future and world Jewry. It was clearly, she said, the responsibility of American Jews in their prosperity to help alleviate the plight of wretched millions by aiding in the establishment of a Jewish Palestine. The bond between Jews of different countries could never be broken even though each group owed political allegiance only to the land it lived in, for "the condition of Jews all over the world must inevitably be affected by the condition of several millions of people holding the same religious tenets and springing from the same ancestral stock, however widely they may be separated by seas and continents." "The establishment of a free Jewish state" would not have "the remotest bearing upon the position of American Jews," but Zionism was incumbent upon them for their own sake and for that of their brother Jews. "A home for the homeless, a goal for the wanderer, an asylum for the persecuted, a nation for the denationalized. Such is the need of our generation."*

The writings of Emma Lazarus, the American, played an important part in keeping alive the Zionist impulses of the immigrants of 1881 and succeeding years. The majority of them, it may be fairly said, were so completely absorbed in the difficult business of making a living in the new land that they had little intellectual or organizational energy left for causes other than the immediately urgent one of trade-unionism or association in synagogues and *landsmanschaften*. But there was a saving remnant—passionate Hebraists and "Lovers of Zion" who organized struggling little societies to perpetuate those historic ideals of the Jewish people. It was in New York and Baltimore that the first Zionist† groups were established, and to the little Baltimore group must go at least some of the credit for the fact that native-born Baltimoreans became pioneer and outstanding leaders of American Zionism. In 1888, the Isaac Bar Levinson Hebrew Literary Society of Baltimore was organized by young immigrants, and

---

* All the passages here quoted or paraphrased are from "Epistles to the Hebrews," published in the *American Hebrew* from November 10, 1882 to February 1883. The "Epistle" was reprinted in 1900 by the Federation of American Zionists.

† The term Zionism at this period refers to the pre-political *Hovevei Zion* movement.

Henrietta Szold, the learned daughter of Baltimore's learned Hungarian-born rabbi, read the group a paper on Emma Lazarus and enlisted its members' aid in establishing a night school to teach English, Americanization and other subjects to immigrants. Contacts with the Russians brought Henrietta Szold to Zionism. She had been prepared for it intellectually by her father's attitudes and the training he had given her, but the movement as such first appeared before her in the guise of *Hevrath Zion*, the Zionist association which her Hebraist friends organized in 1893, and into which they drew her and young Dr. Harry Friedenwald, later to be president of the Federation of American Zionists.

In Henrietta Szold, American Zionism found one of its greatest leaders, at once an intellectual and moral guide and an organizer of remarkable practicality and devotion to detail. From the very beginning of her Zionist affiliation, she was certain that Zionism alone could be the salvation of the Jewish people. It was either Zionism or extinction, and since, she wrote, "no one person can do more than fight a little tiny bit of a world problem, I must stick to the Jewish problem." Her contribution through Zionist work to the solution of the Jewish problem has written a notable chapter in modern Jewish history; it includes painstaking service as secretary of the Federation of American Zionists in 1910, and head of its admirable department of education from 1916 to 1920. Above all, it includes the organization in 1912 of Hadassah, the Women's Zionist Organization of America, which has become so powerful an instrument for the upbuilding of Palestine and so great a factor in the life of the American Jewish community itself. Spending most of the last two decades in Palestine, Henrietta Szold has left more of an impress upon the life of the developing Jewish homeland than any other American Jew. She organized the Palestinian Jewish community's health and education services, instituted almost single-handed a modern social service system, and helped create and directed the Youth Aliyah, that magnificently successful children's immigration movement from

Europe to Palestine. The letters and reports she has sent from Palestine in the course of the last two decades* reflect a wise, sensitive and remarkably humane spirit. More than that, they have helped to make Palestine, its problems and achievements real for Hadassah and have had no small effect upon that organization's activities and attitudes. The tragedy of the destruction of German Jewry, the brave beauty of its youth's taking new root in Palestine, have nowhere been described with such poignant understanding as in Henrietta Szold's letters.

The unique personality of Henrietta Szold was to a very large extent molded by her father. Rabbi Benjamin Szold was one of that pioneer group of Central and Western European rabbis whose deep roots in Jewish learning and whose love of Jewish life made them important early American protagonists of the Zionist ideal. They were Zionists at a time when their own "German" congregants were indifferent or antagonistic and the mass of East European immigrants were preoccupied with economic adjustment to their new surroundings. Rabbi Szold's Zionist colleagues included, among others, Bernard Felsenthal of Chicago, Gustav Gottheil of New York, Marcus Jastrow of Philadelphia. It was Rabbi Gottheil's young son, Richard Gottheil of Columbia University, who organized and became the first president of the Federation of American Zionists in 1897, after his return from a trip to Europe during which he had attended the first Zionist Congress at Basle. The Baltimore *Hevrath Zion* and also the Hebrew National Association of Boston had been represented at that historic meeting which under Theodore Herzl's powerful and magnetic leadership made Zionism a consciously political movement and brought it out upon the scene of international history. In America as in Europe, the recruits to political Zionism consisted largely of existing *Hovevei Zion* and Hebraist groups. These endorsed political Zionism's credo, the Basle platform, and

* Many striking excerpts of these are included in Marvin Lowenthal's *Henrietta Szold: Life and Letters,* New York, 1942.

were reinforced by a small number of outstanding American converts to political Zionism, such as Richard Gottheil and Stephen S. Wise.

Thus in 1897, American Zionism, for all that it was still very limited in numbers and influence, acquired a large political purpose, a certain degree of unification and organization, a distinct relationship to the constantly growing world-wide movement. Its first activities were small in scope but invariably characterized by enthusiasm and deep sincerity. At the fourth conference of the Federation in 1901, for instance, the sum of fifty dollars was voted for the National Library in Jerusalem, and an entire session was devoted to the question of the sale of shares of the Jewish Colonial Trust at five dollars a share. Thousands of shares were sold throughout the United States, though the five dollars usually had to be paid in instalments, and with similar zeal, tiny—and sometimes larger—contributions were made to the Jewish National Fund.

The Kishineff pogrom of 1903 evoked a storm of protest in American Jewry, made it for the first time organize its growing strength and realize its relationship to world Jewry. Zionists were active in the demonstrations and relief collections, and Zionism's influence was strengthened and broadened. It was to be further and markedly strengthened by the great new wave of immigration which followed Kishineff and that other violent series of pogroms after the abortive Russian Revolution of 1905. The Zionism which was brought to the American movement by the thousands of adherents it now gained was far more mature and crystallized than that of the earlier immigrants. American Zionism developed: the period between 1903 and the beginning of the World War in 1914 saw the foundation of the Intercollegiate Zionist Organization, the Order Sons of Zion, Hadassah, Young Judaea, the *Mizrachi* or orthodox wing of Zionism, the *Poale Zion* or Socialist wing. The Yiddish press began to be won over to the movement. There was growing sympathy in circles that seemed very remote—Nathan Straus, Louis D. Brandeis became Zionists; Louis Marshall and Jacob H. Schiff helped to support the Hebrew Technical Institute in Haifa and the Agricultural Experimental Station established by Aaron Aaronsohn of Zichron Jacob. As the Marshall and Schiff benefactions indicate, the fresh heroic life of the pioneering Palestine of those early days was beginning to have a definite influence on the attitude of American Jews to Zionism. The *Yishuv* (the Jewish community in Palestine) was very small then, but the seeds of the social, cultural and economic phenomena that were to be the boast of the post-war years were being sown by the daring and inspired young pioneers who settled in Palestine after 1905.

The effect of those modern Palestinian beginnings on a very distinguished American Jewish mind is clearly written down for us to read in Louis D. Brandeis' "The Jewish Problem—How to Solve It," the address he delivered in June 1915 before the Eastern Council of the Central Conference of Reform Rabbis. If American Jews are to be protected from "demoralization which has to some extent already set in" among them, and which is caused by the relaxation of the ancient tradition and discipline, they must, Brandeis argues, be imbued with self-respect. Self-respect can be inculcated "only by restoring the ties of the Jew to the noble past of his race, and by making him realize the possibilities of a no less glorious future . . . and this can be done effectively only through furthering the Zionist movement." The source and inspiration of this reasoning become apparent in the very next paragraph: "In the Jewish colonies of Palestine . . . everyone, old and young alike, is led to feel the glory of his race and his obligation to carry forward its ideals. The new Palestinian Jewry produces . . . great scientists like Aaron Aaronsohn, the discoverer of wild wheat; great pedagogues like David Yellin; craftsmen like Boris Schatz, the founder of the Bezalel; intrepid Shomerim, the Jewish guards of peace, who watch in the night against marauders and doers of violent deeds."*

Aaronsohn and Boris Schatz visited America in the years before the first World War and the influence of their accomplishments was reinforced for American Jews by actual contact with them as personalities. Nahum Sokolow, the brilliant littérateur, scholar and linguist, later to be president of the World Zionist Organization, was in the United States in 1912, and met, among others, Louis Brandeis, then a leading Boston attorney. There was one visitor who came time and again in the period between 1906 and 1914 and who was without doubt the great teacher of American Zionists, one of the chief factors in preparing them for the historic role the first World War was suddenly to thrust upon them. Schmarya Levin was a rare and extraordinarily fascinating personality, a great propagandist with a manner all his own, compact of profundity and scholarship, brilliant wit and cutting humor, an understanding love of European Jewish life and a vision of the Jewish future in Palestine.

THE BRANDEIS LEADERSHIP

In a sense it was the accident of Schmarya Levin's visit to America in the spring and summer of 1914 which changed the course of American Zionist history. In August he left New York for Europe on a German boat, which was compelled by the sudden declaration of war to return to its New York port. Levin was a member of the World Zionist Executive, and since all the other members in their Berlin headquarters found themselves cut off from contact with the Zionists of allied and neutral countries, he took the initiative in organizing American Zionism for leadership. A summons to an extraordinary conference was issued to all American Zionist parties and organizations by Levin for the World Zionist Executive and Louis Lipsky for the American Zion-

---

* Louis D. Brandeis, *The Jewish Problem—How to Solve It*, published by Hadassah, pp. 14, 15.

ist Federation. On August 30, 1914, in a small New York hotel the Provisional Executive Committee for General Zionist Affairs was formed and an Emergency Fund, the goal of which was the then shockingly large sum of $100,000, was instituted to support the Palestinian institutions of the Zionist movement and to carry on Zionist propaganda. These were in essence the functions of the World Zionist Executive, and it was, indeed, American Jewry through the Provisional Committee that saved the *Yishuv* in time of danger and starvation, and that had a very large share in winning Zionism's first great political victory, the issuance of the Balfour Declaration.

The little American Zionist movement had been lifted to a place of central importance in world Jewish history. The leader capable of raising it far above its petty concerns and of fitting it for its new functions appeared suddenly—almost, one might say, providentially. Quite as America under Woodrow Wilson assumed leadership in world affairs, so American Zionism took world Zionist leadership under the direction of Wilson's aid and adviser, Louis D. Brandeis. It was in late middle age that Brandeis, "the people's lawyer," became interested in Jews and the Jewish question: this new interest brought him directly to wholehearted acceptance of Zionism, the basic movement for Jewish survival. Jacob de Haas, whom Herzl had sent from England to be secretary of the young Federation of American Zionists, started Brandeis' Zionist education; Schmarya Levin was his great source of Jewish and Zionist knowledge. But Brandeis' Zionist philosophy was one which he worked out by himself and which has a special and permanent significance as a clear analysis of the organic place of Zionism in American Jewish life.

"My approach to Zionism was through Americanism," he summed it up himself, for "it became clear to me that to be good Americans, we must be better Jews, and to be better Jews, we must become Zionists." This passage, quoted from Brandeis' *The Jewish Problem—How to Solve It,* expresses his central belief. The qualities which had been developed by thousands of years of Jewish life and which were uniquely attuned to the needs and ideals of twentieth century democratic America, could be preserved in American Jews only if they were Zionists. For Zionism alone could imbue them with the living relationship to the past that is never possible except when the past is "the mirror of a glorious future."

How precisely would a Jewish Palestine build the future on the past? Brandeis answered the question in his "Call to the Educated Jew":

"The fruits of three thousand years of civilization and a hundred generations of suffering may not be sacrificed by us. It will be sacrificed if dissipated. Assimilation is national suicide. And assimilation can be prevented only by preserving national characteristics and life as other peoples, large and small, are preserving and developing their national life. Shall we with our inheritance do less than the Irish, the Serbians, or the Bulgars? And must we not, like them, have a land where the Jewish life may be naturally led, the Jewish language spoken, and the Jewish spirit prevail? Surely we must, and that land is our fathers' land: it is Palestine."*

It was only natural that so outstanding an American as Brandeis should have come to grips with the question of dual loyalties. Only loyalties that were inconsistent could not be held simultaneously, he asserted: Zionism is so consistent with American ideals, so essentially democratic, that loyalty to America actually demands that American Jews become Zionists. "Every Irish-American who contributed to advancing home rule was a better man and a better American for the sacrifice involved. Every American Jew who aids in advancing the Jewish settlement of Palestine, though he feel sure that neither he nor his descendants will ever wish to go there, will likewise be a better man, and a better American for doing so."†

* De Haas, Jacob, *Louis D. Brandeis,* New York, 1929, pp. 163, 198, 200.
† *The Jewish Problem—How to Solve It,* cited, p. 13.

Brandeis threw himself into the work of the Provisional Executive Committee with characteristic energy and forcefulness. He gathered able young professional men around him—Felix Frankfurter was one of them—and he influenced them to apply their expert training to the consideration of the post-war problems of Palestine. The masses responded as never before to Zionism, impelled, as Louis Lipsky aptly described it, by "the fever of social responsibility" the war brought "into the very foundations of American Jewish life."*

This new social maturity awoke memories of youthful Zionist feeling in thousands of hitherto indifferent American Jews and brought a multitude of new recruits. Zionism was expanding at a rate that would have seemed incredible just a few years earlier. Leaders of powerful fraternal orders came over to the movement. The widespread popular support of Zionist aims made it easier for Brandeis and Stephen Wise to carry on their work for the Balfour Declaration in Washington. Drafted in London, the Balfour Declaration was revised in New York and Washington, and issued at Downing Street with President Wilson's approval. The work of American Zionists had been invaluable in strengthening the case presented by Chaim Weizmann and his fellow workers in London. Nor was American governmental aid to Zionism limited to support of the Balfour Declaration: the Medical Unit sent by Hadassah to Palestine in 1918 with such momentous consequences for the future health of the country, could never have sailed had it not been for friendly co-operation in Washington, nor could a boatload of food on the S. S. Vulcan have reached the starving population of Palestine.

To American Zionists and the American Jewish masses as a whole, the Balfour Declaration seemed an event of messianic dimensions, and the joyous enthusiasm it aroused was unrestrained. Over 4000 American young men enlisted in the Jewish Legion and took part in General Allenby's victorious Palestinian

* Lipsky, Louis, *Thirty Years of American Zionism*, New York, 1927, p. 247.

campaign. The Emergency Fund became the Palestine Restoration Fund. The $100,000 goal of the Emergency Fund had been many times as large as the sums American Zionists were accustomed to raising, but it was to shrink into insignificance when compared with the achievements of the Palestine Restoration Fund. Three million dollars were raised in 1919—a far cry from the $14,000 collected by American Zionists in 1914. There had been 20,000 *shekel** payers in the United States in 1914; in 1917 there were 150,000; in 1920, 171,000.

Furthermore, Zionist political energies went beyond the securing of the Balfour Declaration to a consideration of the need for adequate presentation to the Peace Conference of the Zionist demands of the majority of American Jewry. It was patently necessary to create a democratically elected representative body to speak for American Jewry. Thus the Zionists, and particularly the Poale Zionists, played an active part in the agitation for an American Jewish Congress. After complicated negotiations and a very lively general election, the American Jewish Congress assembled in Philadelphia in December, 1918. In the name of the three million Jews of America it adopted a resolution approving the Balfour Declaration and urged Great Britain to assume the Palestine Mandate. It elected a delegation to represent American Jewry at the Peace Conference. Julian W. Mack was chairman of the delegation, which included among its eight members Louis Marshall of the American Jewish Committee, Stephen S. Wise, and Nachman Syrkin of the Poale Zion. The delegation practically represented a united American Jewry. At Versailles the delegation presented a formal memorandum to President Wilson asking "that the Peace Conference recognize the aspirations and historic claims of the Jewish people in regard to Palestine; that such action be taken by the Conference as shall vest the sovereign possession of Palestine in such League of Nations as may be

---

* Membership in the World Zionist Organization is determined by the payment of dues, fifty cents, known by the Biblical term *"shekel."*

formed, and that the government thereof be entrusted to Great Britain as the mandatory or trustee of the League." The delegation was then received by Wilson, who expressed his own approval and "the fullest concurrence of our Government and people" with the Zionist plan "that in Palestine shall be laid the foundation of a Jewish commonwealth."

American Zionists, and, in the final analysis, American Jewry as a whole, had played no small part in the political negotiations culminating in the assignment of the Mandate over Palestine to Great Britain and in the express inclusion in the Mandate of the proviso that "the Mandatory should be responsible for putting into effect the [Balfour] declaration . . . in favor of the establishment in Palestine of a national home for the Jewish people."

Effect of the Upbuilding of Palestine

In the great program of Palestinian development which was the central Zionist task of the post-war years, American Jewry was again to occupy an unusually significant place. They furnished a very considerable part of the funds (at least $100,000,000 in contributions and investments) which made possible the large scale immigration and colonization of the last two decades. In doing so, they were themselves drawn increasingly closer to the new pattern of life in Jewish Palestine with its constant and underlying emphasis on co-operative living, on the joy and duty of creative labor, on the revival of the historic language and culture of the Jewish people. Through participation in work for Palestine, new vistas and new values have opened before increasingly large numbers of American Jews. This has been true whether their specific interest is the national land ownership program of the Jewish National Fund; the co-operative and communal colonization sponsored by the *Keren Hayesod* (the Palestine Foundation Fund founded in 1921); the public health system established by Hadassah and the deeply moving and highly effective Youth Aliyah work, in the execution of which it has had a major share since

1935; the co-operative banking, industry and housing, aided by the Palestine Economic Corporation since its inception under Justice Brandeis' influence in 1926; or the ramified activities of the *Histadruth* (the General Federation of Jewish Labor), which is the backbone of the *Yishuv* and the most important single force in its life.

Interest in the development of the Jewish National Home has not been limited to those affirming their allegiance to the Zionist platform. American non-Zionist sympathizers with the program for the upbuilding of Palestine were largely instrumental in organizing the Jewish Agency for Palestine. The Mandate for Palestine had expressly provided—upon the initiative of the Zionist leaders themselves—that the Zionist Organization "take steps in consultation with His Britannic Majesty's Government to secure the co-operation of all Jews who are willing to assist in the establishment of the Jewish national home." Accordingly, after extensive negotiations, the Jewish Agency, including representatives of both Zionists and non-Zionists, was organized at Zurich in August 1929. Louis Marshall was the central figure on the non-Zionist side, and the sentiments he expressed were typical of those of Felix Warburg, Cyrus Adler, and the other American and European non-Zionists who joined the Agency. Their concern for Palestine was rooted in a general warm attachment to Judaism and the Jewish people. "We are Jews," Marshall said at Zurich, speaking of American Jewry, "Jews who respond to every cause in Judaism." The building of a Jewish center should not be a task for Zionists alone, he insisted. It is the duty of all Israel, and "we cannot permit the bankruptcy of the Jewish people. The failure of Palestine would be a disgrace to the Jewish people."

A notable example of the growth of the pro-Zionist feeling among non-Zionists is provided by the changed relationship to Palestine of American Jewish labor circles. Particularly in the textile industries where Jewish workers are most heavily concentrated, more and more trade union members have been drawn into the orbit of Zionism through their sympathy with Jewish labor in Palestine and their admiration for its achievements. Their interest has been expressed largely through the special fund-raising and propaganda activity of the National Labor Committee for Palestine (the Gewerkschaften Campaign founded in 1924). The vision of a labor Palestine had been limited for many years to a small group of idealists. They founded the first American Poale Zion Societies in 1903, 1904, and 1905, and the Jewish National Workers' Alliance in 1908, while the bulk of Jewish labor in America was indifferent and even hostile to Zionism. The concrete achievements of Jewish labor in Palestine worked a miraculous change, symbolized, one might say, by the cordial reaction to Palestine of Abraham Cahan, editor of the *Jewish Daily Forward,* the newspaper which had long been the citadel of the anti-Zionist sentiment of American Jewish workers. There are now tens of thousands of contributors to the Gewerkschaften Campaign, part of them convinced labor Zionists, and others warm sympathizers with Palestinian Jewish labor. In the meantime, the organizations directly affiliated with the Labor Zionist movement have themselves grown in number and influence. The National Workers' Alliance, which is a fraternal insurance order, now has about 19,000 members; the Pioneer Women's Organization, which subsidizes the activities of the Working Women's Council in Palestine, has about 7000 members; the Poale Zion party itself about 10,000, and the League for Labor Palestine, which has attracted many American Jewish intellectuals, about 4000.

Zionist sentiment among orthodox Jews, too, has grown markedly from very small beginnings. For the conventional, rigidly observant Jew, concentrated on retaining his traditional way of life in unfavorable surroundings, it was difficult three or four decades ago to reconcile Zionism with the age-old hope for messianic redemption. The founders of *Mizrachi* were men of courage and vision, and a great part of orthodox Jewry has grad-

ually been conquered by their conviction that the upbuilding of
the Land of Israel in accordance with the spirit of Jewish tradition
is a religious duty of paramount importance. The atmosphere of
most orthodox, as of practically all conservative synagogues and
more and more reform temples, is now permeated with Zionist
emotion, symbol, and activity. Teaching in the orthodox *talmud-
torah* and *yeshivah* is, in most cases, deeply influenced by the
national ideal and revival, quite as are the curricula of the overwhelming majority of other Hebrew and religious schools. Of the
thousands of members in the various groups affiliated with the
Mizrachi movement, a growing proportion in recent years have
been women. The characteristic American phenomenon of the
strong women's organization is seen quite as clearly in American
Zionist life as elsewhere, and the Mizrachi Women's Organization,
with its junior group, is a case in point. Its members, like those
of the other women's Zionist groups—notably Hadassah and
the Pioneer Women—not only support specific projects in Palestine, but carry on an extensive educational program of their own.

The name of Hadassah is by now almost synonymous with the
American woman's contribution to Zionism. In the thirty years
of its existence it has become one of the strongest single communal forces in American Jewish life, and it has often been observed with justice that it has given to the American Jewish
woman even more than she has given to Palestine through it. It
has brought to women in small towns and great cities an enlarge-
ment of intellectual interests, a sense of Jewish dignity, and an
understanding of the importance of Jewish education and tradition. Its 100,000 members have acquired a feeling of communal
responsibility in this country, as well as an attachment to the
Jewish center in Palestine they are helping to build. Many a new
member of Hadassah may feel no more than a vague sympathy
or a philanthropic urge, but she makes her way almost always to
a fuller understanding of Zionism and its relationship to her own
life. Even the details of daily life have been affected. Through

Hadassah's influence, the songs of pioneering Palestine are sung from coast to coast by women many of whom had never before uttered a word of Hebrew. Through imitation of modern Palestine's *Oneg Shabbat* celebration a special educational emphasis has come once more to distinguish Saturday afternoons for thousands upon thousands of American women, returning thus to a long neglected folk tradition.

Superb organization, careful planning of education and program have gone into the making of Hadassah. Its youth group, Junior Hadassah, which subsidizes a number of important Palestinian institutions, is the largest of the Zionist youth organizations, and has by now given a generation of adult Zionists to the movement. Every wing of the Zionist movement has its youth organizations. Besides Junior Hadassah, the General Zionists have Young Judaea, whose clubs include 20,000 boys and girls; Avukah, the intercollegiate Zionist organization; Masada, including mainly young men. There is a recently founded Junior *Mizrachi* women's organization; *Hapoel Hamizrachi,* the league for religious labor in Palestine, has about 11,000 members; and *Hashomer Hadati,* the religious scout group aiming at *halutziut* (pioneering) in Palestine, includes 5000 members. *Halutziut* is the goal, too, of *Hashomer Hatzair,* an independent Socialist Zionist group of 3500 members, and, in less mandatory fashion, of *Habonim,* the youth organization of the American Labor Zionist movement (with over 2000 members). Several hundred American *halutzim,* products of *Hashomer Hatzair* and *Habonim,* have settled in Palestine and become an integral part of the agricultural colonization program of Palestinian labor. The close ties these two youth groups have with Palestine have intensified the effect of Palestinian life on their membership here.

These groups have added scope and vitality to American Zionism, but the pioneer body, the Federation of American Zionists, reorganized in 1918 as the Zionist Organization of America, has maintained a position of preeminence in the movement. Its influence has penetrated the Jewish communities of almost every city and town in the country, while its membership, including the youth groups, is approaching the 100,000 mark.

The Zionist Organization of America played the leading role in bringing Zionism officially before the Congress of the United States; and in 1922, a joint resolution passed by both Houses of Congress declared "That the United States of America favors the establishment in Palestine of a national home for the Jewish people." This statement became the cornerstone of an official American policy toward Zionism, and the views therein expressed were reiterated by every president from Woodrow Wilson to Franklin D. Roosevelt.

. Unlike Hadassah, the Zionist Organization of America adopted no particular project regarding Palestine, instead lending its full support and strength to the existing Zionist funds, first the Jewish National Fund, and, following its establishment in 1921, the Keren Hayesod, the Palestine Foundation Fund. These were later united for fund-raising purposes into the United Palestine Appeal, which has become American Jewry's prime financial instrument for the rebuilding of Palestine.

Any consideration of the influence of Zionism on American Jewry must include the frequent educational tours by Zionist leaders, arranged by all senior and youth Zionist organizations. It must include, also, the publications issued by each of the groups, some of them journals of considerable excellence and importance. There are, too, a number of groups organized for the support of specific institutions in Palestine, the members of which, though not necessarily Zionists, grow increasingly sympathetic with Jewish Palestine through intimate knowledge of, and attachment to, one phase or another of its life. The American Friends of the Hebrew University and the American Committee of the Palestine Orchestra Fund are outstanding examples, and have done much to develop two of Palestine's greatest cultural assets. Mailamm, the American Palestine Music Association, has taken as its purpose the advancement of Jewish music in both the United States and Palestine, endeavoring not only to assist in the development of Palestinian music but also to make it known in America. An important small Zionist group committed to a special purpose in Palestine is the American Economic Committee for Palestine, organized in 1932 to give authoritative guidance to private investors wishing to establish themselves in industry or other fields in Palestine.

The number of organized Zionists has grown constantly in the United States till in 1939 before the last World Zionist Congress there were 268,000 *shekel* payers. But the extent of Zionist influence cannot be measured only by the number formally affiliated with the movement or with organizations directly concerned with work in Palestine. Almost all the *landsmanschaften* and fraternal lodges, including the influential B'nai B'rith, give a measure of moral and financial support to the upbuilding of the Jewish National Home. A Zionist plank is part of the platform of the American Jewish Congress. The Jewish center movement, the Yiddish and Anglo-Jewish press are permeated with Zionism. Through the centralization in recent years of fund-raising for overseas purposes in the United Jewish Appeal, Zionism has reached previously untouched circles in the community. Similarly, since so many Jewish communities make all their philanthropic contributions through Welfare Funds, the boards and contributors of the Funds become perforce familiar with the merits of the various causes appealing to them for aid. Confronted with the dreadful proportions of the refugee problem, many an American Jew, previously far from, or even hostile to, Zionism, has become gratefully aware of Palestine's central place in the absorption of Jewish immigration. Often such awareness leads eventually to a larger sympathy with Zionist aims and efforts.

By a tragic coincidence, the events of 1914 are, in a sense, repeating themselves now. The wheel has come full circle. Once more in the midst of a World War, American Zionism finds itself chief spokesman and chief bearer of responsibility for the world Zionist movement. Late in 1939 the American Zionist bodies established the American Emergency Committee for Zionist Affairs, which had been called for by the World Zionist Congress of that year to meet the situation occasioned by the outbreak of the war. The Emergency Committee has a public relations program of extensive scope: a national American Palestine Committee was established in 1941, composed of close to 1,000 leading Congressmen, editors, ministers, university presidents and other influential persons, all of whom indicated their interest in the establishment of the Jewish National Home in Palestine. At an extraordinary Conference of Zionist bodies, held on May 11, 1942, at the Biltmore Hotel, New York City, a clear statement of the political aims of Zionism today was formulated. It calls for Jewish control over immigration to Palestine, and the establishment of the country as a Jewish Commonwealth. This statement of Zionist policy, referred to as the Biltmore Program, has since been ratified by Zionist official bodies throughout the world.

Much of the burden of preparing the way for the implementation of the Biltmore program falls necessarily upon American Jews. Fortunately, American Zionism of the second World War is not the tiny movement it was in 1914; more than twenty-five years of growth and participation in the upbuilding of Palestine have made it a large and mature force. Fortunately, too, Palestinian Jewry in the acid test of the war is proving itself a source of strength and hope. Its sturdy development during these last difficult years, its eager and self-sacrificing participation in the military effort of the United Nations are impressive proof of its maturity and its ability to play the post-war role that will be incumbent upon it. As American Zionism works now toward the consummation of its aims, it is fully confident that, as Justice

Brandeis prophesied, its own life will be enriched and dignified, its own adherence to Jewish values and democratic belief and practice immeasurably strengthened, by the existence in Palestine of a great Jewish center.

XI

CONCLUSION

—

Oscar I. Janowsky

As a rule, a symposium dealing with social life does not lend itself to co-ordinated conclusions, and particularly so when addressed to the adult reader. For adult education, like college instruction, follows the line of least resistance. Specialists present their views, not infrequently clashing views, and the student, or reader, is invited to shift or judge for himself—to reach his own conclusions. The objective, which is to stimulate thought and independent judgment, is laudable enough. But too often, it is no more than a confession of failure on the part of the educator, be he a member of a college faculty, or the director of a popular forum. Unable to integrate the unwieldy mass of complex social data, or to discern trends in social development, or to harmonize differences in point of view, facts and opinions are thrown at the reader or hearer. Too occupied with everyday problems, often inadequately equipped to weigh evidence or balance judgments, the reader is either confused, or he passively allows his particular bias to be reinforced.

Even casual reading must have revealed that this book is not a series of lectures, nor even a collection of essays. Although a symposium comprising the contributions of experts in their specialized fields, it is an integrated whole, both as regards fundamental assumptions and the composite portrait which has emerged. The book was conceived and planned as a unit. The collaboration of specialists was sought to assure thoroughness of treatment, without sacrificing singleness of purpose.

This purpose, namely, to portray and interpret the complex of institutions and conceptions which concern Jews, *as Jews,* has been pursued with marked success. It is common practice in discussions of American Jewish life either to paint an idealized scene of unity and harmony, or to pronounce pontifically that American Jewry is a babel of voices and must remain so, because the state power of enforcing the will of the majority is not, and cannot be, present. The authors have refrained from such oversimplification, and, on the whole, they have withstood the temptation to sermonize or prophesy. They have described Jewish group life as it is, in all its variety and complexity, and analyzed it with considerable detachment, indicating discernible currents and trends.

To say that the subject matter of the book has unity is not to imply that all contributors agree on every opinion contained therein. Certainly, there are differences in program and point of view. Dr. Pool, for example, defining Judaism as intrinsically religious, would have the synagogue the center and focal point of all Jewish activities, including even philanthropy and defense against anti-Semitism. Other contributors would question both his definition and policy. Nor would all the participants share his views on American Orthodoxy. While fully allowing for diversity, Dr. Berkson believes that the emphasis in Jewish education should be placed on the elaboration of a common Jewish school program. He is particularly opposed to the indoctrination of children with any fixed point of view, be it orthodox, reform, reconstructionist, or secular. Some of the contributors would disagree and might perhaps prefer to see each ideological group work out its own program. Rabbi Steinberg is at pains to present the principal tenets and shortcomings of all significant Jewish ideologies. But the careful reader will discern a preference for Reconstructionism. That preference is not necessarily shared by the other contributors.

In relating the economic activities of Jews to American economic development, Dr. Reich soundly maintains that Jewish occupational distribution is not abnormal. But some of his colleagues would differ with him on the practical consequences of this point of view. One might agree with his basic conception, and yet believe occupational restratification necessary. Similarly, the interpretation presented by this writer respecting the evolution of the American Jewish community, and the role played by the *Sephardic*, German and East European Jews in that evolution, may not be shared by the rest of the contributors.

These and similar variations in opinion and interpretation abound in this volume. And yet it has unity, both unity of structure and of conception. The chapters were visualized from the very beginning as segments of a totality—American Jewry. Each contribution is, therefore, part of the American Jewish scene, in the same sense as the fragments of a mosaic compose a unified pattern. Moreover, in the view of the present writer, there is substantial agreement among the authors of this volume on certain basic assumptions. In other words, they share a common point of view with regard to the fundamentals of Jewish life in the United States. This point of view is reflected in the book, and may be briefly summarized under the following heads:

1. The Jews of the United States constitute a spiritual-cultural group. Despite differences in ideology respecting the essence of Judaism; despite the emphasis implied by membership in various Jewish associations, the overwhelming majority of American Jews regard themselves, and are regarded by their fellow citizens, as an historical people, conditioned by a common past, a common tradition, common memories and a common fate.

2. American Jewry has validity today as a living and creative group, and Judaism, conceived as the totality of Jewish life, is

capable of satisfying spiritual and cultural needs of its members. Jewish identity, therefore, involves participation in Jewish communal life. The authors may differ on the form which the Jewish community is to assume, or on the role to be played by the synagogue in the totality of Jewish life. But all consider an organized community essential, and all would like to endow it with as much unity and meaningful activity as may be feasible.

Identification with the life of the group may range all the way from the full observance of the traditional faith, or active collaboration in cultural agencies, to support of charitable agencies, or merely co-operation in the struggle against anti-Semitism. Jewish identity should be measured by the degree and extent of participation in the distinctive institutions of the group, rather than by accident of birth.

3. Present-day Jewish life is an outgrowth and development of the past. Survival and creativity are, therefore, closely related to the spiritual and cultural heritage of the group. Old values may require reinterpretation to render them meaningful for the present generation, but any attempt completely to sever the thread of continuity with the past must result in stagnation, perhaps even in disintegration. Just as the individual is a product of heredity and environment, so the life of the group is shaped by its history as well as its surroundings.

4. History and tradition provide continuity in time. A sense of kinship with Jews in other parts of the world, and collaboration with them in furthering common spiritual and cultural interests, constitute continuity in space.

This conception of the unity of the Jewish people requires a word of explanation as to what is the relationship between American Jewry and the Jews of other countries. There has been much confusion in the use of the words "nation," "nationality" and "community." The term "nation" signifies a political state. Obviously, the fifteen or sixteen million Jews of the world do not constitute a state. The political allegiance of every Jew is to the country of his citizenship, and American Jews have no interest in the political affiliations of British or German or Polish or Rumanian Jews. Similarly, American Jews would not tolerate any interference whatsoever with their duties and obligations of American citizenship, in the same sense in which American Catholics or those of Irish ancestry would reject political guidance from the Vatican or the Irish Republic. However, the savage persecution of German Jewry, and the denial of rights to Jews in any other part of the world, is of vital concern to American Jews, not only from considerations of humanity, but also because of a positive sense of kinship. Again employing the same analogy, just as the suffering of the Irish peasantry in the nineteenth century disturbed Americans of Irish ancestry, or as the Nazi oppression of Catholics today inevitably arouses American Catholics, so are American Jews affected by the fortunes of Jewish communities abroad.

The word "nationality" is the English equivalent of the French *nationalité* and the German *nationalität*, which connote, not political allegiance, but spiritual and cultural affinity. Since the term "nationality" has not gained wide currency in the United States, the word "people" might perhaps best characterize this conception. The Scotch and Welsh are nationalities or peoples within the British nation. Their political allegiance is indivisible, but they are conscious of specialized cultural loyalties. Likewise, the American Jews, whose political loyalty is exclusively to the United States, recognize a religious and cultural relationship with Jews in other parts of the world. The Jewish religion, folkways, literature, art, music and other expressions of a spiritual and cultural nature are unaffected by political frontiers. They are worldwide and universal. There is, then, a Jewish nationality, or a Jewish people. The term "community" is frequently employed to designate a local body, such as the Jews of a particular town. In its broadest sense, it has the same meaning as the old word "Jewry," namely, the totality of Jewish institutional life of a particular country, i.e., the Jewish community of the United States, or the Jewish community of Great Britain.

5. The point of view of the book is definitely Zionist. The authors believe that a Jewish homeland in Palestine is indispensable today when masses of Jews are homeless and stateless, and would be indispensable if every Jew enjoyed full political and civil equality in every corner of the earth. If the premise is accepted that the Jews are an historical people with a common and distinctive spiritual and cultural heritage; if it is further agreed that this heritage is worthy of preservation, the imperative need of a homeland becomes self-evident. In every civilized country, Jewish culture must perforce be ancillary to the majority culture. In Palestine, however, where the status of the Jews is not that of a minority, the Jewish way of life has already become a primary civilization of the country. Under such favorable conditions, Jewish culture forms will flourish with renewed vigor and fructify Jewish spiritual and cultural life throughout the world.

6. Primarily concerned with the American Jewish community, the book has not made the attempt to elaborate on the relationship of Jews to the larger American community of which they are an inseparable part. But the position of the authors is clear and unequivocal. American Jews are part and parcel of America. They participate fully in the political life of their American homeland. They share in the common effort to achieve national security and economic prosperity. They are thoroughly imbued with the American spirit, and completely identified with American culture and the American way of life.

The Jews, however, differ in religious faith and practice from their Christian fellow citizens, and for the great majority of them religion has broad cultural implications. In other words, Jewishness involves a single, individual political loyalty, but a multiple, yet entirely consistent, spiritual-cultural interest. In so far as the shared American language and culture are concerned, Jews are undistinguishable from other Americans. But in addition to

American culture, Jewish living embraces a parallel or supplementary Jewish culture.

Moreover, this relationship to Americanism involves no special privileges for the Jews. For the authors believe that Americanism does not require a rigid and stultifying uniformity. American life is the richer and more fruitful because of the variegated pattern of its many culture strains. From this point of view, Jewish institutions, and the conceptions which render them meaningful, are an integral part of the American way of life. Organized Jewish living is a segment of American civilization. It is an inseparable ingredient in the totality we call America.

EVALUATIONS OF THE PORTRAIT OF
AMERICAN JEWISH LIVING WHICH THIS
BOOK ATTEMPTS TO REPRODUCE

I

THE JEWISH COMMUNITY AND THE OUTSIDE WORLD

George N. Shuster

—

BISHOP BURNET said of Peter the Great, after that monarch had sojourned in England, that he seemed "designed by nature rather to be a ship-carpenter than a great prince." One somehow fancies that a good many of Peter's subjects would have agreed with the Bishop had their opinions been asked. At any rate, we in our time have a house painter on our hands—very much on our hands; and it is natural that by reason of him our vision of many things should be distorted.

Manifestly, Hitler is in a special way the product of publicity. And that publicity in turn is in large measure attributable to the ruthlessness and cunning of the Nazi pogrom. For the first time in modern history a great state undertook to justify its anti-Semitic excesses. Every kind of argument and emotion was enlisted. It is an axiom that no person and no cause is proof against suspicion. Poor Desdemona is there to prove that. Othello succumbed to propaganda so silly that when it is extracted from Shakespeare's subtle and poetic diction it seems incredibly naive. Therefore one can hardly wonder that otherwise honest and sensible folk have believed the *Protocols of the Elders of Zion* or fancied that Jewish bankers and Jewish communists had entered into an evil alliance.

This present book is an engrossing and extremely valuable attempt to set things right. It quietly invites us to look at the Jewish adventure in the United States as one chapter in the history of immigration. That is how Americans ought to see it. Doubtless they would if they were more accustomed to the study of their nation's history. Unfortunately we have all neglected that. Few acquire any insight into the organic processes which have underlain the growth and development of the United States. Immigration is clearly the most significant of those processes.

Each group of newcomers has had a rather difficult time. The day was when the New England Irish were despised and gouged. Emerson rose nobly to their defense. Hawthorne wrote of their plight with realism and that curious detachment which was characteristic of him. I can remember as if it were an affair of yesterday the air of amused condescension which our Anglo-Saxon neighbors assumed towards us of German ancestry. The Italian epic has even yet a bitter flavor. Were we not certain that nothing good could come out of Southern countries? Once, some years ago, I asked a class of college Freshmen to state who Dante was. A good many answers read, "Some Wop." Such smaller and sturdy groups as the Slovaks have been shunned and ostracized in many communities. In almost every case, the scars show in the second and third generations.

Those who know something of human nature and its history realize that the events just described were natural and normal. If centuries have not sufficed to teach Croats and Serbs how to live side by side in amity, if the Alsatians have even yet not been wholly absorbed either into France or Germany, could we expect everything to go well over here? Indeed, we have labored as a nation under a severe handicap. The Negro problem cannot be left out of any study of our inter-group relations. A color line has been drawn through all that part of our history which is contemporaneous with immigration. If we distinguished between whites and blacks in a radical fashion, why should we not also differentiate between Latin and Teuton? Or between Jew and non-Jew? Many have believed we ought to do so. Racialist literature has often been fed from the United States.

Since in spite of everything we have succeeded rather better than we ought to have expected, it is worth while reflecting for a moment on the reasons why. I think there are three. First, our laws and our institutions enshrine the spirit of democratic living. They posit human equality before the courts and in the legislative assemblies, and their impact on the nation's life has been tremendous. Second, we have been a religious and idealistic people. There is always somebody to rise to the defense of those who have been wronged. The American conscience is sensitive and it counsels action. Third, we are made up of so many different groups that we have perforce had to get along together. No one faction could have its way absolutely, so that compromise was always unavoidable.

Taken by and large, the experience of the Jewish group does not differ essentially from that of any other group. The Jew has been free to choose his employment and his place of residence; to establish his temples of worship and to practice his religion; to educate his children in the manner he deemed best; and to enjoy every privilege of citizenship. Of course one can argue that he has encountered peculiar difficulties. Judaism is a religion with which the prevailing Christianity of the United States has traditionally been at odds; and there can be no doubt that in some quarters the hostility has flared up violently again and again. Jewish ritual observance has likewise to some extent set the Jew apart. Finally, the Jews are an old and distinct people, and the great majority of them can be distinguished physically from their neighbors. But though all these are important matters, they are not nearly so essential as is often supposed.

Let us take the Jewish religion as an example. Hostility to it has been nowhere near so violent as has been the antipathy between Catholic and Protestant. Catholic churches and institutions have been razed by mobs, whereas Jewish synagogues have, so far as I am aware, never been attacked. Rabbis have often been laughed at, but priests have been insulted and defamed. There is a vast American literature about the iniquities of the Papacy, the immoralities of convents, and the perversities of Catholic doctrine. By comparison with it the anti-Jewish output is decidedly mild. Indeed, Christians have rather generally been prone to consider the religion of Judaism socially valuable. Practically none of them know what it is, but they have a vague feeling that a person who goes to the synagogue and eats *kosher* food is not likely to be anti-social.

Accordingly, I like to insist that the Jewish experience in the United States is like every other immigrant group experience. This does not mean that it has been or is tending to become easy. We must bear in mind that we have absolutely no assurance that as a nation we shall emerge from the epic of immigration without a major inter-group conflict. It is, for instance, still possible that the Catholic-Protestant antithesis may some time enkindle violence, or that anti-Semitism may run through the land like fire. The fate of Japanese-Americans during the present war is a pretty somber indication of what Americans can do if they get a chance. Tens of thousands of citizens have been stripped of every right and every opportunity, despite the fact that military leaders demonstrably saw no necessity for what was done. In short, I view the Jewish situation in our midst as always dangerous, but I shall not concede that it is dangerous for private or esoteric reasons.

The Jew is different. The Catholic is different. The Protestant is different. Some persons who aver that the Jew is unpopular everywhere and that there must be some good reason for that unpopularity forget that in a popularity contest they themselves would run a good chance of defeat. Catholics have been driven underground during my life-time in half a dozen countries. Hitler and Franco hate Protestants worse than poison. An Italian is about as popular in Austria as a stray alligator; the English do not like Frenchmen. East of the Rhine, the Jew has in all truth had a particularly tragic time. The persons alluded to above might be astonished to learn the real reasons why that is so. Far be it from me to minimize the tragedy, so many episodes of which I have myself witnessed. But it must be set in historical perspective side by side with the tragedy of the Pole, the Czech, the Ukrainian, the Armenian, and the Greek. To become pathological in one's attitude toward the Jewish experience is to offer the enemy what he wants.

These things having been said, we may venture to suggest quite tentatively that the Jewish "mind" in the United States does at the present time have its special malady. And its special recuperative power. I have no doubt that the principal reason why this is so is that the European background from which the Jewish immigrant emerged was not of one piece. And backgrounds are of sovereign importance. When the Pole thinks of his heritage, he has in mind a landscape identified with a certain kind of culture and with a given sequence of historical events. But when the Jew attempts to describe his past in Europe he must perforce fall back upon his own individual experience. He may visualize Jewish life in Vienna, and in so doing concentrate either upon matters which were specifically Jewish or upon matters which were generically Austrian. In either case, he will find it difficult to live himself into the mood of a Jew who migrated from Kiev or Warsaw. Therefore the Jewish "mind" is not, cannot be, settled or tranquil. It must attempt to achieve the communality which, for example, the French "mind" possesses as a matter of course. And so we are witnessing the great experiment of Zionism, with all that it is and implies.

It is true that it is difficult for an outsider to realize what Zionism means to the great majority of his Jewish fellow citizens. These themselves are far from being in agreement, some talking primarily of a "state" with political and social institutions like those to be found in Western countries, while others have in mind a view of life which (they hope) is slowly finding expression in Palestine. But after having listened to a great deal of comment on the subject, I feel that what my Jewish friends conceive of as Zionism can best be likened to the vision of the Church which haunted the mind of Francis of Assisi. He was not Dante, with a grandiose scheme of universal Catholic dominion. Instead the world was to him Umbria, or at least Italy; and he wanted to see mirrored in it the quest for beauty, naturalness, justice, and holiness as these were enshrined in the Christian tradition.

Is not Zionism, too, in its deepest essence a yearning for a place which will manifest to the Jew himself and to the world the virtues of the Jewish tradition? Its protagonists may not wish to be "orthodox" in aught else than the broad sense of fidelity to oneself. But little by little there does rise on the hallowed soil something like reverence incarnate—reverence for the spirit and the heart, the faith and the hopes, the impulses and convictions, the tragedy and the glory, of the Jewish people. I used to wonder in a quite materialistic way why Jews were willing to risk their means and their very persons in what seemed a dangerous gamble against the deep-rooted antipathies of the Near East. Now I know that it is not at all a gamble. Even if Zion should crumble into dust by reason of defeat or conquest, it will remain in history as an achievement and a discovery. The Jew will know always that in Jerusalem he found the Lord and himself.

In days when we of the non-Jewish world could afford to be superficial, we assumed that Jews were a sort of close-knit clan the members of which were sworn to support one another under all circumstances. Now we are prone, perhaps, to overestimate the differences between Jews. The Coughlinite sunders "believing" from "atheist" Jews. Others (of whom I shall confess to being one) are consciously or unconsciously given to putting Jews into various categories of a geographical or cultural kind. We catch ourselves wondering whether So-and-So is a Russian or a Polish

Jew. To some extent these tendencies are natural and are, perhaps, to be preferred to the older disposition to lump all members of the Jewish group together. But they are dangerous nonetheless, because they tempt us to ignore the unity of Judaism and to stress the disparity of nationalistic origins.

For me the unity as well as the genuine diversity of Judaism is the gift of the Synagogue. All else seems a legacy of bad science. Looking for Jewish sap in family trees in order to condemn the tree is just as futile and fatuous an operation, I think, as attempting to set up a community of Celts or Nordics. The traveler in modern Germany will have seen not a little of this endeavor. He will have noticed with amazement the effect of peroxide on feminine hair, and have read while his sides ached the racist speculations of Herr Walther Darré. When all is said and done, even the Nazis cannot prove Jewish blood from any other documents than birth certificates.

If your grandmother went to a Synagogue, you are a non-Aryan; if she went to Church, you are an Aryan. There is no other test even in Nazi genealogical science. True enough, some people "look Jewish." But I have seen a girl named Shapiro fail to get a job which she obtained fifteen minutes after she said her name was Sheridan. Please do not misunderstand me. Leaving the Synagogue is no way to get over being Jewish. Catholicism and Judaism have this in common, that it is frightfully difficult to wash one's hands of them. Hitler, despite all his dread apostasy, bears unmistakable traces of Christianity. The emancipated or apostate Jew (of whom there is no dearth, of course) betrays his origin in Judaism by every sentence he utters against it. Generations are needed to wipe out the Church or the Synagogue. And it seems to me, at least, that those generations peter out. Perhaps some different experience has been garnered in Russia under Communism, but what I have said certainly seems to hold true of the Western World.

Can we not say, then, that the unsettled Jewish "mind" is the product of varieties either of religion, or of the manifold cultures with which religion is associated, or of divergent ways in which Jewishness is stressed by those who seek to rid themselves of the tell-tale traces of the Synagogue? This unsettlement would matter relatively little if it did not coincide with the challenge of Hitler to the democratic and religious ideals of our world. To win out over him we must somehow forge unity of spirit and of purpose —unity of dedication to the personalist life. He knows that this is difficult to do, that his mechanized and mechanical pseudo-unity has a head start. He reckons with and foments Jewish unsettlement even as he does Christian unsettlement. Yes, he counts on Jewish disarray in order to achieve his ultimate aim, which is the dissolution and destruction of Christianity.

I am bold enough to believe that this Nazi objective will not be reached because, although Hitler estimated very shrewdly the effect of the blow he would strike at Judaism, he failed to measure the recuperative powers of Judaism. But those powers are in all truth extraordinary. When the story of the European Jew face to face with Hitler is written some day, it will have much to relate of weakness and bad judgment, but it will have much more to tell of really incredible strength. And here in the United States Judaism has profited intellectually and spiritually by the menace. It is far stronger and healthier today than it was in 1930. I am sure that nearly every Christian who has made an honest effort to observe developments feels that. There is new life in Jewish institutions. The significance of the Jewish tradition is daily being revealed anew. Emotion is giving way to intelligence, and emotion is always the sign which betrays unsettlement. There are great rabbis in American Israel today. There are great writers and scholars. There are splendid young people.

Above all, there are Jewish institutions. In the United States living is not enriched by the diversity of dialect, costume and domestic arts which keeps regionalism alive in Europe and (alas) prepares the soil on which national cleavages thrive. With us stale and unprofitable monotony is overcome by reason of the fact that each immigrant group brings to maturity forms of activity and thought—whether in worship or discussion, artistic endeavor or community expression—which are properly its own. Thus Anglo-Saxon New England has conserved its town meeting and its free universities, its village commons and its omnipresent consciousness of the sea. The Pennsylvania German cultural landscape is as unmistakably individual as is the farm-dotted river valley which these Germans turned into home. And surely we see emerging from many efforts a recognizable Jewish American communal life. The Synagogues are, to anyone who knows them, hearths beside which the spirits of men and women find comfort and healing, strength and challenging courage. Much hard work has created the American Jewish school, the greatest achievement of which to date is perhaps the saving of the Hebrew language and literature. But to an outsider, who must perforce speak of all such matters diffidently, knowing that his knowledge is too slight to be of any value, the foremost of American Jewish institutions is the home. That is precious because it is simple and genuine. I never see a Jewish home but I think of Proverbs, that wisest and mellowest of all the Books of the Old Testament. By comparison with those riches, what does it matter whether Jews are not wanted in some clubs and hotels? Or that some colleges have quotas? Or that some Jews—like some Christians—are rotters? To be sure, nobody can guarantee the safety of any minority even in America. But I think the Jew can now begin to breathe more easily than some other groups can, for there are clear signs that, come what may, he will save his soul.

I deem it a privilege to have contributed to this book because I believe it one such sign. It is self-searching and generous. It has vision. We cannot ask more of any book or any people.

THE NATIONAL BEING AND THE JEWISH COMMUNITY

—

Horace M. Kallen

I AM asked to make an "evaluation of American Jewish living." This is a peculiarly disagreeable and thankless task for a Jew, far more trying than simply to "look at the record," to describe and to analyze, and to draw a "composite portrait," as do the authors of this book. That, naturally, delineates the healthy inwardness of "Jewish living" in the United States. It calls attention also, as it should, to certain "evaluations of Jewish living" which premise considerable doubt of the value of "Jewish living" whether as something in itself and for itself, or as a cause having consequences to the living of people who are not Jews. Such "evaluations" assume a certain duress upon the Jew to justify his existence and thus question, if they do not challenge, his right to exist. Among individuals, potential suicides have such an attitude toward themselves; they are persons whose lives are so burdened, insecure and fear-ridden, that they have to argue themselves into keeping up the struggle to live rather than flee anywhere, even to death, for relief. They know what they do not want; but they do not know what they want. As consequence, instead of simply living and growing, they are constantly examining themselves, "evaluating." Jews, since the Emancipation, have evinced a con-

siderable propensity toward such self-examination and self-justifi-
cation both in their private lives and as members of their Jewish
communities, the inclination increasing with distance from the
psychic center and nearness to the psychic boundaries of "Jewish
living." The more marginal the Jew—that is, the greater the number and variety of his relationships, actual and probable with non-
Jews—the greater his feeling of insecurity and his urge to "evaluate" his existence as Jew; the more deeply aware he is of "the
Jewish problem." He may think of himself as merely the innocent
victim of anti-Semitism through "the accident of birth" and refuse
all other connection with his fellow Jews; he may associate himself
with "Jewish living" in any higher degree, from contributing to
Jewish philanthropies, membership in a Jewish social club, membership in a reform congregation, membership in an orthodox
congregation, membership in a Jewish fraternal order or other
definitely Jewish secular association, membership in a Zionist unit,
membership in the American Jewish Congress, to full participation, via all the forms of consent and dissent, in the entire institutional organization of Jewish interests. Whatever his degree of
participation, he will be disposed to seek justification for his
Jewishness as his relationships with non-Jews widen and multiply;
more than a member of any other community, he will feel a com-
pulsion to "evaluate."

Many, by no means reconcilable, explanations are offered for this
state of things. The basic one, which seems to me alone indicated
by the record, is sometimes denied and usually ignored, belittled
or glossed over by emphasis on derivative, on secondary and occasional causes. This is the effect on Jewish relations due to the
singular and universal meaning of the word *Jew* everywhere in
the Christian world. This meaning does not come from what
actual Jews actually are, from what they actually do or say, or
from where and how they live. It is the same where actual Jews
are entirely unknown and where Jews are well-known; where
there are no Jews whatever, and where there are millions. Indeed where Jews are numerous and are well-known, direct

experience tends to modify this meaning which is the same for rich and poor, for educated and unlearned, for masses and classes. It sets men in certain attitudes toward persons to whom the word *Jew* is applied. So long as such persons are called Poles, Czechs, Texans, Russians, Belgians, Scots or what have you, no particular emotion is aroused and no fixed denotation is communicated. The plain people of the Christian world might not even know what those words stood for. But call the very same Poles or Czechs or Texans *Jew* and they are shut out and cut off; the epithet draws an emotional ring around them; it bounds them as a "minority" and in feeling permanently excludes them from and stands them against "the majority." The feeling may be expressed in overt acts or it may not. The material and spiritual conclusion to which it is the premise are the notorious Nuremberg laws; its initiation is the system of Christian beliefs, acquired in childhood, regarding the origin, the nature and the destiny of man in which the idea *Jew* has a leading role. As Pastor Martin Niemöller declared in a sermon designed to insult the Nazis with the deadly insult of identifying them with Jewry, the Jewish people "bears a curse throughout the history of the world . . . because it rejected Him [Christ] and resisted Him to the death . . . the Jews brought the Christ of God to the Cross."*

Among all Christian sects which are open to the influences of the philological, historical and social sciences, the dogma embodied in these expressions is undergoing revision. But the process has not yet reached the point of dissipating the sentiment of discomfort and aversion which the word *Jew* arouses in general Christian usage. Psychologically, it has the same effect as a direct perception

---

* Niemöller, Martin, *Here Stand I,* Chicago, 1937. See also Gilmour, Right Rev. Richard, Bishop of Cleveland, *Bible History,* New York, 1881; Schuster, Ignatius, *Illustrated Bible History of the Old and New Testaments,* St. Louis and London, 1912; Hart, Rev. Charles, *A Shorter Bible History,* New York, 1920. For the sources, growth and employment of the dogma, consult Parkes, James, *The Conflict of the Church and the Synagogue,* London, 1934; Campbell, W. A., *The Crucifixion and Resurrection of Jesus,* London, 1933; *The Cornerstone of Christianity,* La Salle, Ill., 1938; Gibbon, Edward, *The Decline and Fall of the Roman Empire,* London, 1788, Chapter XV; Moehlmann, Conrad H., *The Christian-Jewish Tragedy,* Rochester, N. Y., 1933.

of skin color or other traits of "race"—this even among pundits who know well enough that no scientific anthropologist can regard the Jews as a race. Thus a midwestern psychologist named J. F. Brown permits himself to write: "Almost every one can clearly differentiate . . . between a Negro and a white Indo-European and even between a white European and a Jew."* Such notions are projections of motor-sets established in childhood; not observations, not facts, but unconscious prejudices formulated in stereotyped ideological fictions. When such fictions are given a logical form which rationalizes the prejudice without identifying it as a prejudice, all sorts of secondary explanations are drawn into the rationalizations: race, manners, conduct, economics, politics. Now one is made the base, and now another, and in each case an argument is developed which regularly proves that the Jew is the source of whatever trouble a society encounters. So easy is it to arouse and to mobilize the avertive sentiment attached to the word *Jew* that Jews continue to be the cheapest and most available scapegoats in Christian history.

"My Jews," said Hitler to Rauschning, "are a valuable hostage given me by the democracies. Anti-Semitic propaganda in all countries is an almost indispensable medium for the extension of our political campaign. You will see how little time we shall need in order to upset the ideas and the criteria of the whole world, simply by attacking Judaism." In *Mein Kampf* he wrote, "In the year 1918 there was absolutely no systematic anti-Semitism . . . Only very slowly did things begin to turn for the better. Unsuccessful as was our Guard and Watch League, its service in again opening up the Jewish Problem was great nevertheless. Later, the National Socialists transformed the Jewish Problem into the ruling passion of our great nationalist movement." Events have shown that Hitler's judgment was not wrong. Everywhere, consistently, anti-Semitism has proved an effective "Christian front" for the assault on democracy. Hitler, as Lord Davies wrote

* *Psychology and the Social Order*, New York, 1936, p. 122.

some time ago in *The Manchester Guardian,* has chosen to make
the Jewish people his special target, to identify the Jews with
democracy and democracy with the Jews: he and his crew never
stop prating about "degenerate Jewish democracy." They have
made the Jewish people, as Lord Davies said, "the personification
of the issues involved in this world-struggle." This is the greatest
honor which the Jews have received from friend or foe since
Christianity was established as the prevailing religion of the
Western World.

II

Nor are the enemies of democracy mistaken in making their
assault upon the Jews the spearhead of their assault upon democracy. At the time democracy came into effective being, with
the American and the French Revolutions, the Jews of the world
were in fact living shut out and cut off legally, physically, socially
and spiritually. The ghetto walls were the physical embodiment
of the psychological alienation of Christian from Jew, which kept
the Jews immutably an excluded "minority" and permitted no
Jew to be a neighbor, no neighbor to be a Jew. The rise and
growth of democracy did not, because they could not, put an end
to the psychological alienation, but did make its embodiment in
the structure of society more and more difficult, and its expression in human relations less and less substantial or approvable.
The democratic principle is that Jews can be neighbors, neighbors
can be Jews. The democratic faith opened the gates of the ghetto
that had locked the Jews in and shut them out for thirteen centuries. And during the one hundred and fifty years between 1791,
when the National Assembly of the French voted equal liberty for
all the Jews of France, and 1941, when the fascist "Christian"
government of France imposed Hitler's Nuremberg laws upon
the French, the generations of the Jews of the world have been so
identified with the struggle for liberty that they have become,

according to Mr. Stanley High,* the very incarnation of the spirit of liberty and therefore have every tyrant for their enemy.

Be this as it may, in terms of the inner life of Jews and Jewry, liberty had far from an identical meaning. To many sensitive and articulate spirits, of whom Moses Mendelssohn was the early type, the roads it opened seemed to be all away, and if he himself did not wander far, his children and his children's children did. Willy-nilly his "evaluations" pointed to the Jewish being as the misfortune which Heine called it: the road to freedom was a road of flight; the road of conversion, of reform, of ignoring and forgetting, thus changing oneself from a Jew to a "non-Aryan"; then of a bitter hatred of the Judaism which one reformed or was converted from, or ignored and forgot; and finally an irrepressible animosity against those who would not or could not flee the disaster of being Jews and therein remain somehow so different from their neighbors that the latter refuse to accept them for neighbors. The whole purpose of freedom became to abolish the difference. The end and means of democracy was to be assimilation; whatever else "Americanization" might mean, it would mean the disappearance of the Jew as Jew. His existence cannot be justified. There is nothing in Judaism whose survival is worth the struggle. "We do not want, we do not need, to perpetuate the Jewish Problem," these Jews assure their fellow-citizens. "In truth we are in no way different from you, and if you give us a chance you shall see all the seeming differences disappear, and us as like you as if there had never been any Jews in the world. Not we, but the Jews who persist in their Jewishness make the Jewish Problem. If they did not struggle as they do to survive as Jews, there would not be any problem. . . . We assure you that we understand full well that the task of the minority is to dissolve itself in the majority."† Surer of what they do not want

---

* High, Stanley, "Jews, Anti-Semites and Tyrants," *Harper's Magazine,* June, 1942.
† The latest exposition of this typical attitude from an authoritative pen is "Red, White and Blue Herring," by Judge Jerome Frank, the *Saturday Evening Post,* December 6, 1941.

than of what they want, such Jews do not inquire, who, what, is "the majority" in which they hope to lose themselves.

To this question there is one answer whose moral and political significance is peculiarly symptomatic of the times. It is an answer which accepts the fundamentalist Christian interpretation of the Jewish being and rejects the tempering of that interpretation which is due to science and democracy. According to the answer, nothing can ever diminish anti-Semitism. It has a permanent case against the Jews of our own times. In seeking the fellowship of the men of these times, the wicked times of science and of democracy, the Jews more than ever reject God and betray man. Because of the democratic liberties of the body and soul of man, the world has abandoned faith and piety for free thought and scientific method, the works of the Lord for mechanical skills and machine production, the scarcities of the spiritual life which were the glory of the Middle Ages, for the economy of abundance in thoughts and things which is the degradation of our own time. Thus the western world is given over to unrighteousness, materialism and corruption. The Jews, in turning from the fasts and the fastness of the ghetto to these fleshpots of freedom, have turned more than ever from God to ungodliness. They have taken on the age's materialism and corruption and improved upon them; they have become the most debased of moderns, who reject God, do unrighteously and corrupt commerce, youth and art. Spiritually and materially they would be safe, if not saved, in the ghetto.*

* This "evaluation of Jewish living" has recently received wide publicity in the *Saturday Evening Post* of March 28, 1942. The author is a Jew himself said to have found salvation, not in the ghetto he recommends, but in the fashionable neo-Thomism of the day. See Mayer, Milton, "The Case Against the Jews." For an exposition of the animus against science and democracy which this article rationalizes, see Hook, Sidney, "Milton Mayer: Fake Jeremiah," in *The New Leader*, April 4, 1942. For the actual *facts* regarding the impact of American Jews on the political and moral economy of the nation, see the *Fortune* magazine study, *Jews in America*, New York, 1936; Roth, Cecil, *Jewish Contributions to Civilization*, Cincinnati, 1940; Ross, Irwin, "Labor, Capital and Co.," *Harper's Magazine*, May, 1942; Healy, W., and Bronner, A. F., *Delinquents and Criminals*, New York, 1926; Illinois Crime Survey, *The Juvenile Delinquent*, Chicago, 1929; High, Stanley, "Jews, Anti-Semites and Tyrants," in *Harper's Magazine*, June, 1942; Kallen, H. M., *Culture and Democracy in the United States*, New York, 1924; *Judaism at Bay*, New York, 1932; "National Solidarity and the Jewish Minority," *The*

With very little addition, this "evaluation" might also be Hitler's, or that of any totalitarian dictator who employs anti-Semitism as the spearhead of his attack against human freedom, and possesses, as Sidney Hook showed, all the logical and moral stigmata of the totalitarian propaganda. Although it has a similarity to certain extreme forms of Judaist fundamentalism, its premise is a hatred of Judaism and its conclusion is a flight from it. Like its opposite, it postulates the elimination of the Jew from contact with the modern world, but by psychic segregation instead of assimilation.

III

That no American can accept such an evaluation of the national being goes without saying. That, if he is truly American, he must reject both the segregationist and assimilationist evaluation of the Jewish—or for that matter, any other—community's part in the national being, is not so naturally obvious, but logically just as inevitable. It is not so naturally obvious, because there often obtains among Americans a certain confusion of mind as to what the nation's being truly is, and how majorities and minorities are related to one another in the national life. Only when we have a clear and distinct idea of their dynamic in the doctrine and discipline constituting the American way of life can we rightly evaluate "American Jewish living."

Now so far as the American way is a doctrine, that is, a system of beliefs on which conduct is postulated and justified, we have it in a comparatively few documents such as the Declaration of Independence and the Constitution, Lincoln's Gettysburg Address, Emancipation Proclamation and Second Inaugural, Washington's Farewell Address, Jefferson's First Inaugural. These are the outstanding books of the Bible of America. They figure most frequently in the school texts, they are the most widely quoted and ceremonially read. They are the vehicles of the American faith.

Annals of the American Academy of Political and Social Science, Philadelphia, September, 1942.

The future is likely to add to the list Woodrow Wilson's addresses defining the American purpose in the first World War and Franklin Roosevelt's, defining American purposes in the second World War.

The propositions of the Declaration of Independence are the postulates upon which all the later affirmations rest. To understand the ideal of human relations which these propositions are intended to convey, it is necessary to remember that, when the Declaration was made, the world was everywhere caste-dominated and class-ruled; that some men were free, but most were serfs and slaves; that some ways of life and thought were privileged; that all who differed from the privileged were penalized solely because they were different; that the ideal and the law were conformity and submission to the ruling powers in faith, in morals, in politics, in study, in occupation, and in all similar matters; that those who failed to conform were degraded, shut out and cut off, existing on sufferance instead of by right; that the Jews were of all the variant groups in the countries of the Western World, the most completely shut out and cut off.

To this state of things the Declaration enters an absolute and final *non possumus*. In affirming that *all* men are created equal, and that the rights of *all* to life, liberty and the pursuit of happiness are *unalienable,* it accepts human beings as they are, with all the variety and multiplicity of faith, of race, of sex, of occupations, of ideas, of possessions; and it affirms the equal right of these different people freely to struggle for existence and for growth in freedom and in happiness as different. It repudiates the presumption that any individual or society may demand of the neighbor a justification of the latter's existence. Emerson expressed this repudiation in another way when he declared: "As long as any man exists there is some need of him: let him fight for his own." The American way of life, then, may be said to flow from each man's unalienable right to be different, as this is enchanneled in the American Constitution, especially the Bill of Rights and the subsequent Amendments. If these forbid Congress to make certain laws, they forbid Congress to penalize difference.

The discipline which gives to this doctrine of equal liberty for different people body and movement as a way of life, an organization of doing, feeling and thinking, operates in the political order as equal suffrage regardless of faith, occupation, race or sex, as the base of government of the people, for the people, by the people: in the economic order as free enterprise: in religion as freedom of conscience: in the arts and sciences as freedom of inquiry, research and expression: in education, as the free public school from kindergarten to the university; and throughout these domains of the common life in freedom of association into sects, parties, corporations, trades unions, fraternal orders and whatever other groupings individual Americans choose to come together in. Each such group, if it be reasonably stable, tends to form, within the framework of the national being, a doctrine and discipline singular to itself, with its own characteristic vocabulary and habits of speech and song; its own tradition of competency, heroism, legend and tale; its own architecture, suitable to its purpose and function; its own preferred diet; its own ceremonial occasions and forms of play. That which interests a New Englander in New York, a New Yorker in Florida, a Floridian in Chicago, a Chicagoan in Texas, a Texan in the Northwest, the Northwesterner in New England, are these characteristic differences which make one region important to another. But occupational groups, like, say, the doctors and the lawyers and the teachers, the carpenters and the machinists and the plumbers, the musicians, the stockbrokers, the bankers and the actors, also develop and maintain the characteristic differentiae which identify them as a group—in the Middle Ages they were often called Nations—and which constitute the cultures of their group. These differentiae cross all boundaries, so that American doctors, for example, may as doctors have more in common with doctors in China or England or Russia than with men of other occupations in America; American painters and musicians *qua* painters and musicians may have more interests in common with musicians and painters in Mexico or India or Norway or Brazil than with floorwalkers or clergymen or what have you in the United States. And so on, to any organization of a group interest that can be named, including that of the national interest itself. For the nation obviously has more interests in common with democracies abroad than with organizations inimical to democracy at home.

Now the national being rests upon the co-operative and competitive relationships of these voluntary associations and consists in the free trade of goods and services between them. Their connecting links are their members. While each association—be it a state, a region, an occupation, a religious or cultural community, etc.—is an autonomous culture-complex with a way of being singular to itself, any or every member of the association is, as a rule, also a member of a good many others. The member of the Bar or of a Tradesunion is at the same time a citizen, a member of a family, a church, a political party, a fraternal order, a social club, a consumer society, an alumni association, a patriotic, a philanthropic, an athletic, a burial or other society. Each is a different way of his being together with other people. He is the bond which unites the societies with one another. His relation to each varies in firmness and intensity. Some, like those to his father and mother, are not easily dissolved; others are loose and tenuous; but ultimately all are voluntary, and like his citizenship result from his choice and rest on his consent. The freer the social order in which he lives, the smoother and simpler is his movement in and through the associations which combine into this order. His relations are not fixed by status; they are not coerced to any inevitable sequence or hierarchy, but are liquid and mobile. This mobility of relationships is what gives its characteristic quality to the national living. Of this quality the consummation is Cultural Pluralism. For its diverse and ever-diversifying members are united with one another in and through their differences, and the singularity of our culture is the orchestration of those manifold differences—*e pluribus unum*—into the common faith which makes Liberty the foundation of Union, Union the guarantee of Liberty, and Democracy the fusion of the two in the common way of life.*

Where this fusion tends to be efficacious and consequential, "majority" and "minority" have neither the fixity of form nor the continuity of existence which we are disposed to expect from our having used these expressions in connection with religious and cultural groups. It is exactly the overthrow of such fixations and permanencies that the Democratic Revolution won, and it is precisely the restoration of such invidious status that the Nazis and the Fascists have murderously accomplished. In their Servile State they permit parts but no parties. Whether in politics, economics, religion, science or culture, they war upon the right to be different; the differences they cannot destroy they degrade and penalize. Free societies, on the other hand, know that the free interaction of differences is the surest way to right and truth, and they make discussion and division the instrument of decision. Consequently, "majority" and "minority" mean to free men associative and functional relationships of groups and individuals, not constitutive organs of unchanging societies. When you take together *all* the people who are *"we the people"* as one Association, any and every lesser combination of the people, no matter how large, is a minority, and "we the people" is but the orchestration of such minorities into the singularity of the national being. Every individual by himself alone is a "minority"; every association of individuals by itself alone is a "minority." A "majority" comes into existence only as the combination of such

---

* See Kallen, H. M., *Culture and Democracy in the United States*. Hoskins, Harold B.: "American Unity and Our Foreign Born Citizens," *The Annals*, March, 1941: "As many speakers and writers have begun to suggest, our American ideal should not be expressed in terms of a 'melting pot' with its somewhat mournful implication of uniformity, but rather in terms of an orchestra, in which each racial group, like an orchestral choir, contributes its special different tone to the rich ensemble of the whole." P. 158.

"minorities." But the combination is meaningful as a "majority" alone in relation to some particular interest or issue about which there has been discussion and which has been decided by division. It always remains open to the "minority," to endeavor to win so many members of the majority to its point of view as to convert "the minority" into "the majority." Where there is no issue to be decided, "majority" and "minority" are either meaningless or carry a totalitarian implication.

Obviously there can be no sense in speaking of "the medical minority" or "the dancer minority" or the "baker minority" except in relation to a division of "we the people" on an issue calling for decision by all. So, when the experts speak about "the Jewish minority" they may mean that non-Jews are more numerous than Jews, which is no news; they may mean that in a division on an issue the Jews as Jews stand alone, which is news but not true; they may mean that groups whose members are small and powers few are somehow inferior and have no rights which groups consisting of larger numbers need respect. This expresses a point of view that had been general before the Democratic Revolution; it recurs not infrequently among democrats, and is a prime dogma of tyrannical societies which democracies must combat with all their hearts and strength.* Such a meaning of "minority" reveals nothing about the doctrine, the discipline and the dynamic import of "Jewish living" for the national being. These are as unrelated to size as is the practice of medicine or any other art to the avoirdupois of the practitioner. They are variable configurations of passions, principles and aspirations nourished upon custom, upon tradition, and upon education, and implemented in an economy which ranges from birth to burial and diet to divinity, and is embodied as a going concern in an indefinite number of varying associations whose emulative rivalries take the form of a

---

* "For it is evident that no democracy can long survive which does not accept as fundamental to its very existence the recognition of the rights of its minorities." Franklin D. Roosevelt to the National Association for the Advancement of Colored People, June 25, 1938.

number of struggles to win a majority in the Jewish group. The conflicts and agreements of these struggles emerge in the Jewish press and literature, in the Yiddish and Hebrew and sometimes in the English theater and concert hall, over the radio, in the culture of the *kosher* kitchen, in the theological resultants of sectarian controversy, in the forms of philanthropy, in the confrontation of Zionists and anti-Zionists, "Congress" and "Committee," and the like. Within the boundaries drawn by anti-Semitism, participation in this Jewish living is voluntary. Those abandon it who will, those share in it who desire. And it is likely that, because of the challenge of anti-Semitism, the sharer's is the braver, hence happier part; at least, he chooses to affirm and to defend his integrity, and as a man and a citizen to vindicate the equal liberty of his Jewish difference. Certainly this is more consonant with the national being alike as doctrine and as discipline. They establish the existence and freedom of this difference as unalienable right, equal with that of non-Jews, calling for neither apology nor justification. Even without fruitful consequences to the common life, the mere fact that it is there, that it is one more variety in the dynamic whole, is, like the addition of another taste or sight or sound, an enrichment, a contribution to abundance, spiritual and material. If against the assimilationist the American spirit affirms the right to be different, against the segregationist it affirms the right of free association of the different with one another. But it points also to a certain prior community of the Jewish group with the national being. This community is established in and through the Old Testament, which contributes so largely to the singularity of the Jewish psyche: Lecky wrote that "the Hebraic mortar cemented the foundations of American democracy."* But furthermore, the Jewish community, like every other composing the national being, serves as a psychological locale for voluntary social experimentation, for invention and discovery, as such, in-

* *History of Rationalism in Europe*, II, p. 168.

volving more limited risks than a nation-wide adventure would. Thus the Jewish locale has been an area of trial and error in employer-employee relations, in philanthropy, in education, in literature and in the arts. What was started in the Yiddish theaters of the East Side more than once was perfected—or corrupted—on Broadway; what began as a protocol on relations between Jewish employers and Jewish employees on women's wear, has become the initiating precedent in the national growth toward industrial democracy; what began as an effort to help immigrant "coreligionists" cheaply and efficiently, has contributed to the formation of the theory and practice of scientific charity, and so on. And it is not possible to call these developments more an Americanization of Jewry—even of the Jewry of Palestine—than an enrichment of the American way by Jewish contributions. "American Jewish living" makes an impression of a healthy symbiosis with the diverse other forms of living whose interaction orchestrates the Union we call America, and whose combined utterance is the American spirit. Like its neighbors, the community of Jewish living has a character of its own, a singularity which works as a reservoir and a breeding place of the Jewish difference. This its men and women of genius carry beelike from the nest which nurtured them to the national scene, there to serve as a fertilizing contribution to the commonwealth of things and ideals. Louis Brandeis and Ben Cardozo; David Lubin, Nathan Straus and Julius Rosenwald; Sidney Hillman and David Dubinsky; Emma Lazarus; Robert Nathan and Sholem Asch; Edna Ferber and Gertrude Stein; George Kaufmann, Elmer Rice, Clifford Odets, S. N. Behrmann; Aaron Copland and George Gershwin; Leon Kroll, Maurice Sterne, Max Weber, William Gropper—I mention only a few of the long lists of jurists and business men, playwrights, composers, painters, tradesunionists, who are figures of my lifetime. There are many others, in every walk of life—virtuosos and inventors, physicians and architects, chemists and psychologists, merchants, engineers, whom *Who's Who* counts—all children or grandchildren of a ghetto that has ceased to be a ghetto because its walls have been breached and its gates opened, so that the life of the nation flows through it, and its life flows and mingles in the national stream, in a confluence where the free flow of each is the expanding life of both.

So I close my "evaluation of American Jewish living." I have not studied to make it either "judicial" or "scholarly." I have been concerned first and last to set down the ideals which any evaluation I could make would have to use for measure, and to signalize what, in terms of the national being, these measures of the Jewish community would come to. I have done so. What I have said can be valid only for those Americans whose faith in democracy is a fighting faith, and for those American Jews who are resolved to stand up in the armies of democracy as the democratic faith requires, freely and boldly as Jews.

SELECTED BIBLIOGRAPHY

Daly, Charles P., *The Settlement of the Jews in North America* (edited by M. J. Kohler), New York, 1893.

Very good descriptive material on early American Jewish history.

Elzas, Barnett A., *The Jews of South Carolina*, Philadelphia, 1905.

Ezekiel, H. T., and Lichtenstein, G., *The History of the Jews of Richmond, Va.*, Richmond, 1917.

Gutstein, Morris, A., *The Story of the Jews of Newport: 1658-1908*, New York, 1936.

Good examples of serious history of local Jewish communities.

Friedman, Lee M., *Early American Jews*, Cambridge, Mass., 1934.

Interesting biographical material on a considerable number of American Jews, chiefly of the seventeenth and eighteenth centuries.

Joseph, Samuel, *Jewish Immigration in the United States from 1881 to 1910*, New York, 1914.

Analysis of the causes and course of Jewish immigration from Eastern Europe.

Lebeson, Anita L., *Jewish Pioneers in America: 1492-1848*, New York, 1931.

The author is well acquainted with the sources, and the copious excerpts included in the volume help reproduce the atmosphere of early Jewish life in the United States.

Levinger, Lee J., *A History of the Jews in the United States*, Cincinnati, 1930.

Good elementary introduction to the history of the Jews in the United States.

Linfield, Harry S., *Statistics of Jews: 1931*, New York, 1931.

———, "Jewish Communities of the United States: Number and Distribution of Jews of the United States in Urban Places and in Rural Territory," *The American Jewish Year Book*, Vol. 42 (5701), Philadelphia, 1940, pp. 215-266.

———, "The Jewish Population of the United States," *The American Jewish Year Book*, Vol. 43 (5702), Philadelphia, 1941, pp. 654-673.

The most exhaustive and most dependable statistical estimates of Jews in the United States, prepared by Dr. Harry S. Linfield, who has served as Special Agent of the United States Census Bureau and conducted, in 1926 and 1936, the part of the United States Census of Religious Bodies dealing with the Jews.

Sachar, Abram Leon, *A History of the Jews*, revised edition, New York, 1940.

Sachar, Abram Leon, *Sufferance Is the Badge*, New York, 1939.

Each book contains a well-written chapter on American Jewish history.
Wiernik, Peter, *History of the Jews in America*, New York, 1931.

Particularly helpful for an understanding of the East European Jews.
Wolf, Simon, *The American Jew as Patriot, Soldier and Citizen*, Philadelphia, 1895.

Contains information on Jewish participation in the armed forces of the
United States. For the first World War, see Leavitt, Julian, "American
Jews in the World War," *The American Jewish Year Book*, Vol. 21
(5680), Philadelphia, 1919, pp. 141-155.

Chapter II—Judaism and the Synagogue

The references for Chapter II and Chapter IX are closely related and have
therefore been combined. See Bibliography for Chapter IX.

Chapter III—Jewish Education—Achievements and Needs

Berkson, Isaac B., *Theories of Americanization*, New York, 1920.

A discussion of the problem of the cultural adjustment of minority groups
in the United States on the basis of a philosophy of democracy, with
special reference to the Jewish group. Proposes the Community Theory
of Adjustment, and presents a program and curriculum for a Jewish
community school center.
Chipkin, Israel S., *Twenty-Five Years of Jewish Education in the United
States*, New York, 1937.

A brief, inclusive statement of the progress made in Jewish education
during the last generation. States the main facts of organization and
attendance, and describes the major types of schools and educational
tendencies.
Dinin, Samuel, *Judaism in a Changing Civilization*, New York, 1933.

A broad survey of the various theories of Jewish life and survival, both
religious and cultural, and of democratic conceptions of adjustment to
American life. Application is made to the problem of creating an
American Jewish school curriculum along socially progressive lines.
Dushkin, Alexander M., *Jewish Education in New York City*, New York,
1918.

The first comprehensive analysis of the Jewish educational situation in
the United States. A source for the history and development of Jewish
education and the early work of the Bureau of Jewish Education.

Gamoran, Emanuel, *Changing Conceptions of Jewish Education,* New York, 1924.

A study in the problem of Jewish educational adjustment, with emphasis on the content of instruction and Jewish values. Contains a discussion of the principles of a Jewish curriculum in America.

Kaplan, Mordecai, M., "The Meaning of Jewish Education in America," in *Judaism as a Civilization,* New York, 1934, Chap. XXXI.

A statement of the function of the American Jewish school from the point of view of the reconstructionist conception of Jewish life as a rounded civilization. The main aims of Jewish education are discussed from the point of view of (1) participation in Jewish life; (2) understanding and appreciation of the Hebrew language and literature; (3) the practice of Jewish patterns of conduct, both ethical and religious; (4) the stimulation of artistic creativity in the expression of Jewish values.

Jewish Education.

This quarterly journal contains many useful articles. The following are especially recommended:

Brilliant, Nathan, "The Progressive Reform School," Oct.-Dec., 1935;

Dushkin, Alexander M., and Honor, Leo L., "Aims and Activities of Jewish Educational Organizations in America," Oct.-Dec., 1933;

Gamoran, Emanuel, "The Curriculum of the Future Jewish Sunday School," Jan.-Mar., 1933;

Golub, Jacob S., and Honor, Leo L., "Some Guiding Principles for the Curriculum of the Jewish School of Tomorrow," Oct.-Dec., 1932;

Kohn, Eugene, "Foundations of a Cultural Program of the Jewish Community," Jan.-Mar., 1936;

National Council for Jewish Education, "Re-evaluating Jewish School Curricula," January, 1924;

Neumann, Fannie R., "A Modern Jewish Experimental School—In Quest of a Synthesis," Jan.-Mar., 1932;

Nudelman, Edward A., "Outline of Curriculum of Chicago Jewish Sunday Schools," Apr.-June, 1934.

CHAPTER IV—THE CULTURAL SCENE: LITERARY EXPRESSION

Fleg, Edmond (ed.), *The Jewish Anthology* (*trans. by Maurice Samuel*), New York, 1933.

Selections in prose and verse from Jewish writers of twenty-five centuries.

Lazarus, Emma, *Poems of Emma Lazarus—2 volumes,* Boston, 1889.

Leftwich, Joseph (ed.), *The Golden Peacock,* Cambridge, Mass., 1939.

An anthology of Yiddish poetry translated into English. The largest number of the poets are Americans.

Lewisohn, Ludwig, *Israel,* New York, 1925.

A description of a journey to Palestine and a discussion of Zionism and allied problems.

———, *Rebirth: a book of modern Jewish thought,* New York, 1935.

Selections from the writings of significant Jewish thinkers edited by Ludwig Lewisohn.

Mersand, Joseph, *Traditions in American Literature,* New York, 1939.

A study of Jewish characters and authors in American literature from colonial times to the present day, with copious bibliographies.

Schwarz, Leo (ed.), *A Golden Treasury of Hebrew Literature,* New York, 1937.

A collection including short stories, plays, poetry and essays selected from Jewish authors of all countries, from Biblical times to the present. Many American writers are included.

———, *The Jewish Caravan: Great Stories of Twenty-five Centuries,* New York, 1935.

Chapter V—Hebrew in Jewish Culture

Bavli, Hillel, "The Growth of Modern Hebrew Literature," in Sampter, Jessie (ed.), *Modern Palestine,* New York, 1933, pp. 328-348.

The best brief account in English.

Engelman, U. Z., "The Strength of Hebrew in America," in *Menorah Journal,* March, 1929.

Katsh, Abraham I., *Hebrew in American Higher Education,* New York, 1941.

A statistical study with introductory chapters.

Lapson, Judah, "A Decade of Hebrew in the High Schools of New York City," in *Jewish Education,* April, 1941, pp. 34-45.

An excellent survey by one closely associated with the project.

Lewittes, M. H., "Hebrew Enters New York High Schools," in *Menorah Journal,* Spring, 1938.

Neumann, J. H., "American Literature in Hebrew," in *Menorah Journal,* December, 1917.

Raisin, J. S., *The Haskalah Movement in Russia,* Philadelphia, 1913.

Describes the rise of modern Hebrew literature and its social orientation.

Raskin, P. M., *Anthology of Modern Jewish Poetry,* New York, 1927.

Contains translations from Hebrew and Yiddish, as well as English poems.

Spiegel, Shalom, *Hebrew Reborn,* New York, 1930.

A very well written history of modern Hebrew literature from its beginnings to the period of the first World War.

Waxman, Meyer, *A History of Jewish Literature,* Vol. IV, New York, 1941. The most comprehensive history of Jewish literature in English. Contains summaries of the contents of many of the books described.

CHAPTER VI—STRUCTURE OF THE JEWISH COMMUNITY

Bernheimer, Charles S., "Jewish Americanization Agencies," in *The American Jewish Year Book,* Vol. 23 (5682), pp. 84-111.

Bogen, Boris D., *Jewish Philanthropy,* New York, 1917.

A history of Jewish charities and their organization.

"Community Councils, their Organization and Objectives," in *Proceedings* of the General Assembly of the Council of Jewish Federations and Welfare Funds, New York, 1938, pp. 34-54.

Engelman, Uriah Z., "Medurbia" (Buffalo, N. Y.), in *Contemporary Jewish Record,* August, 1941, pp. 339-348 and October, 1941, pp. 511-531.

Feibelman, Julian B., *A Social and Economic Study of the New Orleans Jewish Community,* Philadelphia, 1941.

Ginzberg, Eli, *Report to American Jews on Overseas Relief, Palestine and Refugees in the United States,* New York, 1942.

Hartford Communal Study Committee, *Hartford Jewish Communal Study, 1937-1938,* Hartford, 1938 (mimeo.).

Karpf, Maurice J., *Jewish Community Organization in the United States,* New York, 1938.

A standard work on types of organizations, activities, and problems.

Kohs, Samuel C., "Jewish Content in Jewish Social Work," in *The Jewish Social Service Quarterly,* September, 1936, pp. 99-113.

Kraft, Louis, "Goals of Jewish Community Organization," in *The Jewish Center,* March, 1939, pp. 2-7.

Mandelbaum, David G., "A Study of the Jews of Urbana," in *The Jewish Social Service Quarterly,* December, 1935, pp. 223-232.

Minneapolis Council of Social Agencies, *Minneapolis Jewish Communal Survey,* New York, 1936 (mimeo.).

Papo, Joseph M., "The Jewish Community of Duluth," in *The Jewish Social Service Quarterly,* December, 1941, pp. 219-231.

Robison, Sophia M., "Some Characteristics of Trenton and Passaic Jews. A Summary of a Report," in *Jewish Social Studies,* July, 1940, pp. 249-254.

Rontch, I. E., "The Present State of the Landsmanschaften," in *The Jewish Social Service Quarterly,* June, 1939, pp. 360-378.

Selekman, B. M., "Federation in the Changing American Scene," in *The American Jewish Year Book,* Vol. 36 (5695), pp. 65-87.

Taylor, Maurice, *The Jewish Community of Pittsburgh, December 1938,* Pittsburgh, 1941 (mimeo.).

Chapter VII—Economic Trends

Davidson, G., "The Jew in Agriculture in the United States," *The American Jewish Year Book,* Vol. 37 (5696), pp. 99-134.

Fagen, Melvin M., "The Status of Jewish Lawyers in New York City," *Jewish Social Studies,* Vol. 1, pp. 73-104.

"Fortune," Editors of, *Jews in America,* New York, 1936.

A series of articles on the participation of Jews in American economy.

Goldberg, Jacob A., "Jews in the Medical Profession—A national survey," *Jewish Social Studies,* Vol. 1, pp. 327-336.

Graeber, I., and Britt, S. H., *Jews in a Gentile World,* New York, 1942.

Chapter XV by Jacob Lestchinsky—a general discussion of the position of Jews in the economic life of America.

Chapter VIII by Samuel Koenig—a detailed analysis of the socio-economic structure of the Jewish community in Stamford, Conn.

Jewish Occupational Council, *Patterns of Jewish Occupational Distribution in the United States and Canada,* New York, 1940.

Levine, Louis, *The Women's Garment Workers,* New York, 1924.

An excellent detailed account of one of the most important segments of trade union organization among Jewish workers.

Levinger, Lee J., *The Jewish Student in America,* Cincinnati, 1937.

———, "Jews in the Liberal Professions in Ohio," *Jewish Social Studies,* Vol. 2, pp. 401-434.

Loft, Jacob, "Jewish Workers in the New York City Men's Clothing Industry," *Jewish Social Studies,* Vol. 2, pp. 61-78.

McGill, Nettie Pauline, "Some Characteristics of Jewish Youth in New York City," *The Jewish Social Service Quarterly,* Vol. 14, pp. 251-272.

Meyer, Henry J., "The Economic Structure of the Jewish Community in Detroit," *Jewish Social Studies,* Vol. 2, pp. 127-148.

Perlman, Selig, "Our Economic Arena," *Menorah Journal,* Vol. 22 (1934), pp. 1-12.

An analysis of current economic trends and their effects on Jewish life in America.

Rosen, Irwin, "Professional Careers for Jewish Youth," *The Jewish Social Service Quarterly,* Vol. 15, pp. 343-357.

Ruppin, Arthur, *The Jews in the Modern World,* London, 1934.

A general treatment of economic and social conditions of modern Jewry including some discussion of American Jewry.

Zubin, Joseph, *Choosing a Life Work,* Cincinnati: Commission on Jewish Education, Union of American Hebrew Congregations, 1937 (mimeo.).

A very detailed study of conditions in professions, especially as they affect Jewish youth. Contains a comprehensive bibliography.

CHAPTER VIII—ANTI-SEMITISM

Bernstein, Herman, *The Truth About "The Protocols of Zion,"* New York, 1935.

A thorough study of the notorious forgery.

Curtis, John S., *An Appraisal of the Protocols of Zion,* New York, 1942.

A scholarly analysis by a Gentile.

Graeber, I., and Britt, S. H., *Jews in a Gentile World,* New York, 1942.

Sociological approach to the problem of anti-Semitism. Especially valuable are several case histories of communities, and the excellent chapter by Miriam Beard: "Anti-Semitism—Product of Economic Myths."

Levinger, L. J., *Anti-Semitism in the United States,* New York, 1925.

Sociological analysis of anti-Semitic developments of the first World War period.

Lewisohn, Ludwig, *Upstream; An American Chronicle,* New York, 1922.

A sensitive account of the impact of social and cultural snobbery on a Jewish-born intellectual. A case history of a cosmopolitan spirit driven back to his cultural roots by anti-Semitism.

The New Universal Jewish Encyclopedia, see article on Anti-Semitism, Vol. I, pp. 341-410.

This gives a good account of the rise of modern anti-Semitism in the various countries, and gives very specific information about the prejudice organizations in the United States. Well illustrated.

Philipson, David (ed.), *Letters of Rebecca Gratz,* Philadelphia, 1929.

A good picture of Jewish life in America, covering the period 1808-1866. Also reveals pioneer work of prominent Jewish families in extension of the frontier.

Pinson, Koppel S. (ed.), *Essays on Anti-Semitism,* New York, 1942.

The analytical studies of Part II by Weinryb, Wechsler and Marcus are more directly trained on our problem and more helpful than the essays in the Graeber-Britt symposium.

Samuel, Maurice, *The Great Hatred*, New York, 1940.

An interesting attempt to explain anti-Semitism as a mass phobia resulting from the Gentile's maladjustment to Christianity, and the expression of this frustration by acts of aggression against the Christ-source—the Jews.

Stonequist, E. V., *The Marginal Man*, New York, 1937.

Very competent study of cultural conflicts leading to cultural hybridism, assimilation and self-hate, with good use of Jewish group for illustrative material.

Strong, Donald S., *Organized Anti-Semitism in America*, Washington, 1941.

Especially valuable for the study of 121 anti-Semitic organizations. The rise and fall of these groups are related to the major social developments in America.

Valentin, Hugo, *Anti-Semitism*, New York, 1936.

Probably the best book on the subject available in English.

Veblen, Thorstein, *The Theory of the Leisure Class*, New York, 1899.

A splendid exposition of the manner in which folk-ways and economics act upon each other and make for those invidious distinctions which are the stuff of prejudice.

CHAPTER IX—CURRENT PHILOSOPHIES OF JEWISH LIFE AND CHAPTER II—JUDAISM AND THE SYNAGOGUE

Agus, Jacob B., *Modern Philosophies of Judaism*, New York, 1941.

An account of several of the most significant contemporary Jewish theologies, including a full statement on Reconstructionism and a critique of it.

Eisenstein, Ira, *Creative Judaism*, New York, 1936.

A vivid and readable abstract and restatement of Kaplan's *Judaism as a Civilization*.

Friedlander, M., *The Jewish Religion*, 7th edition, London, 1937.

A presentation of Judaism from the viewpoint of Orthodoxy.

Gordis, Robert, *The Jew Faces a New World*, New York, 1941.

A series of essays treating with aspects of the contemporary Jewish problem from the point of view of conservative Judaism tinged with the reconstructionist attitude.

Hirsch, S. R., *The Nineteen Letters of Ben Uziel*, New York, 1899.

A statement of the orthodox position by one of the founders of modern Orthodoxy. First published in 1836.

Jung, Leo (ed.), *The Jewish Library*, 1st—3rd Series, New York, 1928-1930-1934; 4th Series, *Judaism in a Changing World*, New York, 1939.

A series of essays and articles on Jewish problems in the light of the orthodox position.

Kaplan, M. M., *Judaism as a Civilization*, New York, 1934.

A critique of all the current philosophies of Jewish life and the classical statement of the reconstructionist position.

Kohn, Eugene, *The Future of Judaism in America*, New Rochelle, 1934.

An analysis of modern Judaism in the light of the reconstructionist position.

Levinthal, Israel H., *Judaism, An Analysis and an Interpretation*, New York, 1935.

A series of essays on the contemporary Jewish problem from the point of view of conservative-to-orthodox interpretation.

Levy, Beryl H., *Reform Judaism in America*, New York, 1933.

A history and critical analysis of reform Judaism in America.

Philipson, David, *The Reform Movement in Judaism*, revised edition, New York, 1931.

A history of classical reform Judaism in America by one of its founders and first proponents.

Stern, Horace, "The Synagogue and Jewish Communal Activities," *The American Jewish Year Book*, Vol. 35 (5694), pp. 157-170.

CHAPTER X—ZIONISM IN AMERICAN JEWISH LIFE

De Haas, Jacob, *Louis Dembitz Brandeis*, New York, 1929.

This chief source book on Brandeis' development as a Zionist contains almost all his Zionist writings and addresses.

Doniger, S. (ed.), *A Zionist Primer*, New York, 1917.

An early and influential source book for American Zionists.

Labor Zionist Handbook, New York, 1939.

An introduction to Labor Zionism in America.

Lesser, Allen, "Emma Lazarus, Poet and Zionist Pioneer," in *Menorah Journal*, Spring, 1938, pp. 212-226.

Lewisohn, Ludwig, *Israel*, New York, 1925.

An American Jewish writer's pilgrimage from the background of assimilation in America, through Europe, to the new Palestine.

Lipsky, Louis, *Thirty Years of American Zionism*, New York, 1927.

Reminiscences by one of the leading figures in American Zionist history.

Lowenthal, Marvin, *Henrietta Szold, Life and Letters*, New York, 1942.

The development of American Zionism, of the Hadassah organization, and of the growing Palestinian community are mirrored in the eight decades of Henrietta Szold's rich and full life.

Rosenblatt, Samuel, *This Is the Land,* New York, 1940.

Presents the viewpoint of the religious Zionist movement in America.

Sampter, Jessie (ed.), *Modern Palestine,* New York, 1933.

A valuable symposium on Zionism in Europe and America and on the concrete realities of Palestine.

Shubow, Joseph S. (ed.), *The Brandeis Avukah Annual,* New York, 1932.

A collection of articles dealing with many phases of Zionist thought and history.

CONTRIBUTORS TO THIS VOLUME

I. B. Berkson has made notable contributions to Jewish and general education. Engaged for more than fifteen years in Jewish educational work in the United States, he was invited in 1928 to direct the Hebrew school system of Palestine. He served until 1935, and during 1931-1935, he was also a member of the Jewish Agency for Palestine. On his return to the United States, he directed the 1936 survey of Jewish education in New York City, made under a grant from the Friedsam Foundation. Dr. Berkson is the author of *Theories of Americanization; Preface to an Educational Philosophy;* and a forthcoming book entitled *Education Faces the Future.* He is Lecturer in Education at the College of the City of New York.

Margaret G. Doniger has been associated with Hadassah educational work for twenty years, and during the past five years she has served as chairman of the National Education Committee. During that time, her efforts have been directed toward broadening the scope of the educational program of Hadassah. This book is the result of those efforts.

Abraham G. Duker is editor in the Research Institute on Peace and Post-War Problems of the American Jewish Committee. He is associate editor of *The Reconstructionist* and associate chairman of the editorial board of *The Jewish Social Service Quarterly.* Until recently he was managing editor of the *Contemporary Jewish Record.* He is the author of *Jewish Survival in the World Today;* of *The Situation of the Jews in Poland;* and of articles which have appeared in the *Hebrew Union College Annual, Current History, Kirjath Sepher, Jiwo Bleter,* and the *Contemporary Jewish Record.*

Abraham S. Halkin is assistant professor of Hebrew at Brooklyn

College and instructor in Bible and Jewish History at the Teachers Institute of the Jewish Theological Seminary. He is the author of *Moslem Schisms and Sects;* of *Samaritan Polemics Against the Jews;* and of articles which have appeared in various journals.

Oscar I. Janowsky is associate professor of history at the College of the City of New York. He is the author of *The Jews and Minority Rights; People at Bay;* and (with Melvin M. Fagen) *International Aspects of German Racial Policies;* and of articles on minorities published in several books and periodicals.

Horace M. Kallen is professor of philosophy and psychology in the graduate faculty of the New School for Social Research in New York City. An outstanding authority in the fields of philosophy and psychology, he is one of the few Jews in American academic life who has actively concerned himself with Jewish problems and Jewish movements. Among his numerous books are, *The Philosophy of William James; Frontiers of Hope; Individualism, An American Way of Life; A Free Society; The Decline and Rise of the Consumer; Culture and Democracy in the United States; Why Religion; The Book of Job as a Greek Tragedy; Zionism and World Politics;* and *Judaism at Bay.* His new book, *Art and Freedom,* will be published in October, 1942.

David de Sola Pool is an outstanding figure in Jewish religious and communal life. He has been Rabbi of the Spanish and Portuguese Synagogue, *Shearith Israel,* in New York City, since 1907, and President of the Union of Sephardic Congregations since its organization in 1929. His communal activities have been numerous and varied. He was one of the three American representatives of the Zionist Commission to Palestine (1919), and served as regional director for Palestine and Syria of the Joint Distribution Committee (1920-1921). During the first World War, he was one of the organizers of welfare work among American Jewish soldiers and sailors, and today, he is Chairman of the Jewish Welfare Board Committee on Army and Navy Religious Activities. Dr. Pool's writings include the preparation and editing of six volumes of *Sephardic* liturgy; a book entitled *The Kaddish*; and numerous articles in general as well as Jewish journals.

Nathan Reich is assistant professor of economics at Hunter College, and a recognized authority in his field. He was assistant editor of the Encyclopaedia of the Social Sciences. His book, *Labour Relations in Republican Germany,* was awarded the E. R. A. Seligman Prize by Columbia University; and in 1940 he won a Guggenheim Fellowship. Dr. Reich has written on Jewish as well as general economic problems.

Sulamith Schwartz is editor of the *Hadassah Newsletter.* For two years she was president of Junior Hadassah. She has done educational work for the Jewish National Fund and has lectured widely in the United States. During 1938 and 1939, she was Palestine correspondent of *The Jewish Frontier,* and she has written for *The Palestine Review, The Palestine Post, Davar,* and other publications.

George N. Shuster is President of Hunter College. He has a nationwide reputation as an educator and as a political and religious journalist. He was Head of the Department of English at Notre Dame, and for twelve years served as managing editor of the *Commonweal.* Among his publications are *The Catholic Spirit in Modern English Literature; The Catholic Spirit in America; The Germans;* three books of fiction; and numerous articles.

Milton Steinberg has attained distinction as rabbi, author and lecturer. He is Rabbi of the Park Avenue Synagogue in New York City, and has taught classical languages at the College of the City of New York (1924-1925), and Jewish history and religion

at the Teachers Institute of the Jewish Theological Seminary
(1926-1928). He is divisional chaplain (lieutenant colonel) in the
New York Guard, and his Jewish communal activities include
membership on the publications committee of the Jewish Publication Society, the National Commission of the Hillel Foundation,
the Jewish Welfare Board Committee on Army and Navy
Religious Activities, the public relations section of the Emergency
Committee on Zionist Affairs, and the Jewish Education Committee of New York. Rabbi Steinberg is author of *The Making
of the Modern Jew;* of a philosophical novel entitled *As a Driven
Leaf;* and of articles which have appeared in various journals. He
is a member of the editorial board of *The Reconstructionist.*

Marie Syrkin is associate editor of the *Jewish Frontier.* She has
written on literary themes, educational and political problems and
Zionism for numerous periodicals, including *The Menorah
Journal, Common Ground, The Protestant Digest* and the *World
Digest.* Her translations of Yiddish verse have been included in
various anthologies, notably Mark Van Doren's *Anthology of
World Poetry.*

Jacob J. Weinstein has had occasion to study Jewish life, and to
observe Christian-Jewish relationships in various parts of the
country. He was director of Hillel Foundation at Austin, Texas,
and advisor to Jewish students at Columbia University in New
York City. He served as rabbi in San Francisco, where he was
also director of the School for Jewish Studies. A member of the
editorial boards of *Jewish Frontier, Opinion, Jewish National
Monthly,* and *The Reconstructionist,* he has contributed to these
and other journals. He is at present Rabbi of the *Kehillat Anshe
Maarib Temple* in Chicago.

INDEX

Aaronsohn, Aaron, 238-9
Adjustment, see Jews, Adjustment of
Adler, Cyrus, 50, 245
Adult Education, 60, 139-143, 148, see
    also Education
Agency, Jewish, see Jewish Agency for
    Palestine
Agrarization, 176-7
Agriculture, 172-3, 176-7
Agudath Haadmorim, 137
All day school, see School, all day
Allocation committee, 152, 154, 155
Amalgamated Clothing Workers
    Union, 174
America First movement, 196
American Academy for Jewish Re-
    search, 142
American Aryan Folk Association, 194
American Association for Jewish edu-
    cation, 67
American Committee of Palestine
    Orchestra Fund, 248a
American democracy, VIII, 274-7
American Economic Committee for
    Palestine, 248b
American Emergency Committee for
    Zionist Affairs, 249
American Federation for Polish Jews,
    144
American Friends of the Hebrew
    University, 156, 248a
American Gentile Protective Associa-
    tion, 194
American Jewish Committee, 24, 142,
    158-9, 181, 243, Year Book,
    142, 153
American Jewish Congress, 24, 117,
    142, 148, 158-9, 160, 180, 243,
    248b, 271
American Jewish Historical Society,
    29, 30, 142
American Jewish Joint Distribution
    Committee, see Joint Distribu-
    tion Committee
American Jewish life, see Jewish com-
    munity in U. S.

American Jewish Year Book, 142, 153
American Jewry, see Jewish community
    in U. S.
American Ort Federation, 156
American Palestine Committee, 249
American patriotism
    and assimilation, 210-2
    and Jewishness, 206-7
    and Zionism, 240-1
American Pro-Falasha Committee, 156
American Protective Association, 186
American Vigilant Intelligence Federa-
    tion, 194
American Zionism, see Zionism in U. S.
American Zionist Federation, see Fed-
    eration of American Zionists
American Zionist Medical Unit for
    Palestine, 242, 244, 247-8
Americanism, see Americanization
Americanization, 14, 24-6, 37, 82, 97,
    100-1, 136, 145, 257, 275, 284
    and Judaism, 207, 210-1, 227
    and Zionism, 240-1
    Philosophy of, 208-12, 241, 275
Anglo Jewish poets, see Poetry in Jew-
    ish literature
Anglo-Jewish press, see Press
Anshe Chesed, 31
Anti-Defamation League, 159, 192
Anti-Semitism, 7, 18, 57, 100, 103, 108,
    146-7, 159, 179, 183-204, 221,
    254, 261, 271, 273, 276-7, 283
    and Communism, 189
    and Economic conditions, 171-81,
    192-3
    and Occupations, 171-72
    and Palestine, 202-3
    and World War I, 188-9, 224, 239,
    278
    and World War II, 95-6, 200-1
    in Colonial period, 184-5
Anti-Semitism
    and Zionism, 222-3
    Organized movements of, 186, 189-
    90, 193-6

305

Anti-Semitism—(*Continued*)
  Pattern of, 183-97
  Psychology of, 199-200
  Roots of, 197-201
  Solution to, 201-4
Anti-Semitism
  Weinstein, J. J., 183-204
Apostasy, 43
Appraisal of the Protocols of Zion
  Curtis, J. S., 189
Arbeiter Ring, see Workmen's Circle
Arbitration, 23
Artisans, *see* Working Classes
Arts, 120-21, 255
  Collections, 140
Asch, Sholem, 118, 120, 284
Assembly of Orthodox Rabbis, 137
Assimilation, 24-6, 51, 82, 97, 104-5, 277
  in Colonial period, 29-32, 184-5
  of Hellenism, 60
  Philosophy of, 208-12, 241, 275
Association of Hungarian Jews of America, 144
Auslander, Joseph, 114
Auto-emancipation, by Pinsker, 233
Autonomy, national, 224-5
Avukah, 248

Balfour Declaration, 126, 240, 242-4
Baltimore
  First Zionist group, 234
Basle platform, 236
Bavli, Hillel, 131
Behrman, S. N., 109, 284
Benderly, Samson, 68, 69
Benet, William Rose, 115
Benjamin, Judah P., 186
Berkowitz, I. D., 127
Berkson, I. B., 252
  Jewish Education, 56-91
Berlin, Irving, 93
Bernheimer, Charles S., *A Review of Studies of the Jewish Welfare Board During the Past Decades* in *The Jewish Center,* Sept., 1940
Bernstein, H.
  The Truth About the Protocols of Zion, 1935, 189
Beth din, 61
Beth haknesseth, 54, 61
Beth hamidrash, 61
Beth hasefer, 61

Biakik, Chaim Nachman, 61, 126
Bible, 20, 36, 43-4, 50, 56-7, 62-5, 72-3, 75, 77, 118, 123-4, 128, 139, 269, 283
  and Colonial America, 184
  Proposed courses of study in, 89
Bibliography, 289-98
Biltmore Program, 249
Bilu movement, 10
Bitzaron, Hebrew monthly, 127
Bloch, Ernest, 120
Blood libel, 191
B'nai B'rith, 21, 129, 135, 146, 157, 159, 248b
  organized in 1843
B'nai Jeshuran, 31
Board of Delegates of American Israelites, 157
  founded in 1859, 24
Bodenheim, Maxwell, 113-114
Bolshevism
  and Jews, 188-90
Brainin, Reuben, 125, 127
Brandeis, Louis D., 17, 24, 150, 238-242, 245, 250, 284
  de Haas, J., *Louis D. Brandeis,* 241
  Jewish Problem—How to Solve it, 238-41
Brinig, Myron
  Singerman, 100
B'rith Abraham, *see* Independent Order of B'rith Abraham
Bunker Hill Movement, dedication of, 17
Bureau of Jewish education, 68-70, 130
Bureau on Jewish Employment Problems, 151
Burial, 20, 30, 187
Burlesque, 109

Canada Jewry, *see* Jewish community in Canada
Cardozo, Benjamin, 284
Caspary, Vera
  Thicker than Water, 100
Catechism, 62
Census of religious bodies, 11, 36
Center Workers, 149
Central conference of American Rabbis
  organized in 1889, 138
  Pittsburgh program of, 45-6
  Year Book, 138, 1937, 219
Charity, *see* Philanthropy

Charleston, Jewish community of, 20, 33, 111
earliest reform movement, 45
Chipkin, Z. S.
Twenty-five years of Jewish Education in U.S., 1937, 72
Chovevi Zion, see "Lovers of Zion"
Christian Front, 194
Christian-Jewish Tragedy
Moehlmann, C. H., 272
Church and State, 5, 34, 40
Citizenship and Judaism, 206, 207, 255
and Zionism, 223-4, 240-1
Civil War, 15, 16
and Anti-Semitism, 185-6
Cohan, Abraham, 119, 246
The Rose of David Levinsky, 96, 97
Cohen, Morris, 120
Collectivization of American economy, 178-190
Columbus, 3
Committee on Economic Adjustment, *Industrial Classification of Jewish Gainful Workers in New York City*, in Conference on Jewish Relations 1938, 163, 168
Communists, 76
and assimilation, 211
and Jews, 189
Community, Jewish, *see* Jewish Community; Jewish Community in U. S.; Jewish Community in Palestine
Community centers, 141, 147-50, 248b
Conclusion, Janowsky, O. I., 251-257
Conference on Jewish Relations, 142
Congregations, Jewish, *see* Judaism, Synagogue, Temples
Congress Weekly, The, 117
Conservative Judaism, 49-51, 53, 214-16
and Zionism, 215
Institutions of, 138
Contemporary Jewish Record, 117
Contributions of Jews, *see* Jewish contributions
Contributors, 301-4
Copland, Aaron, 284
Coralnik, A., 120
Council of Jewish Federations and Welfare Funds, 153
General assemblies, Proceedings, 153

Council of Jewish Federations and Welfare Funds—(*Continued*)
Organized in New York City 1932, 152
Year Book of Jewish Social Work 1942, 151
Cultural Pluralism, 202, 203, 280-85
Cultural Scene, The
Syarkin, Marie, 92-121
Culture, Jewish, 20, 22, 57, 84, 92-121, 197, 203, 228, 244, 256
Agencies of, 139-43
and Hebrew, 122-33
Drama, 108-11
Essay, 107-8
Evaluation, 92-5
Novel, 96-107
Philosophy, 221-6
Poetry, 111-6
Press, 116-8
Role of Yiddish literature, 118-20
Sciences and arts, 120-1
Culture, *see also* Education; Hebrew language and literature; Jewish literature; Yiddish language and literature
Current Philosophy of Jewish Life in America
Steinberg, Milton, 205-230
Curriculum of Jewish education, *see* Education curriculum
Curtis, John S.
An Appraisal of the Protocols of Zion, 1942, 189
Customs, *see* Folkways; Ritual

Daly, Charles P.
Settlement of the Jews in North America, 1893, 30
Day, a Yiddish daily, 119
De Haas, Jacob, 240
Louis D. Brandeis, 1929, 241
Dearborn Independent, 190, 192
Defenders of the Christian Faith, 194
Democracy, 11
and Anti-Semitism, 201-4
and Jews, 274-7
Denominationalism, religious, 20
Department of Synagogue and School Extension of the Union of American Hebrew Congregations, 141
Depression
and Anti-Semitism, 192-3

Deutsch, Babette, 113, 114
Dewey, John, 57-60
Diaspora Nationalism, 224-225
Discrimination, 106-157
    and Anti-Semitism, 198-204
    and Depression, 193
    and Unions, 180-1
    in Colonial period, 184-5, 267
    Economic, 171-8, 179-81
    Religious, 12
    Social, 186-7
Domnitz, E., 132
Doniger, G., xii, *Preface* ix-xii
Drama in Jewish Literature, 108-11
Dropsie College of Hebrew and Cog-
    nate Learning, 140
Dubinsky, David, 284
Duker, Abraham G.
    Jewish Survival in the World Today,
        x, 143
    Structure of the Jewish Community,
        134-160

East Side of New York, 97-9, 101, 110
Eastern European Jews of, *see* Jews,
    Eastern European
Ecclesiastes, 92, 93
Economic conditions, 161-82, 253
    Abnormality of, 171-7
    Adjustment to, 12-14
    and Anti-Semitism, 171-2, 77-8, 192-
        3, 198-9
    Characteristics of American Jewry,
        162-3
    Discrimination, 171-181, 192-3
    Distribution, 163-167
    in U. S., 162-9
    Occupational trends, 169-77
    Vocational guidance, 181-2
Economic trends
    Reich, Nathan, 161-82
Editor's Note
    Janowsky, O. I., xii
Edmondson, Economic Service, 194
Education, 20, 33, 38, 41-2, 47, 50, 55,
        56-91, 128, 252
    and Survival, 56-57
    Bureau of Jewish education, 68-70
    Common School program, 76-91
    Cultural agencies, 139-43
    Curriculum, 56, 67, 76-91
    In America, 64-76

Education—(*Continued*)
    In Medieval times, 61-63
    Meaning of, 56-62
    New Tendencies, 62-64
    Origins, 64-66
        German-Jewish, 65; East European,
            65; Spanish-Portuguese, 64
    Proposed course of study, 88-91
    Statistics, 65-6, 70-1, 73-4, 78
    Traditional education, 60-62
    Types of school, 70-6
        All Day School, 73-74
        Hebrew Week Day, 70-72
        Sunday School, 72-73
        Yiddish Culture School, 75-76
Efros, Israel, 131-132
Einhorn, David, 45
Einstein, Albert, 94
Eisenstein, I. D.
    Otzar Yisrael, 125
Elders of Zion, Protocols of, see Proto-
    cols of Elders of Zion
Eliot, George, 112
Elks, 146
Ellis Island, 95, 102
Emancipation, 206, 221, 270
    and education, 62
Employment, 151, 176, 179, 181
    and Anti-Semitism, 171-172
    distribution of, 161-162
    trends in, 169-179
Enlightenment, 63, 123, 124
Epistles to the Hebrews, 234
Epstein, 132
Epstein, Judith G., xi
Equality, 11, 12, 17, 180, 181, 256, 262
Essay in Jewish literature, 107-108

F. P. A., 93, 115
Farmers, 151, 172-3, 176-7
Fascism, *see* Nazism and Fascism
Fearing, Kenneth, 113-114
Federal Council of the Churches of
    Christ in America, 192
Federation of American Zionists, 235-
    7, 240, 248
Federation of Jewish Charities, 21, 52,
    67, 149, 152-3
Federation of Jewish Men's Clubs and
    Women's League, 138

Federation of Lithuanian Jews, 144
Federation of Orthodox Rabbis, 137
Feinstein, M., 132
Felsenthal, Bernard, 236
Female Hebrew Benevolent Society, 135
Ferber, Edna, 99, 107, 284
  So Big, Cimarron, Fanny Herself, 99-100, 104, *A Peculiar Treasure*
Finances
  Jews in, 169
Fineman, Irving, 107
  Hear, Ye Sons, 106, *Dr. Addams,* 107
Folkways, 48, 49, 53, 57, 72, 120, 202, 219, 224, 227, 255
Ford, Henry
  Dearborn Independent, 190, 192
Fortune, eds., *Jews in America,* 1936, 168-9, 276
Forums, 128, 141
Forward, a Yiddish daily, 119, 246
France Jewry, *see* Jewish Community in France
Frank, Jerome
  "Red, White and Blue Herring," the *Saturday Evening Post,* Dec. 6, 1941, 275
Frankfurter, Felix, 242
Franklin, Benjamin, 16
Fraternal Orders, 19, 22, 135-6, 145-7
  and Zionism, 242
Fraternities, 147, 187
Free Sons of Israel organized in 1859, 135
Freiheit, a Yiddish daily, 119
Freud, S., 94
Friedenwald, Harry, 235
Friedlander Classes, *see* Israel Friedlander Classes
Friedlander, Israel, 68
Friends of New Germany, 193

General Federation of Jewish Labor in Palestine, 245
General Jewish Council, 159-160
German-American Bund, 194, 195
German-Hebrew Benevolent Society, 135
German versus *East European Jews,* 18-19
Germany, Jews of, *see* Jews, German
Gershwin, George, 93, 284

Gewerkschaften Campaign, *see* National Labor Committee for Palestine
Ghetto, 19, 33, 37, 43, 95, 122, 274, 276, 285
Ginsburg, S., 132
Glantz, Rudolf
  "Jews in Early German-American Literature," in *Jewish Social Studies,* April, 1942, 185
Glass, Montague, 102
  Potash and Perlmutter, 98
Gold, Michael, 102, 104, 114
  Jews Without Money, 101
Goldberg, Isaac
  Major Noah, 1936, 232
Gordon, J. L., 124
Gottheil, Gustav, 236
Gottheil, Richard, 236-7
Graeber, I., and Britt, S. (eds.)
  Jews in a Gentile World, 1942, 197
Gratz, Rebecca, 184
  Letters, 185
Gratz College, 140
The Great Hatred
  Samuel, Maurice, 108
Greek Letter fraternities, *see* Fraternities
Greenberg, Hayim, 120
Gropper, William, 284
Guiterman, Arthur, 116

Habonim, 248
Hadassah, Women's Zionist Organization of America, ix, xi, 142-3, 235-7
  Education Advisory Committee, xi, xii
  Medical Unit, 242, 244, 247-8
  National Board, xi
  National Education Committee, xii
Hadoar, Hebrew daily, later weekly, 127, 128
Hadoar Lanoar, bi-weekly children's supplement to *Hadoar,* 128
Haivri, Hebrew weekly, 125
Halkin, Abraham S.
  Hebrew in Jewish Culture, 122-3
Halkin, Simon, 132
Halper, Albert, 102
  On the Shore, 100, *The Foundry,* 100, *Union Square,* 100
Hapoel Hamizrachi, 248

Hashomer Hadati, 248
Haskalah, see Enlightenment
Hatikvah, 47, 125
Hatoren, Hebrew monthly, 127
Hays, Mortimer, xii
Hebrew Benevolent Society, 135
Hebrew College and Teachers' Training School of Baltimore, 140
Hebrew College of Boston, 140
Hebrew in Jewish Culture, Halkin, A. S., 122-33
Hebrew language and literature, 36, 42, 53, 54, 56, 57, 64, 65, 66, 67, 68, 70, 72, 73, 74, 75, 77, 79, 84, 92, 112, 140, 225, 283
  and Conservative Judaism, 49
  and Jewish culture, 122-33
  and Orthodox Judaism, 35, 42
  and Reconstructionism, 49, 226
  and Reformed Judaism, 43-4, 217
  Background, 122-5
  Enlightenment, 123-4
  Hebrew in Palestine, 124-5
  Hebrew Poetry, 131-2
  Hebrew Prose, 132
  in America, 122-33
  Proposed course in, 90-1
  See also Jewish literature
Hebrew Language in secondary schools and colleges, 78, 130-1
Hebrew movement in America, 125-33
Hebrew poetry, 131-2
Hebrew press, *see* Press
Hebrew prose, 132
Hebrew Sheltering and Immigrant Aid, *see* HIAS
Hebrew speaking circles, 125
Hebrew Teachers' Seminary of Cleveland, 140
Hebrew Technical Institute in Haifa, 238
Hebrew Theological College of Chicago, 140
Hebrew Union College, 21, 139
  established in 1875, 64
  Graduates of, 47
Hebrew University in Jerusalem, 127, 156, 249
Hebrew Week Day school, *see* Schools, Hebrew week day
Hecht, Ben, 109
  A Jew in Love, 103

Heder, 42, 63, 65, 66, 71, 75, 135
Heine, Heinrich, 93, 112, 118, 275
  Hebrew Melodies, 93
Hellenism, 60
Hellman, Lillian, 93, 109
Hendrick, Burton J., 192
  World's Work, 190
Henrietta Szold
  Lowenthal, Marvin, 236
Herzl, Theodor, 154, 232, 233, 236, 240
Herzliah Hebrew Academy of New York City, 140
HIAS, 150
High School, *see* Schools, Secondary
High, Stanley
  "Jews, Anti-Semites and Tyrants," *Harper's Magazine*, June, 1942, 275, 276
Hillel Foundation, 129, 142, 143, 159
Hillman, Sydney, 284
Hirshbein, Peretz, 120
Histadruth, see General Federation of Jewish Labor
Histadruth Hanoar Haiuri, 129
Histadruth Ivrith, 127-29
Historical background
  Janowsky, O. I., 1-27
Hitler, 100, 104, 107, 108, 115, 176, 193, 196, 199, 201, 261, 267-8, 273-4, 277
Hoffenstein, Samuel, 116
Hook, Sidney, 120
Houtz, Philip
  "Current Theories and Techniques in Fund-Raising," *The Jewish Social Service Quarterly*, June, 1942, 153
Hovevei Zion, see Lovers of Zion
Hurst, Fannie, 98, 102
  Humoresque, 98

I, the Jew
  Samuel, M., 100
Imber, N. H.
  Hatikvah, 125
Immigration, 1-27, 135-6
  recent German, 153
  restriction, 10-11, 42, 191
Independent Order B'rith Abraham, 135, 146
Independent Order B'rith Sholom, 146
Independent Order Free Sons of Israel, 146

Industrial classification of Jewish Gainful Workers in New York City, 163, 168
Industrial Defense Association, 194
Industrial distribution, 163-171
Industrialism, 9, 22, 23, 102
Industries, 167-169, 171-177
  Garment industry, 168-9, 174-5
Inquisition, 3
Institute on Jewish Affairs, 142
Institutions, 18-26, 34-42, 134-60, 255-268
  Courses of study, 89
  Cultural, 139-43
  Historic account, 134-43
  Landsmanschaften, 144-5
  Overseas relief, 154-6
  Philanthropic, 150-4
  Rebuilding of Palestine, 154-6
  Religious, 136-8
  Representative body of, 156-60
  Social and recreational, 143-56
  Welfare, 150-4
  Zionist, 244-50
Integration of Jews, *see* Jews, Adjustment
Intercollegiate Zionist Organization, 237
Intermarriage, 34, 51
International Jew, 190
International Ladies Garment Workers Union, 174
International Workers' Order, 76, 146
Intolerance, *see* Tolerance
Isaacs, S. M., 50
Isolationist, 188, 196
Israel, 60, 61
  Concept of, 83
  Preservation of, 61
  Redemption of, 206
Israel Friedlander Classes, 141

Jacobs, Rose G., xi
Janowsky, Oscar I., xii
  Conclusion, 251-257
  Editor's note, xii
  Historical background, 1-27
Jastrow, Marcus, 236
Jefferson, Thomas, 12
Jew
  Definition of, 271-4
  interpretation, 252-7

Jew—(Continued)
  Relation to American Community, 262-9
Jewish Agency for Palestine, 155, 245
Jewish Agricultural Society, 151
Jewish Alliance of America, 157
Jewish Book Week, National Committee for, 142
Jewish Center, a quarterly, 148, 149
Jewish Centers, 71
Jewish Colonial Trust, 237
Jewish community
  proposed course of study for, 88
Jewish Community and the Outside World
  Shuster, G. N., 262-9
Jewish community in Canada
  Occupational distribution, 167, 171
Jewish community in France, 274-5
Jewish community in Palestine, 127, 238, 240, 245, 284
Jewish community in Russia, 155, 171, 176, 188-9, 211
Jewish community in U. S., 1-27, 134-160
  Agencies for relief and Palestine, 154-6
  and American way of life, 277-85
  and democracy, 274-7
  and Judaism, 28-55
  and Zionism, 231-50
  community centers, 147-50
  cultural agencies, 139-43
  Cultural Pluralism, 280
  East European element, 9-11
  Economic conditions, 161-82
  Education, 64-76
  Evaluation, 261-85
  Evolution of, 19-26
  Fraternal orders, 145-7
  German element, 7-9
  Hebrew culture, 122-33
  Historic account, 136-8
  Institutional life, 18-24
  Integration, 11-18
  Landsmanschaften, 144-5
  Literary achievements, 92-121
  Philanthropic and welfare agencies, 150-4
  Philosophy of, 205-26
  Relation to American life, 24-6, 256-7
  Religious institutions, 136-8

Jewish community in U. S.—(*Cont.*)
Representative body, 262-70, 156-60, 243
Sephardic, 3-7
Social and recreational establishments, 143-56
Jewish contributions, 15, 17, 105, 203
in Hebrew, 122-33
in Literature, 92-121
in Science and Arts, 120-1
Jewish Culture, *see* Culture
Jewish Culture Council, 130, 131
Jewish education, *see* Education, Jewish
Jewish Education, Berkson, I. B., 56-91
Jewish Education Committee, 130
Jewish Education in U. S.
Chipkin, I. S., 72
Jewish Frontier, 117
Jewish genius, 92, 94, 120-121, 284-5, *see also* Culture, Jewish literature
Jewish group life, *see* Jewish community in U. S.
Jewish history, 57, 60, 231, 254
and Anti-Semitism, 183-4
in Curriculum, 56, 62-3, 66, 72, 74-7
Proposed course of study, 89
Jewish Institute of Religion, 139
Jewish Journal and Daily News, see Morning Journal
Jewish journalism, *see* Press
Jewish Labor Committee, 159
Jewish Labor Federation, *see* General Federation of Jewish Labor in Palestine
Jewish learning, 20, 22, 33, 41, 47, 63, 77, 84, 139-40, 143, *see also* Education
Jewish Legion, 242
Jewish life in the U. S., *see* Jewish community in U. S.
Jewish literature, 66, 92-121
Drama, 108-11, Essay, 107-8
Evaluation, 92-5, Novel, 96-107
Poetry, 111-6, Press, 116-8
Role of Yiddish literature, 118-20. *See also* Hebrew language and literature, culture, Yiddish language and literature
Jewish music, 43, 120
Jewish National Fund of America, 155, 237, 244

Jewish National Homeland, *see* Palestine
Jewish National Worker's Alliance, 75, 140, 146, 246
Jewish Occupational Council, 151
Jewish Occupational Council. *Patterns of Jewish Occupational Distribution in the United States and Canada*, 1940, 164, 166, 170
Jewish Occupational Council
Baltimore Jewish Youth, 1940, 170
Some Characteristics of, 408
Jewish periodicals, *see* Press
Jewish population, *see* Jews, Statistics of population
Jewish Press, *see* Press
Jewish problem, 99, 101, 104, 105, 106, 107, 143, 271, 273, 275
Jewish problem, How to solve it
Brandeis, L. D., 238-9, 240-1
Jewish Publication Society, 141, 142
Jewish Reconstructionist Foundation, 138
Jewish representative body, *see* Representation of Jews in U. S.
Jewish State, *see* Palestine, Nationality and Nationalism, Zionism
Jewish Statistical Bureau, 142
Jewish survival, *see* Survival
Jewish Survival in the World Today
Duker, A. G., x, 143
Jewish Teacher, a periodical, 67
Jewish Telegraphic Agency, 142
Jewish themes, *see* Jewish literature
Jewish Theological Seminary of America, 49, 139, 230
Jewish rights, 4, 148, 210, 224, 255-6, 262, 271-282
defense of, 24, 157-9, 203
In continental America, 5, 11, 12
in Soviet Union, 256
Jewish scholarship, *see* Jewish learning
"Jewish War," 196
Jewish War Veterans, 147
Jewish Welfare Board, *see* National Jewish Welfare Board
Jewish Welfare Board, 149
Jewishness
definition of, 271-4
interpretation, 252-7
philosophy of, 206-7
Jewry, *see* Jewish community in U. S.

Jewry, conservation, *see* Conservative Judaism

Jewry, Orthodox, *see* Orthodox Judaism

Jewry, reformed, *see* Reform Judaism

Jews, Adjustment of, 16, 24-6, 83, 95, 99, 104, 150, 187, 197
  Economic adjustment, 12-14, 167-177, 171-77
  Integration of Jews, 11-18
  Political adjustment, 11-12
  Social and cultural adjustment, 14-18

Jews after the war
  Niebuhr, Reinhold, 202

Jews, Anti-Semites and Tyrants
  High, Stanley, 275-6

Jews, Cultural adjustment, 14-18

Jews—Eastern European, 7, 9-11, 14, 20, 22, 23, 24, 25, 26, 40, 186, 231, 253
  and education, 65, 67-8
  and Fraternal orders, 145
  and Hebrew culture, 124, 132-133
  and Institutions of, 134-135
  and Landsmanschaft, 144
  and Orthodoxy, 37
  and Reform, 47
  and versus German, 18-19

Jews, Economic conditions, *see* Economic conditions

Jews, Galician, 23

Jews, German, 7-8, 13-15, 20-23, 26, 158, 253
  and Education, 64-5
  and Reform Judaism, 43-8
  In Colonial period, 185
  In World War, 188
  Institutions of, 134-5
  versus East European, 18-19

Jews in a Gentile World
  Graeber, I., 197

Jews in America, by Fortune, 168-9, 276

Jews in industry, *see* Economic conditions

Jews in the armed forces, 15

Jews in Russia, *see* Jewish community in Russia

Jews in U.S., *see* Jewish community in U.S.

Jews, Polish, 23, 175-6, 190

Jews, Rumanian, 23

Jews, Russian, 16, 23, 188-9

Jews, Sephardic, 8, 15, 19, 20, 22, 26, 31, 111, 253
  and education, 64-65
  and Hebrew culture, 125
  contributions, 16
  Institutions of, 134-135
  Origin and growth, 3-7

Jews, Social conditions, 14-18

Jews, Statistics of, *see* Statistics

Job, 92, 93

Job placement, 151, 181

Johanan ben Zakkai, 60

Joint Distribution Committee, 144, 155

Joseph Rabbi Jacob of Vilna

Joshua ben Gamala

Journalism, *see* Press

Judaism, 16, 20-1, 26, 28-55, 61, 112, 147, 205-30, 252-3
  and Americanism, 210-1
  and Education, 61-2
  and Nazism, 267-8
  and Zionism, 221-2
  Census of religious bodies, 11, 136
  Conception of, 206-7
  Conservation, 49-51, 214-6
  Hostility to, 263-5
  Orthodox, 34-43, 212-4
  Outlook, 51-5
  Philosophy of Assimilation, 208-12
  Philosophy of Survival, 212-21
  Reconstruction, 48-9, 226-30
  Reformed, 43-8, 216-9

Judaism and the Synagogue
  Pool, D. De S., 28-55

Junior Hadassah, 248

Junior Mizrachi, 248

Juvenile delinquency, 150

Kallen, Horace, 120
  Culture and Democracy, 276, 281
  Judaism at Bay, 276
  National Being and the Jewish Community, 270-85
  National Solidarity and the Jewish Minority, 276

Kaplan, Mordecai M., 68, 147, 226
  Chairman of Jewish community study, xi, 65

Kaufman, George S., 93, 109, 284

Kehillah, 65

Keren Hayesod, see Palestine Foundation Fund

Keren Kayemeth Le Yisrael, *see* Jewish National Fund
Kinsley, Sidney, 109
  Men in White, 109
Klein, Abraham M., 115
  Design for Medieval Tapestry, 115-16
  Haggadah, 116
  Hath Not a Jew, 115
Knights of Pythias, 146
Know-Nothing, 186, 190
Kober, Arthur, 111
  Having a Wonderful Time, 110
Kohanski, Alexander S., and Jacobs, Maurice
  Fraternal Orders and Fraternities in *The Universal Jewish Encyclopedia,* Vol. IV, 1941, 147
Krall, Leon, 284
Kraus, Michael, xii
Ku Klux Klan, 17, 186, 190, 192

Labor, 191
  and renaissance of Hebrew, 124
  and Zionism, 245-6
Labor unions, *see* Trade Unions
Labor Zionist movement, 76, 85, 117, 140, 141, 146, 225, 245-6, 248
Landsmanschaften, 21, 23, 135, 144-5, 248b
  overseas relief, 154-6
Lapson, Judah, 130, 131
  "Proceeding of the Sixteenth Annual Conference of the National Council for Jewish Education in Jewish education," in *Jewish Education,* January, 1942, 80
Lawson, John Howard, 109
Lazarus, Emma, 2, 3, 11-15, 235, 284
  and Zionism, 233-4
  The Dance to Death, 113, 114, 115, 235, 284
  The New Colossus, 111
  Songs of a Semite, 112
League for Labor Palestine, 246
League of Nations, 243-4
Learning, *see* Jewish Learning
Leavitt, Julian
  "American Jews in the World War" in *The American Jewish Year Book,* 1919, 15
Lebenson, Micah, 124

Lebeson, A. L.
  Jewish Pioneers in America, 1931, 19
Leeser, Isaac, 50
Lehrer Seminar, 75
Leivick, 93, 118, 119, 120
  The Golem, 119
  The Yellow Badge, 119
Levin, Meyer
  The Old Bunch, 100
Levin, Schmarya, 239-40
Levinger, L. J.
  A History of the Jews in U.S., 12
  The Jewish Student in America, 1937, 171
Levinson, Baer, 124, 234
Levy, Newman, 116
Lewisohn, Ludwig, 94, 105, 107
  Israel, 231
  Renegade, 105
  The Island Within, 105, 106, 231
  Upstream, 105, 106
Libraries, 140
Life Magazine, April 13, 1942
  Review of Anti-Semitic organizations, 194
Lilienblum, Moses, 124
Linfield, H. S., xii
  Jewish population in U.S. in the *American Jewish Year Book,* Vol. 43, 1941, 11
  State population census by Faith, 6
Lippmann, Walter, 93, 116
Lipsky, Louis, 239, 242
  Thirty Years of American Zionists, 1927, 242
Lisitzky, E., 132
Lopez, Aaron, 13
Lovers of Zion, 63, 233, 234, 236
Lowell, A. L., 190, 192
Lowenthal, Marvin
  A World Passed By, 108
  Henrietta Szold: Life and Letters, 1942, 236
Lubin, David, 284

Mack, Julian S., 24, 158, 243
Madison, James, 12
Magnes, J. L., 65, 68
Mailamm, 248a
Manch, Mordecai, 124
Mandate, *see* Palestine Mandate
Mapu, A., 124
Marranos, 3, 20

Marshall, Louis, 69, 158, 238, 243, 245
Marx, Karl, 94
Masada, 248
Masons, 146
Massena, N. Y.
  disappearance of child, 191
Masses, see Working classes
Maximon, 132
Meller, Sidney
  Roots in the Sky, 100
Mendelssohn, Moses, 274
Mendes, H. Pereira, 49
Menken, Adah Isaacs, 111
Menorah Association, 141, 142, 143
Menorah Journal, 142
Merchants, 13
Messianism, 111, 246
  and Reform Judaism, 46
Michelson, Albert, 120
Middle classes, 14, 19, 63, 172, 185, 187
  non-Jewish Middle classes and anti-
    Semitism, 195
Miklat, Hebrew Monthly, 127
Mikrah, see Bible
Mikveh Israel, Philadelphia, 16
Minority rights, see Jewish rights
Mission theory, 217-18
Mizrachi, 225, 237, 246-7
Mizrachi Women's Organization, 247
Moehlmann, Conrad H.
  The Christian-Jewish Tragedy, 1933,
    272
Moise, Penina, 111
  Hymns Written for the Use of
    Hebrew Congregations
Morais, Sabato, 50
Morning Journal, a Yiddish daily, 119,
    137
Morris, Nathan
  The Jewish School, 1937
Morris, Robert, 15

Nathan, George Jean, 120
Nathan, Robert, 114, 284
  Road of Ages, 107
National Academy for Adult Jewish
    Studies, 141
National Association of Jewish Center
    Workers, 149
National Being and the Jewish Com-
    munity
  Kallen, Horace M., 270-85
National Braille Institute, 151

National Council for Jewish Education,
    67
National Desertion Bureau, 151
National Federation of Temple Brother-
    hoods, 138
National Federation of Temple Sister-
    hoods, 138
National Federation of Temple Youth,
    138
National Home, see Palestine
National Home for Jewish Children,
    Denver, 151
National Jewish Hospital at Denver,
    151
National Jewish Welfare Board, 149
  Annual Report, 1941, 148
National Labor Committee for Pales-
    tine, 246
National Library in Jerusalem, 237
National Refugee Service, 156
  established in 1939, 153
National revival, see Palestine
National Union for Social Justice, 194
National Workers' Alliance, see Jewish
    National Workers' Alliance
Nationality and nationalism, 221-6, 233,
    241, 271-80
  and Hebrew, 124-5
  and Jewish community, 271-85
  and Judaism, 206-8
  and Reform Judaism, 44, 46, 47, 108,
    126
  and Renaissance, 68
  definition of, 254-6
  Diaspora nationalism, 224-5
Nativist, 17
Nazism and Fascism, ix, 93, 107, 115,
    119, 155-6, 159, 255, 261, 267-8
  against Christianity, 198
  organizations in U. S., 193-6
Needle industries, 13, 174-5
  strikes, 23
Ner Maaravi, a Hebrew monthly, 125
New Amsterdam, Jewish community
    in, 3, 4
New Deal, 193, 195
Newport, Jewish community of, 5, 13,
    33
New York, Jewish Community of, 3,
    12, 20, 35, 51
  First Zionist group, 234
  Occupational distribution, 163-7

New York, Jewish community
of—(*Continued*)
schools, 70-1, 74-5
seminaries in, 40-1, 139-40
New York Stock Exchange, 169
Niebuhr, Reinhold
"Jews After the War," *The Nation*,
Feb. 21 and 28, 1942, 202
Noah, Mordecai Manuel, 232
Goldberg, I., *Major Noah*
Non-Zionists, 245-6
Nordau, Max, 46
Notes and News, 153
Novel in Jewish literature, 96-107
Numerus clausus, 191
Nuremberg laws, 272, 274

Occupations, 161-82
Abnormal distribution, 171-77
and Anti-Semitism, 177-78
distribution, 163-7, 253
Training, 151
Trends, 169-71
Vocational guidance, 181-2
Odets, Clifford, 109, 111, 114, 284
Awake and Sing, 110
Oglethorpe, James, 5, 6
Old Testament, *see* Bible
Oneg Shabbat, 42, 248
Opinion, 117
Oppenheim, James, 113-14
Order Sons of Zion, 146, 237
Organizations
anti-Semitic, 186, 189-90, 193-6
fraternal, 135-6, 145-7
Landsmanschaften, 144-5
philanthropic, 15-4
religious, 136-8
United Jewish representation, 156-60
Veterans, 147
Organized Anti-Semitism in America
Strong, David, 194-5
Orphan asylums, 135
Ort Federation, *see* American Ort
Federation
Orthodox Judaism, 31, 34-42, 53-4, 212-
14, 252
and education, 42, 66
heterogeneity, 39
institutions of, 136-8
Philosophy of survival, 212-21
Overseas relief, *see* Relief, overseas

Palestine, 3, 10, 24, 68, 69, 72, 76, 108,
115, 128, 134, 148, 158, 222,
223, 266
Absorptic capacity, 202
Agencies for building of, 154-6
Agrarian resettlement, 176
American contributions to, 244-50
and Anti-Semitism, 202-3
and Conservative Judaism, 49, 215
and Hebrews, 124-7
and Orthodoxy, 37
and Reconstructionism, 49, 228-9
and Reform Judaism, 45, 46, 217-18
and the Synagogue, 55
as a Jewish Homeland, 231-6, 241-3
Proposed courses in, 90
Social experiment in, 85
Palestine Economic Corporation, 245
Palestine Foundation Fund, 155, 244
Palestine Jewish Community, *see* Jew-
ish Community in Palestine,
and Palestine
Palestine Mandate, 126, 155, 243, 244,
245
Palestine Restoration Fund, 243
Parker, Dorothy, 93, 116
Parochial schools, *see* School, all day
Patriotism and assimilation, 210-12
and Zionism, 240-1
Paul Reveres, 1941
Peace and post-war problems, 142
Peace conference at Versailles, 24,
158-9
and Zionism, 243
Peddlers, 21, 185
Penn, William, 6
Pennsylvania, Jewish community of,
5, 6, 12
Philadelphia, Jewish community of, 6,
20
Philanthropy, 16, 19-21, 24, 135
agencies, 68-9, 152-3, 154-7
Philipson, David, Ed.
Letters of Rebecca Gratz, 1929, 185
The Reform Movement in Judaism,
1907, 46
Philosophies of Jewish Life, 205-30
Diaspora nationalism, 224-5
of Assimilation, 208-12
of Citizenship and Judaism, 206-7
of survival, 212-21
Reconstructionism, 226-30
Zionism, 221-4

Pinsker, Leon, 233
Pinski, David, 120
Pioneer Women's Organization, 246, 247
Pittsburgh program of 1885 of Central Conferences of American Rabbis, 45, 46, 216
Poale Zion, 75, 76, 237, 242, 243, 246
  See also Labor Zionist movement
Poetry in Jewish literature, 111-16
Pogroms, 10, 112, 124, 154, 157, 233, 237
Polonies Talmud Torah, 64
Pool, David de Sola, 252
  Judaism and the Synagogue, 28-55
Pool, Tamar de Sola, xi
Poverty, 22, 150
Prayers, 20, 43
Preface
  Domiger, Margaret G., ix-xii
President's Committee on Fair Employment Practices, 180
Press, 23, 116-18, 249
  Hebrew press, 125, 127
  Yiddish press, 119-20, 126, 237
Proceedings of the General Assembles of the Council of Jewish Federations and Welfare Funds, 153
Pro-Christian American Society, 194
Pro-Falasha Committee, *see* American Pro-Falasha Committee
Professional services, 163, 164, 165
Professions, 14, 181-2, 187
Progressive Order of the West, 146
Proletarian novelists, 100-1, 104, 119
Proletarian poets, 114-15
Proletariat, *see* Working classes
Proletariat, industrial, *see* Working classes
Propaganda, 200
Protocols of the Elders of Zion, 189, 190, 262
Provisional Executive Committee, 240, 241
Psychology and Anti-Semitism, 199-200
Publicists, *see* Press
Publishing, 141-42

Rabbi Isaac Elchanan Theological Seminary and Yeshivah College, *see* Yeshivah College

Rabbinical Assembly of America and Conservative Judaism, 49
  organized in 1901, 138
Rabbinical Council of America
  organized in 1923, 41, 137
Rabbis, 31-3, 156, 264, 268
  organization of, 137-8
  orthodox, 34-42
  reformed, 43-8
  union of, 41
Racial and religious minorities, 190
Raphael, Morris, 50
Reconstruction, 154-6
Reconstructionism, 48-9, 138, 226-30, 253
  Program of, 228-9
Reconstructionist, The, bi-weekly Journal, 138
Red, White and Blue Herring
  Frank, Jerome, 275
Redemption of Israel, 89, 107
Reform, religious, *see* Reform Judaism, 21, 22
Reform Judaism, 43-8, 216-19
  and Zionism, 44, 46-8
  German language, 45, 53
  German spirit, 45
  Hebrew language, 44
  Institutions of, 138
  Music, 43
  Pittsburgh program of 1885, 45, 46
  reaction against Reform, 46-7
  return to tradition, 48
  Synagogue modified, 44
  Temples, 25
Reform Movement in Judaism, The
  Philipson, David, 46
Refugees, 153, 155, 196
Regelson, A., 132
Reich, Nathan, 253
  Economic Trends, 161-82
Relief, overseas, 38, 148
  Agencies for, 68-9, 152-3, 154-6, 157
Religion, 23, 224-5, 255, 267-8
  and assimilation, 207-12
  and Hebrew, 122-3
  and survival, 212-21
  Conservative, 49-51, 214-16
  Hostility to, 263-5
  Institutions of, 136-8
  Observances, 34

Religion—(*Continued*)
  Orthodox, 34-42, 212-14
  Outlook, 51-5
  privileged, 12
  Proposed course of study, 84
  Reconstructionism, 48-9, 226-30
  Reform, 43-8, 216-19
Religious liberty, 6
Religious reform, *see* Reform Judaism
Representation of Jews in U. S., 156-60
  at Peace Conference, 242
Research Institute of Peace and Post-
    War Problems, 142
Restoration, *see* Zionism
Retail trade, 21
Revolution, American, 7, 11, 15
Revolution, Russian of 1905, 10, 237;
    of 1917, 188-9
Reznikoff, Charles, 115
  Kaddish, 115
  Memoriam: 1933, 115
  Rashi, 115
Rhode Island, 4
Ribalow, M., 127, 132
Rice, Elmer, 109, 284
  Counsellor at Law, 109
Richmond, Jewish community of, 6, 20
Rise of David Levinsky
  Cahan, A., 96, 97
Ritual, 18, 20, 22, 43-4, 54, 263
  conservative, 50-1
  in colonial period, 28-33
  orthodox, 40
  reconstructionism, 228, 229
  reform, 43-8, 217
Roosevelt, Franklin D., 270
Rosenbloom Teachers' Training School
    of the Hebrew Institute of
    Pittsburgh, 140
Rosenfeld, Paul, 120
Rosenwald, Julius, 284
Roth, Henry
  Call It Sleep, 101, 102

Sabbath, 36, 38, 46, 75
Sabbath School Union, 64
Sackler, Harry
  Festival at Meron, 107
Salomon, Haym, 15
Sampter, Jessie, 116
  The Book of the Nations, 116
  The Emek, 116
  Modern Palestine, 1933

Samuel, Maurice, 108
  I, The Jew, 108
  The Great Hatred, 108, 198
  You Gentiles, 108
Satire in Jewish literature, 109
Scapegoat, 192, 193
Schatz, Boris, 238-9
Schechter, Solonn, 49, 50, 215
Schiff, Jacob, 69, 158, 238
Scholarship, Jewish, *see* Jewish Learn-
    ing
School, program of, 76-91
  and democracy, 80-1
  proposed course of study, 88-91
  relation to American life, 76-82
  relation to Jewish group life, 82-3
  relation to religion, 84
  relation to social problems, 85-7
Schools, All day, 73-4
Schools, elementary, 61
Schools, experiment, 80
Schools, Hebrew week-day, 70-1, 77, 79
Schools, High, *see* Schools, Secondary
Schools, secondary, 78, *see also* Yeshivah
Schools, Sunday, 65, 66, 72-3, 77, 79
Schools, types, 70-6
  All-Day school, 73-4
  Hebrew Weekday school, 70-2
  Sunday school, 72-3
  Yiddish culture school, 75-6
Schools, Yiddish, 75-6, 79
  National Workers Alliance, 75
  Poale Zion, 75
  Sholem Aleichem Folk, 75
  Workmen's Circle, 75
Schulberg, Budd, 104
  What Makes Sammy Run?, 103
Schwartz, A. S., 132
Schwartz, Dalmon
  Shenandoah, 115
Schwartz, Sulamith
  Zionism in American Jewish Life,
    231-50
Science, 120-1
Sefer Hashanah, 128
Self-criticism, 103, 203, 208, 210
Seminaries, 40-1, 139-40
Sephardic Jews, *see* Jews, Sephardic
Shaw, Irwin, 109
  The Gentle People, 100
Shekel, 243

Shevilei Haohinuch, Hebrew Quarterly, 128
Shift of population, 172
Sholem Aleichem, 118
Sholem Aleichem Folk Shulen, 75
Shomerim, 238
Shore, 132
Shulhan Aruch, 36
Shuster, George N.
  The Jewish Community and the Outside World, 262-9
Silberschlag, Eisig, 132
Silkiner, B. N., 131
Silver Shirts, 194, 195
Singer, I. J., 118, 120
Smolenskin, P., 124
Social democracy, *see* Democracy
Social institutions, *see* Institutions
Social insurance, 23, 145
Social Justice, 17
Social problems,
  proposed course of study, 85-7
Social reform
  of Labor unions, 175
  Roosevelt administration, 192
Society for the Promotion of Craft and Agriculture among the Jews, *see* American Ort Federation
Socio-economic distribution, *see* Economic conditions
Sokolow, Nahum, 239
Songs of a Semite
  Lazarus, E., 112
Song of Songs, 92
Soviet Union, 155, 176, 188
  and assimilation, 211
  and Jews, 171
Spanish-Portuguese Jews, *see* Jews, Sephardic
Spinoza, Baruch, 94
Stamford, Conn., studies of Jewish occupation, 169
Statistics
  Community centers, 148
  Congregations, 136-8
  Educational, 65-6, 70-1, 73, 74, 76, 78
  Fraternal orders, 146
  Fraternities, 147
  in armed forces, 15

Statistics—(*Continued*)
  occupational distribution, 163-7
  origin, 3-12
  population, 6-7, 8, 10-11
  Students of Hebrew, 130
  Synagogues, 38-9
  Welfare agencies, 151, 153
Statue of Liberty
  Sonnet at the base, 2
Stein, Gertrude, 113, 284
Steinberg, Milton, 252
  As a Driven Leaf, 107
  Current Philosophies of Jewish Life in America, 205-30
Sterne, Maurice, 284
Stiles, Ezra
Straus, Isidor, 13
Straus, Nathan, 13, 238, 284
Strong, Donald S.
  Organized Anti-Semitism in America, 1941, 194-5
Structure of Jewish Community
  Duker, A. G., 134-60
Strunsky, Simeon, 93
  Topics of the Times, 116
Students, 170-1
Stuyvesant, Peter, 4
Survival, ix, 108, 179, 207, 210, 211, 275
  and assimilation, 208-12
  and education, 56-7, 60, 61, 69, 77
  and Jewish community, 254
  and Zionism, 221-4
  Philosophies of, 212-21
  See also Assimilation
Synagogue, 20, 28-55, 60, 141, 220, 252, 254
  Centers, 53, 147-50
  Conservative, 49-51
  educational function of, 62, 139-43
  Fees, 29
  in communal life, 134-5
  institutions of, 136-8
  Orthodox, 34-42
  Reconstructionist, 48-9
  Reform, 43-8
Synagogue Center, The, a quarterly, 138
Synagogue Council of America, 55, 138
Syrkin, Marie
  The Cultural Scene, 92-121
Syrkin, Nachmann, 243
Szold, Henrietta, xi, 68, 235-6

Talmud, 60, 61, 62, 63, 66, 139
Talmud Torahs, 23, 65, 70, 71, 72, 73,
  78, 84, 247
Tchernowitz, Chaim, 127
Teachers, 64-7, 69
  organizations of, 67
  and courses of study, 84
Teachers' Institute and Seminary College of Jewish Studies, 140
Teachers' Institute of the Rabbi Isaac
  Elchanan Seminary, 140
Teachers seminary, Jerusalem
Teachers training schools, 66, 75, 140-1
Temples, 21, 23, 43, 44, 46, 47, 52, 54,
  55, 139, 141, 147
Theatre, Experimental, 109
Theatre, Jewish, 23
Theatre, Yiddish, 120
Theological academies, 62
Tolerance, 4, 5, 11, 16, 17, 201, 203-4
  and Anti-Semitism, 183-4
  movements of intolerance, 186, 189-
  90, 193-6
Toleration, see Tolerance
Torah, 53, 60, 61, 62, 79, 83, 84, 186,
  214
Totalitarianism, ix, xi, 196, 203
Touro, Judah, 16
Trade, 12, 13, 163-7
Trade unions, 23, 126, 135, 159, 174-5
  and discrimination, 180-1
  and Zionism, 245-6
  placement policies, 79
  social reform, 175
Traders, 21, 163, 184
Tradition, xi, 69, 72, 76, 80, 105, 106,
  206, 247, 254, 268
  and assimilation, 208-12
  and conservation, 214-15
Trenton, N. J., studies of Jewish occupations, 169
Truth About the Protocols of Zion
  Bernstein, H., 189
Twersky, T., 132

Unemployment
  and anti-Semitism, 198
Union Hebrew Prayer Book, 73
Union Hymnal, 47
Union of American Hebrew Congregations, 21, 157
  Dept. of Synagogue and School Extension, 141

Union of American Hebrew Congregations—(Continued)
  not affiliated with, 53
  organized in 1873, 138
Union of Orthodox Jewish Congregations of America, 39
  Founded, 40
  organized in 1898, 137
Union of Orthodox Rabbis, 40, 137, 156
United Galician Jews of America, 144
United Hebrew Brothers, 146
United Hebrew Charities, 152
  organized in 1874 in N.Y.C., 67
United Jewish Appeal, 55, 156, 160, 248b
United Palestine Appeal, 155, 156
United Rumanian Jews of America, 144
U. S. Constitution
  First Amendment, 12
  See also Jewish rights
U. S. Dept. of Commerce
  Census of Religious Bodies, 1936,
  Bulletin #72, Jewish Congregations, 11, 136
United Synagogues of America, 50, 141
Untermeyer, Louis, 113, 114
  Caliban in the Coal Mines, 114
  "Jewish Spirit in Modern American
  Poetry" in Menorah Journal,
  August, 1931, 113-14
  Roast Leviathan, 114
Urbanization, 51, 162

Valentin, Hugo
  Anti-Semitism, 1936, 197
Veterans, see Jewish War Veterans
Virginia, Jewish Community of, 6
Vocational adjustment, 181-2
Vocational guidance, 151, 181-2

Wallenrod, 132
Warburg, Felix, 245
Weber, Max, 284
Weidman, Jerome, 104
  I Can Get It for You Wholesale, 103
  What's In It for Me?, 103
Weinstein, Jacob J.
  Anti-Semitism, 183-204
Weismann, Chaim, 242
Welfare agencies, 150-154
Welfare Board, see National Jewish
  Welfare Board

Welfare Funds, 40, 52, 151-152, 248b
  and financial support of centers, 149
White-collar classes, 181
"White Shirts," 194
Williams, Roger, 5
Wilson, Woodrow, 240, 242, 243, 244,
  278
Wise, Isaac M., 21
Wise, Stephen S., 24, 158, 237, 242, 243
Women's Zionist Organization of Amer-
  ica, see Hadassah, Women's
  Zionist Organization of Amer-
  ica
Working Classes, 14, 19, 55, 71-79, 143
  and philanthrophy, 154
  and Yiddish schools, 63, 75-76
  educational courses, 140
  poverty of, 12, 13, 32, 37, 38, 46A,
    48, 52, 56, 75, 83, 150
  proletarian writing, 100-1, 104, 114,
    115, 119
Workmen's Circle, 75, 76, 140, 146
Workmen's Circle Schools, 75
Works Project Administration
  Yiddishe *Familien un Familie
    Kraisen*, 1939, 145
Works Project Administration, Yiddish
  Writers Project, De *Yiddishe
    Landsmanschaft in New York*,
  1938, 144
"World Alliance Against Jewish Ag-
  gressiveness," 194
World War I, 10, 15, 16, 24, 99, 126,
    145, 147, 154-5, 158, 191
  and Anti-Semitism, 188-189, 224, 239,
    278
World War II, 149, 278
  and Anti-Semitism, 195-6, 200-1
  and Zionism, 250
World Zionist Organization, 239
  Executive, 240

Yehoash, 93, 118
Yellin, David, 68, 238, 239
Yeshiva Isaac Elchanan, 41
Yeshivah, 23, 61-2, 65, 66, 70, 73, 74,
    79, 247
  Yeshivah at Jabneh, 60
  See also Education, Jewish
Yeshivah College, 41, 137, 139
Yeshivat Minhat Areb, 64
Yezierska, Anzia, 98

Yiddish culture school, *see* School,
  Yiddish culture
Yiddish language and literature, 23,
    37, 41, 45, 63, 73, 92, 93, 122,
    211, 225, 283
  Role of, 118-20
Yiddish Lehrer Seminar, *see* Lehrer
  Seminar
Yiddish schools, *see* Schools, Yiddish
Yiddish Scientific Institute, 142
Yishuv, *see* Jewish community in Pales-
  tine
You Gentiles
  Samuel, Maurice, 108
Young Israel, 41, 137
Young Judaea, 237, 248
Young Men's Hebrew Association, 24,
    66
  First in New York, 1874, 21, 71,
    147, 148
Young People's League, 138
Youth, 69, 147, 148
  and employment, 179-80
  and vocational adjustment, 181-2
  education, 140-1
  Hebrew youth movement, 128-9
  occupational trends, 169-71
  Zionism, 248
Youth Aliyah, 235, 244

Zangwill, Israel
  Melting Pot, 97, 104, 105
Zhitlowsky, Hayim, 120
Zionism, x, 63, 111, 127, 136, 154, 221-4,
    231-50, 256, 271
  American contribution to, 244-50
  and American loyalty, 211
  and Americanism, 240-1, 265-6
  and Assimilation, 211
  and Conservative Judaism, 53, 93,
    215
  and Hebrew, 124-6, 129
  and Jewish literature, 105
  and labor, 245-6
  and orthodox Judaism, 36, 246-7
  and Reconstructionism, 49, 228-9
  and Reform Judaism, 44, 47-8
  and World War I, 239-44
  and World War II, 250
  effect in Jewish community, 244-50
  in United States, 232-44
  In Yiddish schools, 76
  non-Zionists, 245-6

Zionism—(*Continued*)
  proposed course of study, 90
  societies, 24
  youth seminars, 143
  See also Hadassah, Labor Zionist,
    Mizrachi
Zionism in American Jewish Life
  Schwartz, Sulamith, 231-50

Zionist Medical Unit, *see* American
  Zionist Medical Unit for Pales-
  tine
Zionist Organization of America, 248-9;
  Provisional Executive Commit-
  tee, *see* Provisional Executive
  Committee
Zukofsky, Louis, 113